Designing the
iPhone User Experience

The Art Institute of San Antonio
10,000 IH 10 West
San Antonio, TX 78230

Designing the iPhone User Experience

A User-Centered Approach to Sketching and Prototyping iPhone Apps

SUZANNE GINSBURG

✦✦Addison-Wesley

Upper Saddle River, NJ • Boston • Indianapolis • San Francisco
New York • Toronto • Montreal • London • Munich • Paris • Madrid
Capetown • Sydney • Tokyo • Singapore • Mexico City

Library of Congress Cataloging-in-Publication Data

Ginsburg, Suzanne.
  Designing the iPhone user experience : a user-centered approach to sketching and prototyping iPhone apps / Suzanne Ginsburg.
       p.   cm.
  Includes index.
  ISBN 978-0-321-69943-5 (pbk.)
  1. iPhone (Smartphone)—Programing. 2. Application software—Development. I. Title.
  QA76.8.I64G56 2010
  005.1—dc22
                                        2010021718

ISBN-13: 978-0-321-69943-5
ISBN-10:   0-321-69943-2

Text printed in the United States on recycled paper at Courier in Kendallville, Indiana.
First printing, August 2010

Editor-in-Chief
Karen Gettman

Senior Acquisitions Editor
Chuck Toporek

Managing Editor
John Fuller

Full-Service Production Manager
Julie B. Nahil

Copy Editor
Barbara Wood

Indexer
WordWise Publishing Services

Proofreader
Christine Clark

Technical Reviewers
Marion Buchenau, Nancy Frishberg, Patrick Jean, Christian Rohrer, Mirjana Spasojevic, Mike Shields, Brian Arnold, Dan Grover, and August Trometer

Editorial Assistant
Romny French

Interior Design and Composition
Bumpy Design

Cover Designer
Chuti Prasertsith

To Mom and Dad,
who have always been inquisitive, supportive, and encouraging.

Contents

Preface

With over 200,000 apps in the App Store, it has become increasingly challenging for app designers and developers to differentiate their apps. The days are long gone when it was possible to crank out an app over the weekend and refine it *after* receiving a few not-so-flattering user reviews. Users now have choices—lots of them. If your app is difficult to use or doesn't meet their needs, finding another one is just a tap away.

To illustrate, consider the ever-growing field of Twitter clients. There are hundreds of variations in the App Store, but only a handful stand out from the pack (such as Tweetie and Twitterific). For most apps, it boils down to one thing: the user experience. The same is true for countless other categories within the App Store; well-designed apps are more likely to attract and retain users. Of course there are other critical aspects of iPhone app development: the coding, the marketing, the customer support. All of the elements must come together.

Designing the iPhone User Experience will help you tackle the user experience part of the iPhone challenge. Three key themes will be reinforced throughout the book: know thy user, the design life cycle, and attention to detail.

Know Thy User

Millions of people depend on iPhone apps to get them to work, find their next meal, and stay in touch with family and friends. Professionals of all kinds also rely on iPhone apps: Doctors look up drug interactions; photographers fine-tune lighting; cyclists find the best routes. To truly understand how apps can fit into their lives, designers and developers must learn how users do things today, what's important to them, and what needs have not been met. FIGURES P.1–P.5 illustrate contextual observations from field interviews, an effective way to uncover user needs. Part Two, "Defining Your iPhone App," will introduce a variety of user research methods.

FIGURE P.1 Child using an iPhone in the yard. It's his mother's phone, but he uses it almost as much as she does! *(Courtesy of Alison Oshinsky)*

FIGURE P.2 The contents of a user's handbag help show how the iPhone fits into the person's life. This person has two phones to keep her work and personal lives separate. *(Courtesy of Michael Massie)*

FIGURE P.3 iPhones aren't just for young people. This lady quickly learned how to use her grandson's iPhone. *(Courtesy of David Pegon)*

FIGURE P.4 A cyclist incorporated the iPhone into his biking routine. *(Courtesy of Marcus Kwan)*

FIGURE P.5 A Volkswagen Beetle owner converted the bud vase into an iPhone holder. *(Courtesy of Nathan Barry, njb@mac.com)*

The Design Life Cycle

Award-winning designs rarely happen overnight; they usually occur only after many rigorous design cycles. To illustrate, **FIGURE P.6** shows how USA TODAY went through at least seven iterations for the article view in its app. These kinds of iterations should happen *before* you launch your app; doing so will save valuable time and money. More important, you may have only one chance to impress your users—you do not want to sell them half-baked ideas.

Part Three, "Developing Your App Concept," will explain how to iteratively design and test your app concepts.

FIGURE P.6 Progression of USA TODAY's article view. Chapter 10, "Visual Design," includes a case study about the USA TODAY iPhone app design. *(Courtesy of Mercury Intermedia)*

Attention to Detail

Most professionals know that attention to detail is important, but hundreds of apps fail to incorporate even the most basic design principles. This lack of attention is not merely an aesthetic issue (which is important); it also affects the way apps function. For example, a news article without proper alignment is difficult to read, and a poorly rendered icon is challenging to interpret. Apps with a razor-sharp attention to detail stand out because they look good *and* perform well.

Part Four, "Refining Your iPhone App," will show you how to make your app shine, from visual design and branding to accessibility and localization.

Mastering these three areas—know thy user, the design lifecycle, and attention to detail—will help set your app apart from the crowd. You may not have an award-winning app overnight, but knowing your users, iterative design, and attention to detail are important first steps.

Audience for This Book

This book is intended for anyone who wants to improve an existing iPhone app or create a new app.

Individuals new to the iPhone should start with Part One, "iPhone Application and Device Overview." This section of the book introduces important aspects of the iPhone and Apple's *iPhone Human Interface Guidelines* (known as the "HIG"). Although the overview will be helpful, you should download the iPhone HIG and read through it at least once so you can familiarize yourself with the terms, concepts, and design principles.[1] If you are already familiar with the iPhone's capabilities and the HIG, feel free to skip ahead to Parts Two, Three, and Four, which jump into product definition, prototyping, and usability testing.

To learn how the book may benefit your specific role, read the following highlights:

- **Entrepreneurs**

  Many iPhone entrepreneurs wear more than one hat: developer, designer, product manager, and more! These individuals will appreciate the "guerrilla" user research methods outlined in the book. They will also enjoy reading the case studies, which show how companies big and small approach user-centered design. As their companies grow, entrepreneurs can use this book to help build their own user experience team of iPhone designers and researchers.

- **Developers**

  Developers who are new to user-centered design will learn how to bring users into their process, from up-front research to iterative design and usability testing. They may use this knowledge to run their own studies or to improve collaboration with designers and user researchers (e.g., internal or outsourced teams). Developers will also appreciate the best practices included throughout the book, particularly those outlined in Part Four, "Refining Your iPhone App."

- **User experience professionals**

  Designers, researchers, and other user experience (UX) professionals will learn how to adapt a variety of user-centered design methods for the iPhone (e.g., how to prototype and test location-based apps). These individuals may be inspired by the range of sketching and prototyping examples in

---

1. iPhone Dev Center, *iPhone Human Interface Guidelines*, http://developer.apple.com/iphone/library/documentation/UserExperience/Conceptual/MobileHIG/Introduction/Introduction.html#//apple_ref/doc/uid/TP40006556-CH1-SW1.

Part Three, "Developing Your App Concept." The best practices outlined in Chapter 9, "User Interface Design," will also be a valuable resource, particularly in the later design stages.

- **Product managers**

  Product managers who work with iPhone designers and developers will find the book valuable on a number of levels. First, product managers may want to participate in up-front user research and usability studies, so it will be helpful for them to learn more about user-centered design methods. Second, product managers may want to understand the rationale behind certain app flow and user interface decisions. References to the HIG and usability principles will provide a common vocabulary and improve team collaboration.

- **QA and customer care**

  Quality assurance (QA) and customer care team members can also benefit from this book. Understanding iPhone task flows and usability issues will help QA folks create test plans and customer care folks create support documentation. Additionally, these individuals may participate in team brainstorming and design review sessions. Having an understanding of the HIG and other iPhone best practices will help them contribute to these sessions.

Definitions

Before we delve into the book details, let's quickly review some design terminology. User experience design and user-centered design are most synonymous with the book's overarching goals:

- **User experience design**

  According to Donald Norman, "User experience design [abbreviated to UX or UE] deals with all aspects of the user's interaction with the product: how it's perceived, learned, and used."[2] In the case of the iPhone, these "aspects" can include everything from the interaction and visual design to the app's performance.

- **User-centered design**

  User-centered design (UCD) gives extensive attention to the needs, wants, and limitations of users at each stage of the design process. This book includes many user-centered design methods, but it's not exclusively dedicated to UCD.

---

2. Donald Norman, *The Invisible Computer: Why Good Products Can Fail, the Personal Computer Is So Complex, and Information Appliances Are the Solution* (MIT Press, 1999).

- **User interface design**

  Strictly defined, user interface (UI) design refers to the design of the "interface" between users and the underlying software. However, in reality, most UI designers think beyond this superficial level to create designs that meet users' needs.

- **Interaction design**

  David Kelley, the founder of IDEO, defines interaction design this way: "Interaction design is using your technical knowledge in order to make it useful for people, to delight someone, to make someone get excited about the new technology they're using."[3] Given its broad scope, this definition is most closely aligned to UX design.

- **Information architecture**

  Information architecture (IA) is the categorization of information into a coherent structure. The term was popularized when vast web sites started cropping up during the dot-com boom. Many people use the term interchangeably with interaction design but the scope is arguably narrower.

What This Book Teaches You

This book provides an end-to-end overview of the user-centered design process, specifically for iPhone applications. After reading this book, you will know how to

- Conduct up-front user and competitive research to inform your app's vision statement, also known as the Production Definition Statement.
- Brainstorm, sketch, and prototype your app concepts. The prototypes covered take many different forms, from simple paper to scripted videos.
- Refine your app's user interface and visual design, using best practices based on established design principles.
- Make your app accessible to individuals with impairments, with specific attention to VoiceOver, the screen-reading software built into the iPhone.
- Localize your app's user experience with an emphasis on language, content, and culture.

While the book is focused on the iPhone and iPod Touch, many of the principles you will learn here can also be applied to user experience design for the iPad. For example, the research methods in Part Two, "Defining Your iPhone App," and sketching and prototyping in Part Three, "Developing Your App Concept," can also be applied to the iPad. Many sections in Part Four, "Refining Your iPhone

---

3. Quoted in Bill Moggridge, *Designing Interactions* (MIT Press, 2007).

App," are also relevant; however, there are some new iPad user interface controls and transitions that are not covered in this book. To learn more, consider reading the *iPad Human Interface Guidelines*.[4]

How This Book Is Organized

This book is organized into four parts, which take you through the process of developing the Product Definition Statement for your app to prototyping and testing your designs with target users. The book concludes with best practices that cover key aspects of the user experience: the user interface, visual design, branding, accessibility, and localization. Case studies are included throughout the book to illustrate how other companies approach user experience design.

- Part One: "iPhone Application and Device Overview"

  The chapters in this part provide the grounding and foundation you'll need for the rest of the book. You'll learn about the *iPhone Human Interface Guidelines*, as well as specifics about the iPhone hardware and what that means for application design teams.

  - Chapter 1: "iPhone Application Overview"

    This chapter reviews applications that clearly fit into Apple's three classic definitions—Productivity, Utility, Immersive—as well as apps that build upon principles set forth in the HIG. The chapter also provides advice on how to choose an application style.

  - Chapter 2: "iPhone Device Overview"

    Here we explore the iPhone device with an emphasis on the technologies and hardware that define the iPhone user experience, such as the multi-touch display, motion sensors, and location information.

- Part Two: "Defining Your iPhone App"

  The chapters in this part discuss the value of up-front research, with an emphasis on user research and competitive research. Case studies are given to illustrate how companies have put these methods into practice.

  - Chapter 3: "Introduction to User Research"

    This chapter reviews a variety of user research methods such as shadowing, field interviews, and diary studies and suggests ways to tailor these methods for your app.

---

4. iPhone Dev Center, *iPad Human Interface Guidelines*, http://developer.apple.com/iphone/library/documentation/General/Conceptual/iPadHIG/Introduction/Introduction.html.

- Chapter 4: "Analyzing User Research"

  This chapter has step-by-step advice on how to effectively analyze your user research. You'll also learn how your findings can be used to create valuable design tools such as personas, scenarios, and user journeys.

- Chapter 5: "Evaluating the Competition"

  Here I introduce a variety of ways to conduct competitive user experience analyses and explain how your findings can help shape your Product Definition Statement.

- Part Three: "Developing Your App Concept"

Once armed with your up-front research findings, you'll learn how to translate these discoveries into design solutions for your own applications. In addition to sketching and prototyping, Part Three explains how to evaluate your app designs through usability testing.

- Chapter 6: "Exploring App Concepts"

  This chapter starts by explaining how to create a design-friendly environment and hold effective brainstorming sessions. The remainder of the chapter discusses ways to illustrate and communicate your early design explorations.

- Chapter 7: "Prototyping App Concepts"

  In this chapter, we look at a variety of iPhone prototyping approaches—paper, software, and video—and I give suggestions for how to choose the best approach for your app.

- Chapter 8: "Usability Testing App Concepts"

  A variety of usability testing methods—ranging from "traditional" tests to the Rapid Iterative Testing and Evaluation (RITE) method and guerrilla testing—are explored in this chapter. It also discusses beta testing and ways to enhance it with traditional usability methods.

- Part Four: "Refining Your iPhone App"

Although user testing is a critical part of the iterative design process, the book also reviews best practices that have emerged in the iPhone space, considering a variety of application styles and categories. Topics covered in Part Four include user interface design, visual design, branding, accessibility, and localization.

- Chapter 9: "User Interface Design"

  In this chapter, I introduce user interface best practices that can be applied across many app types, covering topics such as the first-time user experience, personalization, and feedback.

- Chapter 10: "Visual Design"

  This chapter begins with a discussion of visual structure—grouping, hierarchy, alignment—then explores how color, type, and imagery can reinforce visual structure and create harmonious designs.

- Chapter 11: "Branding and Advertising"

  This chapter focuses on ways to express your brand within your app's design. It also discusses mobile advertising and ways to integrate ads into your designs.

- Chapter 12: "Accessibility and Localization"

  This chapter reviews accessibility on the iPhone, with specific attention to VoiceOver compatibility. Additionally, the chapter explains how to localize the user experience of your app, covering both built-in and custom solutions.

The book wraps up with a look to the future of the iPhone and how its evolution may impact the user experience.

Case Studies

Parts Two through Four contain iPhone app case studies, which show how different companies approach user experience design. Although the methods and tools vary from company to company, these organizations have at least one common goal: the desire to offer the best user experience possible. You'll learn how successful companies manage to deliver on this promise, and you may find ways to bring similar approaches into your own organization.

Here are some highlights from the 13 case studies:

- **Case Study 1: Windspire** (Chapter 4)

  The Windspire app helps users determine whether they have enough wind for a turbine and how much money they could save with one. In the early design phase, the company conducted field research to understand the needs of potential customers.

- **Case Study 2: Aardvark Mobile** (Chapter 4)

  The Aardvark iPhone app lets users ask friends and friends of friends for advice while on the go. The company involved users throughout the design and development process, from early-stage user interviews to late-stage alpha testing.

- **Case Study 3: Foodspotting** (Chapter 6)

  Foodspotting is a visual local guide that helps users find dishes and earn points for spotting foods. Its creators used concept posters, paper prototypes, and simple on-screen prototypes to get user feedback.

- **Case Study 4: Not For Tourists** (Chapter 6)

  NFT helps users navigate and explore cities like a local. Personas and scenarios helped focus the team on the app's core interactions. The scenarios were then used to create storyboards, which were translated into paper and on-screen prototypes.

- **Case Study 5: MUSE** (Chapter 6)

  MUSE is an interface that visualizes your music library as a grid of dots; each dot is a track, and all tracks are playing. It was born out of a desire for a more right-brain tool for navigating music libraries and creating playlists.

- **Case Study 6: Prototyping at Dan4, Inc.** (Chapter 7)

  Dan4 has experimented with many kinds of prototypes—paper, Keynote, video, and more. When choosing a prototype, the company factors in time, budget, and scope but also how the wider development team works and how the prototypes could be reused.

- **Case Study 7: What's Shakin'** (Chapter 7)

  The What's Shakin' app is an egg shaker developed with OpenAL, a cross-platform 3D audio API. Over the course of designing the app, the inventors tested their prototypes with friends, musicians, and local bar patrons.

- **Case Study 8: REALTOR.com** (Chapter 8)

  The REALTOR.com app is for individuals who are searching for a home. After several rounds of sketching and storyboarding, the design team created a paper prototype and conducted usability tests with prospective users.

- **Case Study 9: Sonos** (Chapter 9)

  The Sonos iPhone app lets users access their wireless multi-room music system. In addition to internal design reviews, the team improved their design through usability tests with current Sonos customers, as well as iPhone users who had never heard of Sonos.

- **Case Study 10: FlightTrack** (Chapter 9)

  The FlightTrack app is used to look up and monitor flight information. The initial designs went through several iterations before the team found a solution that effectively addressed their customers' needs.

- **Case Study 11: USA TODAY** (Chapter 10)

   The USA TODAY app lets users access headlines, sports scores, weather, photos, and other content from *USA TODAY*. The final app's design came after dozens of rigorous design explorations.

- **Case Study 12: Voices** (Chapter 10)

   The Voices app lets users record their voice and change it with filters (such as Chipmunk and Fun House). The Voices team paid close attention to app details, adding special touches such as a roving strobe light and quirky background music.

- **Case Study 13: Convertbot** (Chapter 10)

   The Convertbot app is used to convert time, mass, currency, and more. Depth was a really important aspect of the visual design; there were many iterations to make the app "feel" like a real robot.

The case studies appear in the chapters to which they are most applicable and are provided to give you additional insight into how other developers and designers approach iPhone UI design.

NOTE

Some of the case studies have been edited to fit within the confines of the printed book; however, we have compiled full-text versions as a freely download-able PDF file on the book's web site. To download the PDF, go to informit.com/title/9780321699435 and click on the Extras tab.

We'd Like to Hear from You

You can visit our web site and register this book at **informit.com/title/ 9780321699435**. There you will also find any updates, downloads, or errata that might be available for the book.

As the reader of this book, you are our most important critic and commentator. We value your opinion and want to know what we're doing right, what we could do better, what areas you'd like to see us publish in, and any other words of wisdom you're willing to pass our way.

You can email or write me directly to let me know what you did or didn't like about this book, as well as what we can do to make our books better.

When you write, please be sure to include this book's title and the name of the author, as well as your name, phone, and/or email address. I will carefully review your comments and share them with the author and editors who worked on this book.

> **NOTE**
>
> Please note that I cannot help you with technical problems related to the topic of this book, and that because of the high volume of email I receive, I might not be able to reply to every message.

Email: chuck.toporek@pearson.com
Mail: Chuck Toporek
        Senior Acquisitions Editor, Addison-Wesley
        Pearson Education, Inc.
        75 Arlington St., Ste. 300
        Boston, MA 02116 USA

If you would like to contact Suzanne directly, she can be reached via email at **suzanne@iphoneuxreviews.com**.

For more information about our books or conferences, see our web site at **informit.com**.

Acknowledgments

This book would not have been possible without the support of many talented individuals.

The first person who paved the way was Raven Zachary, the president of Small Society. We met when he was presenting on an iPhone panel at the Web 2.0 Summit in the fall of 2008. Raven encouraged me to start my iPhone user experience blog, iPhone UX Reviews (**www.iphoneuxreviews**), which led me to Tim Burks, the founder of the Silicon Valley iPhone Developer Meetup. Tim was impressed with one of my early blog posts and invited me to present at his monthly event. One of my presentations, "An Agile Approach to iPhone Development," caught the attention of Chuck Toporek, who is now my editor at Addison-Wesley.

Chuck recognized the need for a book on the iPhone user experience. At the time there were plenty of iPhone programming books but not one on iPhone app design. Although Chuck and I saw eye to eye on the book's vision, I was uncertain about writing an entire book on the subject. But Chuck, a seasoned editor, had faith in my abilities and encouraged me to submit a book proposal. He has been insightful and supportive throughout the entire process. Other wonderful individuals at Addison-Wesley, including Karen Gettman, Romny French, Julie Nahil, and John Fuller, and copy editor Barbara Wood.

My phenomenal review panel of design and development experts also played a major role in this book. Their comments helped shape the overall organization, direction, and finer details. The design panel included the insightful Marion Buchenau, Nancy Frishberg, Patrick Jean, Christian Rohrer, and Mirjana Spasojevic. The development panel included the esteemed Mike Shields, Brian Arnold, Dan Grover, and August Trometer.

One of my favorite parts of the book is the series of case studies, covering everything from "green" energy to gourmet food. A special thanks to all of the talented designers and developers I interviewed: Alexa Andrzejewski, John Casasanta, Mark Jardine, Ben Kazez, Rob Lambourne, Rusty Mitchell, Margeigh Novotny, Matt Paul, Rob Spiro, Espen Tuft, Bill Westerman, Ilana Westerman, and Cliff Williams. Sincere thanks also go out to George Chen for his insights on mobile advertising, Max Bielenberg for his perspective on prototyping, and Robert Spencer for his advice on gesture interfaces.

Several colleagues and friends informally reviewed my initial proposal and selected chapters. This wonderful group included Nicole Celichowski, Blake Engel, Wendy McKennon, and Rachel Wear. Over the course of writing the book, I reached out to two mailing lists: the Silicon Valley iPhone Developers and IXDA (Interaction Design Association). I appreciate all of the individuals who read and responded to my questions. Also, a big thanks to Michelle Reamy for collaborating with me on user research in the early stages of the book.

My gratitude also goes out to all of the individuals who contributed sketches and photos to the book. In particular, the talented Clive Goodinson was kind enough to create a Pixton comic especially for the book. And Scott Klemmer, Assistant Professor of Computer Science at Stanford, introduced me to a number of his HCI students who were creating iPhone apps. A few of the book's sketches and photos are from current and past Stanford students.

Last but certainly not least, a very special thanks goes out to Lee, who read and commented on the entire manuscript, at least twice! He provided valuable feedback on the content and corrected a semicolon or two.

If I'm missing anyone, I apologize in advance and thank you for your help.

About the Author

Suzanne Ginsburg is a user experience consultant based in San Francisco, California. She helps companies conceptualize and design software. She works with many different kinds of organizations, from established technology companies to small iPhone start-ups.

One of her favorite aspects of user experience design is exploratory user research that helps uncover users' unmet needs and inspires innovation. She has conducted exploratory research for online communities, home networking software, and several iPhone apps. Sketching and prototyping also play a big role in her design process. Suzanne is constantly exploring new approaches and evolving her prototyping toolkit.

Suzanne is most passionate about products that connect people. These projects often involve cross-platform design, which looks at the user experience across the web, desktop, and iPhone. Suzanne is also interested in the field of augmented environments, particularly software that helps users learn about the people, objects, and places around them.

Suzanne is an experienced speaker and writer. She regularly presents at meetups, UX book clubs, and conferences. She also maintains a UX blog, iPhone UX Reviews (www.iphoneuxreviews.com), where she reviews iPhone apps and provides advice on iPhone app design.

Suzanne has a master's degree in user interface design from UC Berkeley's iSchool and an undergraduate degree in business management from Cornell University. You can learn more about Suzanne at Ginsburg Design (www.ginsburg-design. com), her company web site.

Yahoo! Weather; see page 6

CityTransit; see page 10

Mint; see page 12

ProCamera; see page 28

Air Hockey; see page 31

Shazam; see page 34

iPhone Application and Device Overview

Before designing your iPhone app, it's important to acquire a deeper understanding of the *iPhone Human Interface Guidelines*[1] (often referred to as "the HIG"). Apps that follow these guidelines are often easier to learn and use since they are familiar to users.

iPhone designers should also learn about the hardware that defines the iPhone user experience. Having this knowledge may inspire creative app solutions, for example, augmented reality apps combine the compass, GPS, and camera.

The chapters you'll find in Part One are the following:

- Chapter 1, "iPhone Application Overview," discusses the HIG, with an emphasis on the three iPhone application styles: Utility, Productivity, and Immersive.
- Chapter 2, "iPhone Device Overview," switches gears and reviews the iPhone hardware as it relates to the user experience.

By the end of Part One, you should be inspired to create apps that combine the iPhone user interface and hardware in innovative ways.

---

1. iPhone Dev Center, *iPhone Human Interface Guidelines*, http://developer.apple.com/iphone/library/documentation/userexperience/conceptual/mobilehig/Introduction/Introduction.html.

iPhone Application Overview

THE *IPHONE HUMAN INTERFACE GUIDELINES* (HIG) define three different iPhone application styles—Utility, Productivity, and Immersive—to ensure a consistent user experience. These styles are based on visual and behavioral characteristics, the type of information, and the desired user experience.

Before you start designing your iPhone app, read through the application style guidelines included in the HIG. Having a strong grasp of these guidelines will help you understand what's possible within the iPhone framework and how your app may use the framework.

This chapter will review applications that clearly fit into the three classic definitions as well as apps that build upon principles set forth in the HIG. Additionally, the chapter will provide advice on how to choose an application style.

Utility Apps

Utility apps enable users to quickly access a specific type of information or perform a narrowly defined task. Apps well suited to this style include weather, stocks, traffic reports, and sports scores. To illustrate how these apps are used in context, consider the following scenario:

Quick Information Lookup

Sarah, a mother of two young children, owns a MacBook Pro and an iPhone, but she prefers using the iPhone in the morning since it fits into her "flow."

On weekdays she can be found dashing between the kitchen, bathroom, and bedrooms as she gets the children ready for school. She turns to a weather app when deciding what the children should wear that day: Does she need to pack an extra jacket? An umbrella? Sunscreen?

This scenario shows how users with limited time may turn to a Utility app to help them accomplish a task as quickly and efficiently as possible. They may have only a few seconds to spare, so there is no time to create an account, enter preferences, and so on.

Characteristics of most Utility apps include

- Minimal setup
- Simple flows and layouts
- Standard user interface elements

Now, let's take a look at each of those characteristics.

MINIMAL SETUP

Utility apps are typically ready to use when first launched; thus setup processes are unnecessary or kept to a minimum. While this behavior is preferable for any app, it's even more critical for Utility apps since they are used for short periods of time. If setup takes longer than the primary task—and the value of the app remains to be seen—users may abandon the app. For example, the ideal weather app would forgo any registration and immediately detect Sarah's current location (with her permission).

SIMPLE LAYOUTS AND FLOWS

Utility apps have easy-to-scan layouts that include only the most essential information. Users may glance at a Utility app for only a few seconds and won't have time to wade through extraneous data or user interface elements. A good rule of thumb is that the app should still be legible from about five feet away. Also, keeping the task flow succinct allows users to quickly accomplish their goals. For example, Sarah can access weather in two steps: Go to the home screen, and tap on the app icon. When the app opens, she can quickly scan it to see the current temperature and the day's forecast.

STANDARD USER INTERFACE ELEMENTS

Utility apps tend to incorporate the standard user interface elements outlined in the HIG: the selected page, the Info button, and the series of dots that indicate additional pages (FIGURE 1.1). Although custom user interface elements may seem more aesthetically pleasing, they may slow Utility app users down since they are less familiar.

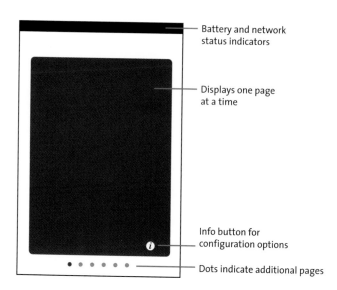

Battery and network status indicators

Displays one page at a time

Info button for configuration options

Dots indicate additional pages

FIGURE 1.1 Utility schematic with standard user interface elements

UTILITY APP TOUR

The Utility application style is predominantly used for "bite-sized" pieces of information like sports scores, stocks, and weather. FIGURES 1.2–1.4 show how ESPN uses the Utility application style for sports scores. Notice how the background color changes depending on the league—NFL, NBA, NHL.

FIGURE 1.2 ESPN NFL scores

FIGURE 1.3 ESPN NBA scores

FIGURE 1.4 ESPN NHL scores

Similarly, the background image of the Yahoo! Weather app changes depending on the time of day and weather conditions. FIGURES 1.5–1.7 show the background images for sun, clouds, and snow; the background color switches to a dark plum shade in the evening. Consider incorporating relevant visual cues into your Utility apps, as they help users process the information more rapidly.

FIGURE 1.5 Yahoo! Weather with sunny graphic

FIGURE 1.6 Yahoo! Weather with cloudy graphic

FIGURE 1.7 Yahoo! Weather with snow flurries graphic

Productivity Apps

Productivity-style apps are more full-featured than Utility apps and encompass everything from social networking to mobile banking. The time spent with these apps varies based on the context and task; for example, a user may spend a few seconds checking for new email messages but several minutes reading the messages. To illustrate how several Productivity apps may be used in context, let's look at another scenario:

Stay Connected

David is a college sophomore majoring in biochemistry. In the morning he wakes to the alarm on his iPhone, which charges on his nightstand while he sleeps.

While lying in bed, he scans through his Facebook and MySpace apps, looking for updates from his friends and family. Next, he checks for emails and reviews his calendar for the day. He relies heavily on the calendar since it has his school and work schedules.

After he has showered and dressed, he walks to the train, often double-checking the train schedule and location using an iPhone app.

This scenario shows how a user may use different Productivity apps to stay connected with family, friends, and work. Although Productivity apps may be used for long durations, the setup process should still be kept to a minimum.

Productivity apps are highly diverse, but most can be identified by the following characteristics:

- Hierarchical structure
- Accelerators and shortcuts

Let's take a look at each of those characteristics.

HIERARCHICAL STRUCTURE

Nearly all Productivity apps have a hierarchical structure composed of list and detail views, as shown in **FIGURE 1.8**. List views contain a scrollable list of items (e.g., text, images, video), as well as tab controls to navigate to other sections of the app. Detail views provide more information on list items and tools related to the items, such as Favorites or Email.

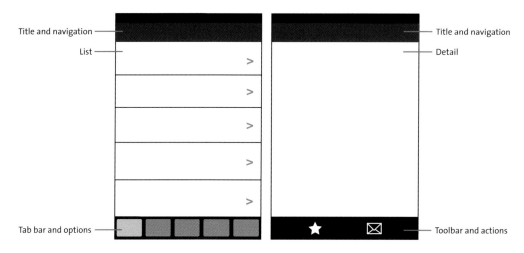

FIGURE 1.8 Productivity schematic including list and detail views

NOTE

Productivity apps such as Facebook and Yelp use a grid to navigate to other sections of the app, not the tab bar. This will be discussed in Chapter 9, "User Interface Design."

ACCELERATORS AND SHORTCUTS

Productivity apps often require text entry for messages, search, or forms. Since these tasks are challenging in a mobile context and further complicated by the small keyboard, your app should minimize text entry as much as possible.

For example, as David views schedules on his way to the train station, it would be much easier if the app could detect his current location and display destinations in a predefined list. When free-form text is required, such as when he is composing an email, the app should provide accelerators to minimize text entry and typing errors. Some of these features, such as spell check, are built into the iOS, and others, such as search suggestions, can be custom-designed. For example, the Google app suggests search matches based on the user's past queries and popular queries on Google, as shown in FIGURE 1.9.

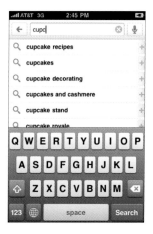

FIGURE 1.9 Google Search suggests search matches as the user types.

PRODUCTIVITY APP TOUR

Although there are thousands of Productivity apps, many of them can be grouped according to high-level user goals. These groupings are helpful when discussing user-centered design, but keep in mind they are not mutually exclusive.

In many cases, one app can help users achieve several related goals. For example, the Foursquare app enables users to "check-in" to places, navigate to places, and connect with members of the Foursquare community (FIGURES 1.10–1.12).

FIGURE 1.10 Foursquare check-in

FIGURE 1.11 Foursquare map

FIGURE 1.12 Foursquare profile

We'll review the following Productivity app groupings:

- Stay connected
- Navigate the world
- Find information
- Transact and track

Stay Connected

One of the primary reasons users have an iPhone is to stay connected with friends, family, and colleagues. Many apps in this category overlap with the iPhone's built-in functionality, specifically the phone, text messaging, and email. Other widely used communication apps, such as Skype, Tweetie, and Facebook, support social networking and collaboration, as shown in FIGURES 1.13–1.15, respectively.

Common features in these apps are

- Message creation
- Message management
- Contact management
- Alerts

FIGURE 1.13 Skype

FIGURE 1.14 Tweetie 2

FIGURE 1.15 Facebook

Navigate the World

With the iPhone's built-in GPS capabilities (iPhone 3G and later) and magnetometer (iPhone 3GS and later), users can locate themselves and get directions to almost anywhere in the world. The Maps application (default on every iPhone device) is perhaps the most widely used mapping app, but there are many niche apps that focus on a particular city, method of transportation, or type of destination, as shown in **FIGURES 1.16–1.18**.

Common features in these apps include

- Maps
- Directions
- The ability to pinpoint your current location
- The ability to find [something] nearby

FIGURE 1.16 Yelp

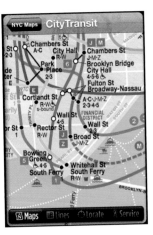

FIGURE 1.17 CityTransit for the New York City subway

FIGURE 1.18 My Starbucks

Find Information

Users turn to information-rich apps for news, entertainment, or reference material. These apps are typically connected to an existing web service but may also download and cache data for offline access. For example, the Dictionary.com app works as a stand-alone app but connects to the Internet for the "Word of the Day" as well as audio pronunciations. FIGURES 1.19–1.21 show a variety of information-rich apps.

Common features in these apps include

- Search
- Bookmarks
- Recents
- Favorites
- Featured content
- Content creation tools (for user-generated content)
- Alerts

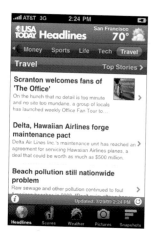

FIGURE 1.19 USA Today

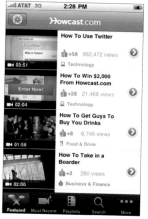

FIGURE 1.20 Howcast

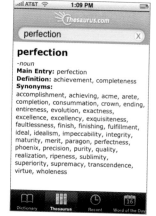

FIGURE 1.21 Thesaurus

Transact and Track

Many banks let their account holders check their account balances and pay bills using dedicated iPhone apps or third-party apps such as Quicken and Mint (FIGURES 1.22–1.23, respectively).

There are also numerous apps for tracking packages (such as FedEx's app, shown in FIGURE 1.24), items for sale, and personal goals such as "to-do" lists, calorie counters, and exercise logs. Alerts, a common feature in this category, can be set for a particular date or milestone.

Common features in these apps are

- Goal settings
- Ability to check current status
- Graphs that show progress over a specified time period
- Alerts

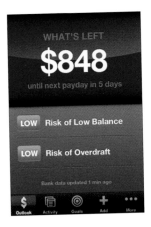

FIGURE 1.22 Quicken

FIGURE 1.23 Mint

FIGURE 1.24 FedEx

The possibilities for Productivity apps are endless. As mentioned earlier in the chapter, the Productivity style may be combined with Utility or Immersive application styles. For example, a video app may offer the ability to *find* videos with the Productivity style but *watch* the videos with the Immersive style. The next section will discuss the Immersive style in more detail.

Immersive Applications

Immersive applications are used to play games, view media, and perform specialized tasks. Users typically turn to games and media apps when they have some downtime, which can last several minutes or several hours. In contrast, task-oriented Immersive apps are used to complete a specific task, such as taking a picture and viewing it via the slideshow. The next scenario illustrates how a task-oriented Immersive app may be used in context.

Perform Specialized Task

About every three or four weeks, Sharon and her assistant receive a new shipment of artwork at her gallery. Although Sharon has a traditional level in the back of the gallery, she finds it easier to use the iHandy app since her iPhone is always in her pocket.

Her assistant typically holds the art in place as Sharon checks its level with iHandy. Afterward, she uses her iPhone to take photos of the art and then views it via the slideshow.

NOTE

While the iHandy Level is listed in the Utility section of the App Store, the application style is Immersive since the app takes over the entire screen and has a fully customized user experience.

Although Immersive applications are relatively diverse, most can be recognized by the following characteristics:

- Focus on the content
- Customized user experience

Let's take a look at each of those characteristics.

FOCUS ON THE CONTENT

Immersive apps may take over the entire screen, including the status bar that displays battery and network information, as is done in many games, movies, books, and musical instruments. This immersion lets users focus exclusively on the primary content. Settings and other controls are within reach, but they may or may not be visible, depending on the app. For example, steering controls are often shown when a driving game is played, but Play and Pause controls are hidden when a movie is being watched. **FIGURES 1.25–1.26** show a YouTube video in these two states.

FIGURE 1.25 YouTube video with controls hidden

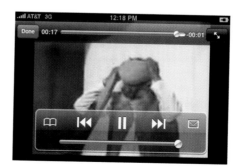

FIGURE 1.26 YouTube video with controls shown

CUSTOMIZED USER EXPERIENCE

Immersive apps often provide a fully customized user experience for which there are no standard controls outlined in the HIG. While it may be tempting to make all of your apps Immersive, be sure the design goals cannot be achieved with a Utility or Productivity application style. As mentioned earlier, incorporating standard controls makes it easier for users to learn and use your app.

IMMERSIVE APP TOUR

Although you can theoretically create any type of app with the Immersive application style, the style is most effective for playing games, viewing media, and performing specialized tasks.

Play a Game

The App Store includes almost every kind of game imaginable: flight simulators, puzzles, role-playing games, board games, and so on. Some of these apps provide simple graphical environments and controls, and others, such as The Sims 3 (FIGURE 1.27), offer multiplayer 3D experiences comparable to stand-alone gaming systems. Another growing area of interest is iPhone games that interact with "real-world" toys such as the Xachi iPhone app (FIGURE 1.28).

FIGURE 1.27 The Sims 3 *(Courtesy of Electronic Arts Inc. © 2009 Electronic Arts Inc. All rights reserved. Used with Permission.)*

FIGURE 1.28 Xachi iPhone app *(Courtesy of Taptic Toys)*

Viewing Media

The most common apps in this category include e-readers and video players, as shown in FIGURES 1.29–1.30. Users often turn to these apps while commuting, traveling, exercising, or during unexpected downtime. The featured content typically takes over the entire user experience, and controls are displayed in an overlay when the user taps the screen. Controls can be customized, but many applications incorporate well-established design patterns, such as Play, Pause, and Stop controls for video content.

FIGURE 1.29 SlingPlayer

FIGURE 1.30 Classics

Performing Specialized Tasks

The Immersive application style is appropriate for many specialized tasks, but a few use cases are popular: sound capture and creation, image creation, and measurement. The iPhone 3GS's built-in Voice Memos app (**FIGURE 1.31**) and More Cowbell (**FIGURE 1.32**) rely heavily on metaphors, but apps such as Convertbot (**FIGURE 1.33**) can sport a customized UI that looks like none of the standard UI controls you'll find in other apps.

FIGURE 1.31 Apple's Voice
Memos app

FIGURE 1.32 More Cowbell
from Maverick Software

FIGURE 1.33 Convertbot
from Tapbots

Choosing an Application Style

Whether you choose one application style or a combination of styles depends on your users' needs, the type of experience you aim to provide, and the app content. As mentioned earlier in the chapter, the Utility style tends to work well with "bite-sized" pieces of information, whereas the Productivity style is appropriate for more structured, hierarchical information. In contrast, the Immersive style is effective when the app has little or no structure, particularly with games.

To illustrate how you might choose an application style, imagine that your app has the following goal: to help users stay physically fit. Technically, all of the application styles can help users achieve this goal (as shown in **FIGURES 1.34–1.36**), but there are notable strengths and weaknesses associated with each style, as shown in **TABLE 1.1**.

The strengths and weaknesses of each application style will vary depending on your design goals, so it's important to evaluate each project accordingly. Also, remember that many apps can contain more than one application style. With the previous exercise app example, it's possible to use the Productivity style along with video instruction (Immersive style) as well as a flattened list of exercises (Utility style).

FIGURE 1.34 A Utility app could have separate screens for each exercise.

FIGURE 1.35 A Productivity app could use the tab bar to access different exercise tools.

FIGURE 1.36 With an Immersive app, users could watch video demos of the exercises being performed.

(Photos in Figures 1.34–1.36 courtesy of Christine Clarkson)

TABLE 1.1 Strengths and Weaknesses of Each Application Style

Style	Strengths	Weaknesses
Utility	Easy to swipe between exercises during a workout.	No overview screen, plus users may get bored with a small set of exercises (ten max).
Productivity	Can provide a full-featured fitness app with many different exercise-related tools.	If lists are too deep, users may find it too difficult to navigate while working out.
Immersive	Video is an established way to simulate a real-world workout experience.	May be challenging to position in the gym; better suited for in-home use.

Summary

Apple's *iPhone Human Interface Guidelines* describe three different application styles: Utility, Productivity, and Immersive:

- Utility apps enable users to quickly access a specific type of information or perform a narrowly defined task.
- Productivity apps are more full-featured than Utility apps and encompass everything from social networking to mobile banking.
- Immersive apps are used to play games, view rich media, and perform specialized tasks.

Choosing an application style depends on your users' needs, the experience you want to provide, and the content. You should evaluate the respective strengths and weaknesses of each type (as shown in **TABLE 1.1**) before determining which application type might be best. Keep in mind that the application styles outlined in the iPhone HIG are just a starting point; apps often include a combination of styles, and many build upon the guidelines to provide differing experiences. ■

iPhone Device Overview

THIS CHAPTER WILL EXPLORE the iPhone device with an emphasis on the

technologies and hardware that define the iPhone user experience, such as

the multi-touch display, motion sensors, and location information.

In addition to explaining what's possible with the device, this chapter will

provide best practices based on recognized usability principles and Apple's

iPhone Human Interface Guidelines. Following these best practices will make

your app easier to use and may expedite its approval in the App Store.

At the conclusion of this chapter, you will understand how the iPhone's

features can improve the user experience of your app. You may also be

inspired to explore and combine these features in innovative ways.

Reviewing the iPhone and iPod Touch's Features

On the surface the iPhone and iPod Touch look like simple devices, but upon closer inspection, their power and sophistication cannot be denied. Inside these devices are capacitive systems that support the multi-touch display as well as other sensors that detect light, motion, and direction. They are also packed with plenty of storage space, RAM, and a GPU (graphical processing unit) capable of rendering OpenGL (Open Graphics Library) graphics. In this chapter, we'll review several features that are central to the user experience of many iPhone apps. Keep in mind that this list is constantly evolving. Visit the Apple web site for the most up-to-date information on both the iPhone[1] and iPod Touch.[2] Features reviewed in this chapter include

The Device Capabilities Framework

One addition you'll find in the iPhone 3.0 SDK and later is the Device Capabilities Framework.[3] This framework enables developers to detect which device the app is being run on, as well as what sort of tasks the device can perform.

For example, let's say that you've built an app for tracking your cycling activity. The app makes use of the GPS and maps, stores start and stop times (and waypoints) along your ride, as well as calculates overall time, distance, and speed. You will want to make sure that the app can run on a particular device. In this case the app will work only on the iPhone 3G and later, since it uses Core Location and MapKit, features not found in the first-gen iPhone or the iPod Touch models. You could run a test when the application begins installation to ensure that the device has GPS capabilities. If it does, the app will install.

While this book won't show you how to use the Device Capabilities Framework in your app, it's nice to know it exists if you are building an app that requires some specific hardware feature. For examples of how to use the Device Capabilities Framework, see *The iPhone Developer's Cookbook, Second Edition*, by Erica Sadun (Addison-Wesley, 2010).

---

1. www.apple.com/iphone/.
2. www.apple.com/ipodtouch/.
3. Mac Dev Center, "UIRequiredDeviceCapabilities," http://developer.apple.com/mac/library/documentation/General/Reference/InfoPlistKeyReference/Articles/iPhoneOSKeys.html#//apple_ref/doc/uid/TP40009252-SW3.

- Multi-touch display
- Light, proximity, and motion sensors
- Location information and compass
- Bluetooth
- Still and video cameras
- Microphone and speaker

Multi-Touch Display

The iPhone's multi-touch display lets users interact with the phone using their fingers. They can achieve these interactions through gestures (specific finger movements) performed on the user interface (**FIGURE 2.1**). Apple has defined a set of gestures for the iOS, but developers can create custom gestures for their applications. The keyboard, an integral part of the iPhone, is also accessed via the multi-touch display.

FIGURE 2.1 A user interacting with the iPhone multi-touch display

Multi-Touch Display Specifications

Screen size: 3.5 inches (diagonal)

Resolution: 480 x 320 at 163ppi (iPhone 3GS and earlier); 960 x 640 at 326ppi (iPhone 4)

Sensor system: The multi-touch display has a capacitive sensing system that contains a protective shield, a capacitive panel, and an LCD screen. When users touch the protective shield, the capacitive panel senses the position and pressure, then transfers the information to the LCD screen below.

NOTE

Activating VoiceOver, an accessibility feature for sight-impaired users, changes the gestures used to control the iPhone.[4] For example, Single Tap is used to read labels associated with UI elements and Double Tap is used to complete actions related to the element. Chapter 12, "Accessibility and Localization," discusses this topic in more detail.

SUPPORTED GESTURES

The iPhone supports eight different gestures, as noted in **TABLE 2.1**. Gesture usage varies based on the application and context. In the Photos app, for example, zoom is enabled in the built-in photo detail view but not when you're looking at a grid of photos. As much as possible, you should keep gestures consistent with those supported by the iOS and outlined in the HIG. Inconsistent gesture usage can lead to frustration, confusion, and usability problems. Users may generate more errors, take longer to complete tasks, and even wonder if your app is broken.

TABLE 2.1 The iPhone's Gestures

Gesture	Action
Tap	To select a control or item (analogous to a single mouse click)
Drag	To scroll or pan (controlled; any direction; slow speed)
Flick	To scroll or pan quickly (less controlled; directional; faster speed)
Swipe	Used in a table-view row to reveal the Delete button
Double Tap	To zoom in and center a block of content or an image
	To zoom out (if already zoomed in)
Pinch Open	To zoom in
Pinch Close	To zoom out
Touch and Hold	In editable text, to display a magnified view for cursor positioning
	Also used to cut/copy, paste, and select text

CUSTOM GESTURES

Apps sometimes include custom gestures to support an interaction not explicitly available in the iOS. Most custom gestures are created for immersive applications such as games, art, or music, as shown in **FIGURES 2.2–2.4**. They may simulate real-world interactions such as swinging a baseball bat or include entirely new gestures created especially for the application. Custom gestures are generally not appropriate for Productivity and Utility applications, as most tasks within these application styles can be accomplished with the gestures supported by the iOS.

If you plan to create custom gestures for your app, read the sidebar "Custom Gesture Tips," contributed by Robert Spencer.

---

4. Apple's "VoiceOver in Depth," www.apple.com/accessibility/voiceover/.

FIGURE 2.2 FlickTunes uses Flick to enable users to play and pause while driving.

FIGURE 2.3 Baseball '09 uses shorter gestures to generate a shorter swing.

(Courtesy of Prof. Robert J. Spencer, Creative Director, Spinfast)

FIGURE 2.4 Cricket uses an upward flicking motion to create a slashing drive.

(Courtesy of Prof. Robert J. Spencer, Creative Director, Spinfast)

KEYBOARD

The multi-touch keyboard can be customized for each task. Common keyboard use cases include search, messaging, filling in forms, and entering URLs.

Search

Search keyboards follow the standard keyboard arrangement for each language, with the exception of a blue Search button that often appears in the Return key position (see **FIGURES 2.5–2.7**). The pane above the keyboard contains the query field(s) and related controls above a transparent gray results area.

FIGURE 2.5 Google Search

FIGURE 2.6 Yelp Search

FIGURE 2.7 NYTimes Search

Custom Gesture Tips

By Robert Spencer, Creative Director, Spinfast

When designing gestures for the iPhone, there are a number of unique issues to consider. The first is what will be hidden under the finger and hand as the gesture is made. This might not be an issue if the screen is static, but when things are moving, as in a game, the finger can obscure quite a large amount of the display. In my sports games I often incorporate this into the challenge of the game, but in many cases the interface might need to be designed to ensure that important information is not obscured.

As in all UI design, I work to simplify gestures as much as possible, but it is important to be very specific about the requirements for a gesture. For example, an "up" gesture may be described as anything that starts at the bottom of the screen and ends at the top, but should an N-shaped gesture be treated differently? It can be algorithmically difficult to differentiate similar gestures even with clarity of the gesture descriptions, so it really pays to be very clear from the start.

It's also important to provide good feedback to users that their gestures are being recognized. For simple gestures such as a Flick to turn pages, it is probably enough to trigger the "page-turning" animation once the gesture is recognized, but for more complex gestures or when finer control is required, I have found that more feedback is required, such as painting a "gesture trail" on the screen. Obviously it is important that the trail match the gesture with very high fidelity and be drawn quickly, so the application needs to reserve sufficient CPU resources to cope with that.

Similarly, it can sometimes be tempting to encourage fast gestures in an effort to capture an indication of velocity, but this approach can easily backfire if the device is unable to detect the gesture correctly. CPU limitations can lead to partial detection of the gesture or sometimes no detection of the touch at all.

Depending upon your application, it might also be necessary to consider other physical issues such as the handedness of the users and the ease of making various gestures (it's easier to slide a finger down glass than straight up, most people hold their devices on an angle, etc.).

In general, however, the focus should be on simplifying the design and iterating on it through testing with real users. The iPhone is capable of detecting very complex gesture systems; the most significant limitation is much more on communicating with the user.

Messaging and Status Updates

Messaging apps typically include the standard keyboard arrangement (as shown in FIGURES 2.8–2.9) with additional "@" and "." buttons when an email address must be entered (FIGURE 2.10). Clicking on the "123" button displays the numeric keyboard, and clicking on the "ABC" button takes the user back to the main keyboard. The layout of the top pane varies among apps. At a minimum, it includes one form field along with Send/Post and Cancel buttons.

FIGURE 2.8 TweetDeck status update

FIGURE 2.9 LinkedIn status update

FIGURE 2.10 NYTimes article shared via email

International Keyboards

The iPhone enables users to add keyboards for other languages and access them via the Globe icon (shown earlier in FIGURES 2.8–2.10 and also in FIGURES 2.11–2.12). Keyboards accessed via the Globe are not necessarily languages; for example, the Genius app enables users to access emoticons as a different language from any app with text entry (FIGURE 2.13).

FIGURE 2.11 Japanese keyboard

FIGURE 2.12 French keyboard

FIGURE 2.13 Emoticon keyboard

Custom Keyboards

Developers can also create custom keyboards, as was done in Parachute Panic, shown in **FIGURE 2.14**. Custom keyboards are most appropriate for games or other creative applications. If you're creating a Productivity or Utility app, in most cases you should stick to the standard keyboard.

FIGURE 2.14 Parachute Panic's custom keyboard

Other Text Entry Features

Other related text entry features include spell check and editing (copy, paste, insert cursor). These features are provided by the iOS, so you don't have to develop custom solutions for your apps. They can be enabled or disabled via the UITextInputTraits Protocol Reference.[5]

Keyboard Usability Issues

Some users find that the keyboard is too small. As a result, they tend to make more text entry mistakes than they would if they were using a traditional keyboard. Although predictive auto-correct can minimize typing errors, it has its own set of usability issues. The control for rejecting recommendations is even smaller than the keyboard keys (**FIGURE 2.15**). Moreover, hurried users are known to accidentally accept an incorrect recommendation. You can try to minimize these issues by incorporating shortcuts and app-specific recommendations as much as possible.

---

5. iPhone Dev Center, "UITextInputTraits," http://developer.apple.com/iphone/library/documentation/UIKit/Reference/UITextInputTraits_Protocol/Reference/UITextInputTraits.html.

FIGURE 2.15 The affordance for rejecting predictive auto-correct recommendations is smaller than the keyboard keys. Note that this is an iPhone standard; this was not introduced by Yelp.

Light, Proximity, and Motion Sensors

In addition to the sensors embedded in the multi-touch display, the iPhone includes light, proximity, and motion sensors that detect the orientation of the device.

AMBIENT LIGHT SENSOR

The ambient light sensor brightens the screen in sunlight and dims the screen in darker conditions. This feature helps the phone conserve display power and improves the battery life. Although the sensor is not currently available through the API, this may change in the future and could lead to innovative context-aware applications.

PROXIMITY SENSOR

The proximity sensor can trigger events when the phone is close to the user's face (about .75 inches away).[6] The built-in phone app uses this sensor to turn off the display when users are talking, thereby preventing them from accidentally interacting with the screen. Similarly, the Google Search app uses the proximity sensor to activate voice search, as shown in **FIGURE 2.16**.

---

6. iPhone Dev Center, "UIDevice Class Reference," http://developer.apple.com/iphone/library/documentation/UIKit/Reference/UIDevice_Class/Reference/UIDevice.html.

FIGURE 2.16 Google Search activates voice search using the proximity sensor.

MOTION SENSOR

One of the most widely used sensors is the accelerometer, also known as a "motion" sensor. The accelerometer can detect the iPhone's orientation and adjust the display accordingly. Perhaps the most practical accelerometer feature is the ability to change the display from portrait to landscape when the iPhone is rotated. Other accelerometer-based features can be found in games, musical instruments, contact management tools, photography tools, e-readers, and pedometers (see **FIGURES 2.17–2.19** for a few examples).

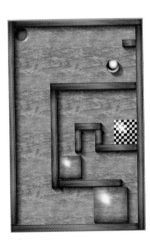

FIGURE 2.17 Marble Maze uses the motion sensor to move the silver ball through the maze.

FIGURE 2.18 Bump uses the accelerometer to detect when the user shakes the device as a way to exchange contact information.

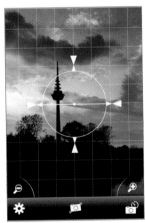

FIGURE 2.19 ProCamera uses the motion sensor to improve image capture.

Location and Compass Information

The iPhone provides location and compass information (at the time of this writing, the compass is available only on the iPhone 3GS and later). Combined, the two features can offer powerful navigation systems.

LOCATION INFORMATION

The iPhone communicates with Earth-orbiting satellites to determine its location. If the phone cannot access any satellites (for example, inside buildings), it uses available WiFi spots or cell towers to help triangulate the iPhone's position. With this location information, users can pinpoint themselves on a map and look up directions to a point of interest (FIGURE 2.20). Although this information is most commonly used for navigation, many social applications (such as Gowalla and Foursquare, FIGURES 2.21–2.22, respectively) also take advantage of this feature.

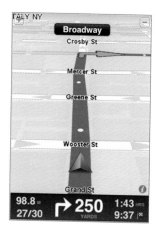

FIGURE 2.20 TomTom

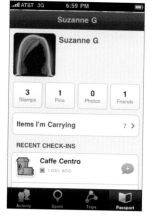

FIGURE 2.21 Gowalla

FIGURE 2.22 Foursquare

COMPASS

The iPhone's compass (technically a magnetometer) can determine the phone's absolute position regardless of its orientation. Three common compass use cases include turn-by-turn navigation, gaming, and augmented reality (AR).

Turn-by-Turn Navigation

Combined with location information, the compass can orient maps correctly and provide turn-by-turn navigation. Apps that leverage these technologies can have features and functionality that rival some in-car navigation systems.

Gaming

With the compass, gaming apps can identify the phone's absolute position and provide more accurate controls. Instead of simply tilting the screen, as is done with the accelerometer, users can physically turn their bodies left and right to control their movements within virtual spaces, as shown in the AirCoaster app in **FIGURE 2.23**.

Augmented Reality

Augmented reality (AR) combines real-world and computer-generated data, taking information retrieval to another level. AR takes full advantage of the iPhone's hardware, including the compass, accelerometer, and GPS location, to show relevant information, typically superimposed on the display, as shown in the Yelp and Starmap apps (see **FIGURES 2.24–2.25**, respectively).

FIGURE 2.23 AirCoaster adapts the coaster ride based on the user's orientation.

FIGURE 2.24 Yelp's Monocle uses augmented reality to overlay business information in the camera viewfinder.

FIGURE 2.25 Starmap lets users get information by pointing at constellations in the night sky.

Bluetooth

NOTE

Bluetooth data transfer is not available on the original iPhone or iPod Touch because of hardware limitations.

Bluetooth enables users to pair their iPhone with compatible headphones or speakers and access audio wirelessly. Additionally, many apps use Bluetooth to transfer data between two iPhone devices when WiFi is slow or not available. Common use cases include exchanging contact information (such as with Bump or LinkedIn) and multiplayer games that leverage GameKit. **FIGURES 2.26–2.28** show a variety of apps that use Bluetooth.

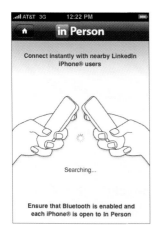

FIGURE 2.26 LinkedIn lets users connect with other LinkedIn members via Bluetooth.

FIGURE 2.27 Bluetooth Photo Share lets users share photos via Bluetooth.

FIGURE 2.28 Air Hockey can be played with a partner over Bluetooth.

Still and Video Cameras

The iPhone enables users to capture and view photos and videos (starting in iOS 3.0, apps can record video on supported devices). The still camera has been integrated into a wide range of photo-related apps that fall into three major groupings:

- Image capture
- Image enhancement
- Image recognition

IMAGE CAPTURE

Apps can use the iPhone's camera API to seamlessly incorporate image capture without leaving the application. For example, a Postman app user may want to capture a photo for a postcard, or a Yelp user may want to capture a photo for a review (**FIGURES 2.29–2.30**).

Of Cameras and iPhones

In addition to offering two separate cameras (front- and rear-facing), the iPhone 4 offers significantly new features over the iPhone 3GS's camera, as noted in this table:

Model	Camera	Video	Graphics Card
iPhone 3GS	3 megapixel with tap-to-focus	30 fps	PowerVR SGX 535
iPhone 4	5 megapixel with tap-to-focus	Rear Camera: 720p HD @ 30 fps Front Camera: Standard VGA @ 30 fps	Apple A4, incorporating the PowerVR SGX 535

FIGURE 2.29 Postman users can use the camera to add a photo to a postcard.

FIGURE 2.30 Yelp users can add photos to reviews.

IMAGE ENHANCEMENT

Image enhancement apps typically combine the iPhone camera with editing tools. For example, Adobe Photoshop's app lets users capture photos and provides several editing options: cropping, exposure, effects (FIGURE 2.31). There are also many apps that specialize in specific types of image enhancements. CameraBag lets users choose a photo and apply effects like "Instant," which looks like a Polaroid, and "1962," which looks like a grainy black-and-white photograph (FIGURE 2.32). ColorSplash, another popular app, converts images to black and white and lets users selectively "paint" colors back into the image (FIGURE 2.33).

FIGURE 2.31 Photoshop   FIGURE 2.32 CameraBag   FIGURE 2.33 ColorSplash

IMAGE RECOGNITION

Image recognition apps use the camera to capture images for analysis. For example, the SnapTell app uses the camera to identify products and look up purchase information (**FIGURE 2.34**), and the USAA app uses the camera to scan checks and deposit them (**FIGURE 2.35**). Future applications may combine the compass and camera, enabling users to point and learn about almost any object in their environment.

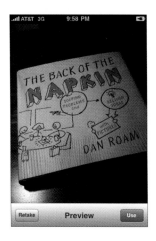

FIGURE 2.3 SnapTell   FIGURE 2.35 USAA

Microphone and Speaker

Microphone- and speaker-related apps (or app features) generally fall into one of five categories:

- Voice and music recorders
- Streaming music services
- Sound recognition and reference tools (e.g., birdcall app)
- Accessibility tools (e.g., voice controls)
- Alerts (e.g., new messages)
- Feedback (e.g., scoring points in games, moving items)

One of the biggest challenges for audio-related apps is how to seamlessly interact with other applications that may already be using the microphone or speaker. For example, what happens if a user is playing music on the iPod while launching a music app? What happens if a user receives a call while using a voice-recording app? These and other design issues will be discussed further in Chapter 9, "User Interface Design." **FIGURES 2.36–2.40** show a variety of audio-related apps.

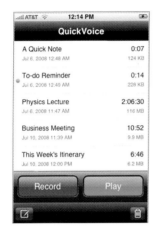

FIGURE 2.36 QuickVoice (voice recorder)

FIGURE 2.37 Pandora (streaming music)

FIGURE 2.38 Shazam (sound recognition)

FIGURE 2.39 iBird Explorer Backyard (sound reference)

FIGURE 2.40 Google Search (Accessibility is one of the defining aspects of voice search.)

Audio Specifications

Frequency response: 20Hz to 20,000Hz

Audio formats supported: AAC (8 to 320 Kbps), Protected AAC (from iTunes Store), HE-AAC, MP3 (8 to 320 Kbps), MP3 VBR, Audible (formats 2, 3, 4, Audible Enhanced Audio, AAX, and AAX+), Apple Lossless, AIFF, and WAV

Summary

The iPhone contains a variety of technologies that enable you to develop compelling user experiences. Some of these, such as the multi-touch display, are relatively new to the mobile space, while others, like the camera, have been built into phones for more than a decade. The iPhone platform has inspired app designers and developers to use these technologies in innovative ways. When designing your own iPhone app, look for ways you can take advantage of the iPhone's unique hardware and software to build new and exciting features. Here are some other things to keep in mind:

- If you run into a user experience challenge, consider ways the hardware combined with software can address the problem; for example, using the camera and image recognition to identify products can reduce text entry errors.

- Before creating custom controls or gestures, make sure the iOS does not have one that meets your needs.

- Remember that certain features are not supported in older versions of the iPhone and iPod Touch. Be sure to communicate this information to users and leverage the Device Capabilities Framework as needed.

In the next part of the book, Part Two, "Defining Your iPhone App," we'll discuss a variety of activities that will help formulate your app vision. ■

Shadowing session; see page 41

Street interview; see page 46

User interview; see page 77

Persona photo; see page 81

Two-by-two diagram; see page 97

Heuristic analysis; see page 102

Defining Your iPhone App

All iPhone app ideas start somewhere—an entrepreneur starts scribbling on some napkins at the local coffee shop, a visionary sketches on a whiteboard, a team has a brainstorm. Regardless of how your app begins, most app ideas are relatively vague at first, perhaps a basic drawing or a few bullet points of things you would like the app to do.

Given the comprehensive suite of tools provided by Apple (Xcode, Interface Builder, and the iPhone Simulator), you may feel compelled to just start coding and then later refine your app's design. While this approach may work for simple apps, most apps can benefit from some level of up-front research and analysis.

Part Two focuses on user research and competitive research since they can lead to qualitative insights and are valuable for both new and existing apps. These are the chapters in Part Two:

- Chapter 3, "Introduction to User Research," will review a variety of user research methods such as shadowing, field interviews, and diary studies.
- Chapter 4, "Analyzing User Research," will then explain how to translate your research findings into valuable design tools.
- Chapter 5, "Evaluating the Competition," will switch gears and focus on competitive analysis.

By the end of Part Two, you should have a solid foundation to begin brainstorming and sketching your app designs.

Introduction to User Research

USER RESEARCH CAN HELP you acquire a deep understanding of your users' needs and how these needs are being met. With this research foundation, you can make informed design decisions throughout the product development process. Moreover, research can reveal opportunities for new apps and inspire innovative solutions that improve upon existing apps.

This chapter will review a variety of user research methods such as shadowing, field interviews, and diary studies and will suggest ways to tailor these methods for your app. After reading this chapter, you should be able to develop and execute a user research plan for your own app. Chapter 4, "Analyzing User Research," will subsequently explain how to interpret user research findings and incorporate them into your app designs.

Common User Research Questions

As you start planning your user research, you may have questions concerning the benefits and costs. Answers to these questions and others are included in this section.

WHAT WILL I LEARN?

The outcome of user research will depend on a number of factors, such as the methods used, the domain explored, and your research goals. Common themes uncovered through early-stage user research include user needs, context of use, perceptions, pain points, language, and norms.

User Needs

At the most basic level, user research will help you understand your users' needs. Questions you may be able to explore include how they do things today, what's important to them, and what needs have not been met. Having this knowledge will help you make both high-level (e.g., overall app concept) and low-level (e.g., screen layout) design decisions.

Context of Use

User research will help you understand the *where*, *why*, and *when* surrounding app usage, such as the environment, time of day, constraints, people involved, motivations, and types of interruptions. For example, FIGURES 3.1–3.2 are from a shadowing session with an art consultant. If a client wants a photo of an art piece or the price converted to another currency, the consultant can slide her iPhone out of her pocket and take care of it on the spot. Rushing off to get her digital SLR camera or calculator would disrupt the sale. Knowing this type of contextual information may help you make design decisions for your own app and may reveal opportunities for innovation.

Perceptions

User research can surface perception-related issues that may prevent users from adopting or using your app. For example, research may indicate that users perceive mobile banking as insecure. As a result, you may want to develop an overall education strategy as part of the app's marketing plan to put users at ease, or emphasize security measures more prominently in your design.

Pain Points

User research often uncovers pain points in the participants' current workflow. Pain points may cause users to completely abandon an app or prompt them to create work-arounds. For example, the art consultant in **FIGURE 3.1** often edits photos before sending them to clients. She tried a few iPhone editing apps, but the features were not comprehensive. One of the apps focused on cropping, another on effects, and so on. As a result, she now downloads photos to her laptop and works on them in Photoshop or iPhoto when she needs to make edits. Insights such as these can present opportunities to improve usability and innovate.

FIGURE 3.1 How an art consultant uses her iPhone to capture images of artwork

FIGURE 3.2 How an art consultant uses her iPhone to convert art prices into foreign currencies

Language and Nomenclature

Learning the language and nomenclature used within a particular domain may influence your app design. For example, if you were designing an app for looking up baseball scores, it would be important to know that scores are tracked according to runs, not points. In contrast, using the term *points* would be appropriate for tracking football or basketball scores. As your design progresses, insights such as these may also impact the tone and voice within your app's user interface.

Norms

Understanding the norms (typical social behaviors) within a user group or domain can also be valuable. User research can reveal which norms to incorporate and what practices to avoid when designing an app. As with language, this knowledge is especially useful for specialized domains. Norms to consider exploring may pertain to workflow, privacy, and more.

For example, a few years ago I worked on a project for one of San Francisco's charter schools. The norms were very different from those of the regular public schools. Students wore uniforms, had longer school days (plus Saturdays and summers), and were thinking about college as early as the fifth grade. If I were to go back and design an app for this school, it would be important to take these norms into account.

HOW IS UP-FRONT USER RESEARCH DIFFERENT FROM USABILITY RESEARCH?

Up-front user research typically informs the product requirements as well as the design. In contrast, usability research generally occurs *after* the product requirements have been defined and an initial design has been established (see Chapter 8, "Usability-Testing App Concepts").

Another way to make this distinction is that up-front research helps answer the question "What should we design?" whereas usability research later asks, "Did we design it right?" and "What do we need to change?"

HOW MUCH IS THIS GOING TO COST ME?

Many companies are reluctant to assign resources when up-front research is recommended. They worry that the research will take several months and cost thousands of dollars. If you outsource a worldwide study with dozens of participants, it's true; your study can cost tens of thousands of dollars. However, small-scale studies may be completed within a two-week time frame and can produce rich insights. If the interviews and analysis are done by your internal team, the only extra costs are travel time and participant payments (approximately $100 per participant for 1.5 hours, but it depends on the participants' skill set and the interview duration). Even travel costs can be eliminated if videoconferencing is a viable alternative.

Two weeks may seem like a long time when a project is starting out, but changing the design after development will almost always take longer and cost more money. If you discover significant design problems after launch, you may need to rewrite large portions of your application. Moreover, you have one chance to make a first impression. A few bad reviews out of the gate can cripple future sales of your app, particularly when there are other apps out there to choose from. In addition, up-front user research explores users' behaviors and motivations, which change slowly; thus, research can be a valuable long-term reference.

TWO WEEKS IS STILL TOO LONG; WHAT ARE MY ALTERNATIVES?

As discussed at various points throughout this chapter, there are ways to simplify user research if you're constrained by time and resources. For example, to shorten the recruiting time, you can search for participants through your friends and family network. Instead of eight participants, you could limit the study to four participants. Including more participants and recruiting outside your network would be better, but some research is better than no research at all. Finally, you don't have to use complicated video-recording setups; notes and photos are sufficient.

Shadowing and User Interviews

This section introduces shadowing as well as alternative types of user interviews. The approach you choose will depend on the type of app, your research goals, and your budget (time and money).

SHADOWING

Shadowing involves the researcher following participants over a certain period of time and recording observations. In contrast to the other methods described in this chapter, the data may be more reliable since observations are captured in situ (in context). This is often referred to as a "sit back" technique, where the researcher may probe with some questions but it's generally undirected. The researcher simply follows participants as they go about their activities.

Context and Duration

Shadowing sessions can take one hour or up to a full day. The context and duration will vary depending on the complexity of the app and your research goals. Imagine that you want to develop an app that enables parents to easily record and share their newborn's special moments. Given that the app may be used in a variety of contexts throughout the day, a full day of observations may be required to get an adequate understanding of the parents' needs. The researcher may start at home, then accompany the parents as they run errands and take the newborn to activities. In contrast, the scope would be much narrower if you were developing an app for museum visitors to learn about museum artwork. Participants could be shadowed in the museum for the duration of their visit.

Privacy

Shadowing for long periods of time can raise some privacy issues for the person being shadowed. It's important for you to establish a rapport with participants before shadowing them. A simple phone call or an informal visit can make a huge difference in making participants comfortable and open during the shadowing.

In addition, participants may need time to attend to their personal affairs in private, or they may request that certain situations not be recorded. Providing participants with shadowing "time-outs" can help alleviate these issues.[1] Researchers may want to informally meet with participants ahead of time to review a privacy policy and address any concerns. Getting permission to publish findings and photos should also be handled in advance of the study. Here is an example of such a permission form, which may also be used for the other interview types in this section:

Permission to Use Comments and Photographs

Subject: [*Brief study description goes here.*]

I grant to [*your company name*] the right to use my comments and take photographs of me and my property in connection with the above-identified subject. I authorize [*your company name*], its assigns, and transferees to copyright, use, and publish the same in print and/or electronically.

I agree that [*your company name*] may use these comments and photographs without my name and for any lawful purpose, including, for example, such purposes as publication/book content, publicity, illustration, advertising, and web content.

I understand I will be paid [*payment amount*] in return for my participation in the above-identified subject.

I have read and understand the above:

Signature: _____

Printed name: _____   Date: _____

Address: _____

_____

---

1. Jan Blom, Jan Chipchase, and Jaakko Lehikoinen, "Contextual and Cultural Challenges for User Mobility Research," *Communications of the ACM* 48, no. 7 (2004).

FIELD INTERVIEWS

Field interviews, derived from anthropological research techniques, involve one-on-one sessions with participants in their natural environments. Interviews are semi-structured, meaning the researcher prepares questions in advance but adjusts the script based on a participant's responses.

In contrast to shadowing, which may involve traveling with participants over the course of an entire day, field interviews typically occur in one place for about one to two hours, excluding travel. Given the limited context and time frame of field interviews, researchers may choose to supplement them with a diary study. Diary studies, discussed later in this chapter, can provide more insight into the participant's context over a much longer period of time.

Context

Choosing one place for a mobile-oriented interview can be a challenge. Ideally, the interview should occur where the app will be used most often, providing researchers with a better understanding of the context of use. For example, with the museum visitor app, holding interviews at the museum would enable participants to easily refer to exhibit information and explain what works or doesn't work well for them. If the interviews were held at an off-site location, it would be harder to reference such information and understand the museum context. Additionally, it would require the users to recall behaviors or memories about the app, which can be less reliable than studying their app usage in context.

Apps that don't have a clear location associated with them may benefit from a diary study combined with a field interview. For example, the diary for new parents may indicate that they spend most of their time at home, at a friend's house, or at the playground. The interview could be held at their home, but the researcher can probe into their activities at the other locations.

INTERVIEWS WITH SUBJECT MATTER EXPERTS

Subject matter interviews typically imply that the participant is the "master" and the researcher the "apprentice." For example, let's say you want to design an app to help users pair a wine with their dinner. Interviewing sommeliers and wine shop owners, as well as some local chefs, would help you understand how experts recommend wine to a customer. These insights can then be used to generate alternative design ideas for your app.

PHONE INTERVIEWS

There is nothing like meeting face-to-face with your experts, but it may not always be possible because of financial or time constraints. Phone interviews are a viable alternative, as are videoconferencing services such as iChat, Skype (**www.skype .com**), or Cisco's WebEx (**www.webex.com**). These alternatives are particularly cost-effective for researchers who want to interview participants in dispersed geographical locations. As with many of the methods previously described, phone interviews may not adequately capture context and behaviors over longer stretches of time, so you may consider pairing phone interviews with a diary study.

STREET INTERVIEWS

In some cases, app creators may find that formal interviewing and recruiting methods are not appropriate for their app. Imagine that you want to create a fashion app that shows what people in your city are wearing and where those items can be purchased. With street interviews, the researcher could stop locals (as shown in **FIGURE 3.3**, an interview conducted in Tokyo) and ask about their approach to fashion, where they shop, and how they put their outfits together. Keep in mind that this method is not suitable for most apps, and people on the street may not respond well to a stranger with a video camera. Having a business card, dressing appropriately, and offering modest incentives (such as a coupon code for your app) can help garner trust and interest.

FIGURE 3.3 Street interview in Tokyo, Japan *(Courtesy of Brandon Reierson Photography)*

FOCUS GROUPS

Focus groups typically involve six to ten participants who are asked to share their thoughts about a particular idea or product. The sessions are moderated by a leader who introduces the topic and encourages conversation around specific themes (hence the term *focus*).

Participant feedback may be used to shape product direction, develop a marketing plan, or create advertising campaigns. Focus groups have their merits, but they are not frequently used in the user-centered design process. One of the main criticisms is that participants are heavily influenced by the other members in the group. In addition, in contrast to observational methods, focus groups rely on what people *say* they do, not what they *actually* do in a given situation. However, focus group conversations can be helpful in a generative way, in that the creative brainstorming among well-selected participants can open your eyes to new possibilities.

Since focus groups are based on self-reported data, they are better suited to marketing questions, such as how people would respond to a particular marketing message and why.

Documenting User Interviews

Shadowing and user interviews can be documented in a variety of ways. Some combination of notes, photos, and audio or video is most common.

NOTES

The format of your notes (handwritten or typed verbatim) is typically influenced by the study goals, note taker preference, and resources available. For example, when facilitating on my own, I tend to take typed verbatim notes. However, if a note taker is responsible for verbatim notes, I'll take handwritten notes. Afterward, I'll use the verbatim notes for user quotes and to make sure I didn't miss anything important. More information on these options is discussed next.

Handwritten Notes

Handwritten notes are a good option if verbatim user quotes are not required. They are also effective if a laptop or camera is too intrusive or difficult to use in the study context (e.g., on a commuter train). If you need word-for-word quotes but want something less intrusive, you could pair handwritten notes with an audio recording.

Verbatim Notes

Typed verbatim notes (also known as "approximate" transcripts) are a nice alternative since they contain valuable details and quotes without the extra noise included in an audio or video transcript. If you go with this approach, instruct the note taker to focus on the interview dialogue. The note taker should not be interpreting and adding commentary along the way—interpretation happens after the session.

STILL CAMERA

Researchers should always bring a still camera to user interviews. It is valuable for capturing the participant's computer setup and context of use. Also, I often take an informal participant portrait so I can associate a face with the findings. This photo can be added to the "participant profile," which will be discussed in the next chapter. A high-end camera is not necessary; an inexpensive point-and-shoot digital camera with ample storage should be fine.

AUDIO

As mentioned earlier, audio is an effective backup, especially if you have hand-written notes. You may also want to use audio to reinforce a particular finding or extract a user quote word for word. If you choose to capture audio, make sure your recorder has a good microphone and there's little background noise. For a recent iPhone study, I used a voice-recording app to document a user interview. Halfway through the session, a construction team started jackhammering the sidewalk, right next to the window. Parts of the session were audible, but I mostly had to rely on my notes.

VIDEO

Video is the most comprehensive method for capturing participant behaviors, but it can be impractical when your participant is on the go. For example:

- It's often difficult to get the right angle when traveling in cramped vehicles or other forms of transportation.
- Equipment can be purchased to make the process easier, but the time required to switch or adjust cameras may outweigh the benefits.
- Video recording in a public place may be restricted for security or privacy reasons.
- The amount of time required to analyze video (assume three hours of analysis for every hour of tape) may be too prohibitive.

Because of these limitations, you may decide that note taking and still photos are sufficient. Having said that, if the researcher wants to share findings with a larger team, video or audio can make the results appear more credible and tangible. Also, if you are working alone, having video can relieve you from detailed note taking and allow you to focus on the participant.

Regardless of the medium chosen, the researcher should ask for permission to record the session. Standard templates are available for these types of release forms from the Society for Technical Communication.[2]

Diary Studies

Diary studies shift the burden of data collection onto the participant. Instead of the researcher shadowing participants for an entire day, participants record their activities over the course of one or more days. Consider using a diary study under the following circumstances:

- Participants can easily capture the kind of data you are seeking.
- You need to collect data over a long period of time because the app may be used intermittently.
- You need a nonintrusive way to gather information.

Although this approach can lead to valuable insights, there are some limitations:

- First, participants may not record activities that seem trivial to them but might be of interest to researchers. For example, one participant was so used to downloading her photos to her computer for editing that she omitted this work-around from her diary. It was only when I interviewed her in person that I learned about this extra step.
- Second, since participants are mobile, stopping to document their activities could be disruptive or impractical, such as when they are driving or out to dinner.
- Third, diary studies are less effective at ascertaining the *how* and *why* behind behaviors.

Because of these limitations, researchers often combine diary studies with other methods such as field interviews.

---

2. Society for Technical Communication, "Usability Toolkit," www.stcsig.org/usability/resources/toolkit/toolkit.html.

Duration

Diary study participants may be asked to record their activities for anywhere from a few days up to a month, depending on the app and design goals. For example, if you're developing an app to help people who commute on public transportation, you might ask participants to record their activities for one work week and focus their entries on commuting hours. In contrast, an app for museum visitors may require an entry only for the day of their visit.

Documentation

Diary study participants should be provided with some form of structured input in order to generate the diary content. This "diary entry" form could be done on paper or in digital form and typically captures the specific research areas of interest. For example, the researcher probably doesn't need to know what the participant ate for dinner, but it would be interesting to know that the participant used his or her iPhone to find a takeout menu and call the restaurant.

Here are some sample diary entry questions:

- What was the activity?
- Why did you take this action?
- Where did the activity take place?
- How long did the activity take?
- Were you with anyone?

Mobile researchers have experimented with a variety of diary entry tools over the years, including voice mail, SMS (Short Message Service), photos,[3] and the classic pen and paper. Voice mail enables participants to easily record events while on the go, but they may feel awkward if they need to record an entry in a public place. In the absence of voice-to-text software (such as Dragon Dictation[4]), this approach also requires additional logging by the researcher. SMS alleviates any public awkwardness, but the brevity of the medium can lead to cryptic messages with unfamiliar shorthand notations and lost information. Creating a private Twitter account is another option worth pursuing.

In an effort to address these limitations, researchers at Stanford University experimented with a hybrid approach.[5] They found that diary participants provided

---

3. Rachel Hinman, Mirjana Spasojevic, and Pekko Isomursu, "They Call It 'Surfing' for a Reason: Identifying Mobile Internet Needs through PC Deprivation," *CHI* (2008).
4. Dragon Dictation for iPhone, http://itunes.apple.com/us/app/dragon-dictation/id341446764?mt=8.
5. Joel Brandt, Noah Weiss, and Scott R. Klemmer, "txt 4 l8r: Lowering the Burden for Diary Studies under Mobile Conditions," *CHI* (2007).

more frequent and descriptive diary entries when given the opportunity to enter a snippet in situ and then expand on it later that day using a web-based form.

Ginsburg Design, in collaboration with Reamy Research and Design, took a similar approach for a study exploring overall iPhone usage. Participants used the iPhone's built-in Notepad instead of SMS, and details on the snippets were elicited in person the day after the entries were submitted. This approach enabled the researcher to probe deeper into the entries but required more one-on-one time with participants. **TABLE 3.1** includes the entries from one participant.

TABLE 3.1 Diary Study Entries and Field Interview Clarifications

Activity Recorded in Notepad	Field Interview Clarification	Implications
7am checked weather n emls	Sarah checks her email and weather while getting her kids ready in the morning. She wishes that the weather app let her enter her zip code since San Francisco has microclimates. She tried AccuWeather, but it was too difficult so she deleted it.	Setup should be easy or else user may abandon app.
740 fb and calendar realck	"fb" is Facebook. She likes to check Facebook during her downtime. She loves the app but gets frustrated since many of the web features don't work on the phone.	Users may expect apps to have most features found in their web counterparts; features should be prioritized accordingly.
835 ck time driving		
919 Katy call gym	Sarah's friend Katy called while she was at the gym.	
Txt Katy	She prefers to text while working out since it's less disruptive at the gym.	It would be helpful if users could easily share their communication preference based on their context.
Txt diana working out 1030		
Txt valerie working out		
Chk vmail 1045		
Call valerie 1050		
Calc $ for sitter 110	She uses the built-in calculator to figure out what to pay the babysitter.	Preset calculations could help someone like Sarah.
Chk eml and fb 145		
Pic of the yard 200 sunny		
245 chk eml, added contact, fb break	She wishes it were easier to organize contacts on her phone.	Users may expect apps to behave similarly to their desktop counterparts.

continues

TABLE 3.1 Diary Study Entries and Field Interview Clarifications *(continued)*

Activity Recorded in Notepad	Field Interview Clarification	Implications
300 txt Nic		
Weather 400 going to pickup max		
Got gas car wash eml ck kporg 5 pm	"kporg" is Kaiser Permanente. She uses their web site often but finds it difficult to navigate on her phone. She said, "Zooming drives me crazy."	There is an opportunity for companies like Kaiser to create iPhone apps; it's important to promote the app when users visit the web site via Safari.
Call for annivsitter 5		
Weather on way to dinner 615		
900 txt Nic for SFO arrival		
1015 eml chk weather for nxt day		

SURVEYS

All of the methods previously discussed are based on small sample sizes, which are perfectly adequate for yielding many types of insights about what to build and why. In some cases, however, you may have questions that could benefit from a large number of respondents. Surveys are the most widely used and effective way to reach a large audience and elicit their preferences. Common high-level goals addressed in user surveys include these:

- Assess interest in proposed app features (e.g., Does the user need a camera or location-based services?).
- Assess preference for an overall app direction (e.g., Does the app suit the users' needs?).
- Gather demographic and technographic[6] information.
- Quantify qualitative research findings (useful if you are making critical decisions based on qualitative data and would like to understand the pervasiveness of the findings).

Survey Tools

With the proliferation of low-cost web-based services, such as SurveyMonkey (www.surveymonkey.com), Zoomerang (www.zoomerang.com), and Google Docs (http://docs.google.com), researchers have easy access to a wide range of

---

6. Information on consumer ownership, use, and attitudes toward technology. The concept and technique were first introduced in 1985 by Dr. Edward Forrest in a study of VCR users and later elaborated upon in the article "Segmenting VCR Owners," published in the *Journal of Advertising Research* 28, no.2 (April/ May 1988), 38.

survey creation and analysis tools. Although it may seem trivial to put up a survey, formulating an effective survey with appropriate questions and logic takes time. Moreover, analyzing the data can be even more time-consuming, depending on your research goals. App creators who need more sophisticated analyses may want to work with someone who is well versed in advanced statistics and software, such as SPSS (www.spss.com/statistics).

Caveats

One of the downsides of surveys is that the data is attitudinal and may not accurately predict user behaviors. For example, survey participants may express interest in a particular feature, but there is no guarantee that they will actually use that feature in your app. Because of these limitations, surveys should complement other qualitative user research methods (e.g., field interviews) that can capture user motivations and behaviors.

In addition, surveys do not allow researchers to measure or understand issues that respondents are not really aware of or cannot recognize in their own experience. Many usability problems fall into this category, as do user needs that people have but do not realize. This means that surveys provide a useful piece of the puzzle but not a complete picture.

Choosing a Research Method

Most iPhone apps will benefit from a combination of user research methods; the optimal mix depends greatly on the app, your research goals, and the design phase. As we'll discuss, apps in the very early stages typically focus on observational methods, whereas later-stage apps may include observational methods as well as prototypes.

NO CLEAR APP CONCEPT

Developers without a clear concept may conduct user research to help uncover app opportunities. Even though the company has not formulated an app concept, there should be a well-defined audience or problem space. For example, young children often use their parents' iPhones for taking photos and playing games. Shadowing these parents is one way a researcher could uncover other app opportunities for this demographic. Similarly, a developer may be interested in offering an iPhone solution for small-business owners. To help build that app, the developer should interview a group of small-business owners to better understand their needs.

ROUGH APP CONCEPT

Developers with a rough app concept can use a variety of user research methods. In addition to shadowing and field studies, they may find it beneficial to introduce early app sketches to prospective users. These sketches can be presented in a demo format, where the researcher walks through the sketches and gathers feedback on the ideas. If the concept is not fleshed out at the user interface level, another option is to create a concept video that gives prospective users a feel for the idea. Concept videos are discussed in more detail in Chapter 7, "Prototyping App Concepts." You can see an example of one for a caregiver app online.[7]

EXISTING APP

If you already have an app in the App Store, you should consider doing some additional research before designing a significant new feature or embarking on a redesign. Regardless of the project scope, the research typically incorporates the existing app. For example, it would be valuable to shadow existing customers as they use your iPhone app, or to have them keep a log of their app usage over a specified period of time. The duration will depend on the type of app; for example, a commuter app may require a week of entries, whereas a museum app may need only an afternoon of entries.

Alternatively, you may consider running a benchmark usability study for your app. In such a study you would provide users with a predefined set of tasks and measure their performance. The results of the study may help identify which areas of your app could be improved in a subsequent redesign. More information on usability studies is provided in Chapter 8, "Usability-Testing App Concepts." Another option is to benchmark your app against one of your competitors' apps as discussed in Chapter 5, "Evaluating the Competition."

As part of your benchmark usability study, you should consider giving the participants a survey to assess their interest in prospective app features. The information you gather at this stage can be beneficial for getting a broad reading on prospective features, which you may then want to examine more closely with qualitative research.

Planning Your Research

Regardless of which method (or *methods*) you choose, it's important to create a research plan. Planning may seem like a formality, especially when you have a small team, but researchers need to keep track of many details as they prepare for

---

7. Eldia concept video, www.vimeo.com/2420799.

a study. The plan will help manage all of these details and ensure that your team members are on the same page with regard to the goals and approach. The information for your plan can be gathered at a research kickoff meeting with stakeholders (set aside approximately 1 to 1.5 hours, depending on the study scope). Common elements of a user research plan include

- Purpose and objective
- Study dates
- User profiles
- Methods
- Questions for research
- Roles
- Equipment
- Report contents

Let's take a look at each of these elements.

PURPOSE AND OBJECTIVE

The most important thing you should do as part of your research plan is to write down the purpose of your research along with your objectives. Having the objective in written form and checking your list of questions against it will help keep your study focused and streamlined.

Here are some examples based on the product stages discussed in the previous section:

Example 1: Up-front research

Purpose: Learn how parents currently capture their newborn's special moments.

Objective: Identify how the iPhone can make their approach easier and more enjoyable.

Example 2: During design and development

Purpose: Learn how parents currently capture their newborn's special moments, and get feedback on early iPhone app concepts.

Objective: Uncover additional iPhone opportunities and improve upon early concept sketches.

Example 3: After design and development

Purpose: Learn how parents capture their newborn's special moments with [*your app name*].

Objective: Uncover additional iPhone opportunities and improve upon the existing app.

Having a well-crafted purpose and objective will make it easier to complete the rest of your study planning. In particular, the user profile, method, and questions for research will be largely influenced by the study purpose and objective.

STUDY DATES

Communicating the study dates is important for a variety reasons:

- Setting the dates forces you to start recruiting participants for the study.
- It enables your team members to block out time in their schedules so they can participate.
- If you're considering including a working version of your app, you'll want the designers and developers to plan accordingly (e.g., the timing of the study may allow you to include a new idea they are working on).

As you figure out the study dates, be realistic with regard to the number of user interviews you can complete in one day. You may be traveling to unfamiliar places, interviews can run over because of events beyond your control, and you may find it valuable to debrief with your team between sessions as well as at the end of the day. Plus you'll need to eat at some point.

USER PROFILES

Having well-defined user profiles is perhaps the most important aspect of user research. Consider the profile of an app for parents with newborn children. While this is a good starting point, we can further clarify the profile:

- Can single parents participate?
- What if both parents are back at work; should the nanny or other caregiver participate?
- What if the newborn has siblings; is it important to understand how parents capture their special moments as well?

As you can see, even seemingly straightforward profiles can raise questions that should be addressed in advance. While each study will have a unique user profile (and potentially more than one profile), some user aspects you may want to consider are demographics, background, and technology experience.

Demographics

- **Age.** Are you focusing on specific age groups or are you seeking a mix?
- **Gender.** Is a 50/50 target mix appropriate or another ratio? For example, for the study with newborn parents you may want an equal proportion of the parents and the children to be male and female.
- **Location.** Where should they be located? Only in the United States? Certain states or provinces? City versus suburbs versus rural?

Background

- **Profession.** Are you seeking certain professions (e.g., doctors, lawyers, skilled trades)? Are there professions you want to avoid (e.g., individuals with too much technical or industry expertise)?
- **Education.** Do you want to include a mix of education levels (e.g., high school, college, master's, PhDs)?

Technology Experience

- **The iPhone.** Are new iPhone owners acceptable? How many apps must they have downloaded to their iPhone?
- **Your app.** If you have an app in the App Store, what kind of experience should participants have, or not have, with it? Is it okay if they've used a competitor's app?
- **In general.** Do you want novice users? Sophisticated users? A mix?

NOTE

In some cases it may be appropriate to include one or two "edge case" users who may inspire or push the design direction. For example, this might be effective if you were trying to change how a particular problem is addressed today.

METHODS

Your research plan should specify what methods you will use in your study: shadowing, field interviews, diaries, surveys, and so on. If your team does not have an understanding of these methods, take time to explain them *before* the user research.

You may want to consider having a training session for colleagues who may attend the user research and directly interact with participants. Having a colleague question your approach during a session will make your team look unprofessional; having a colleague question your approach after a session could compromise your hard work. If your team doesn't support your research, it's less likely that the findings will make their way into the actual product.

QUESTIONS FOR RESEARCH

In addition to stating the high-level purpose and objective of the study, it's helpful to list the questions you want to explore when you meet with participants. These questions will help formulate and guide your discussion during the user interviews. Early-stage user research questions typically focus on user needs, but the questions can also be specific to your iPhone app. Consider the purpose and objectives for an iPhone app for parents who want to capture their newborn's special moments. Some questions you might want to ask for such an app could include these:

NOTE

There are often ten or more high-level questions; the previous questions are only an example.

- What types of events do parents typically want to capture?
- What kind of technology do they use?
- What challenges do they face?

ROLES

If you plan to share responsibilities with your colleagues, spend some time clarifying the roles of each researcher. In the case of field interviews, there are generally no more than four people involved: the participant, the interviewer, the note taker, and the observer/videographer. If you have more than three team members, their presence could overwhelm the participant and you might not get the results you're looking for.

TIP

Companies with larger teams may consider taking turns in the observer or videographer role.

If your team has a dedicated researcher, that person will typically lead the user interviews. Alternatively, you should assign the task of interviewing to the team member with the best interviewing and communication skills. Here are some characteristics of skilled user interviewers:

- **Patience.** Participants may take some time to describe a situation, so you need someone who can sit there and patiently wait while people tell their stories.
- **Assertiveness.** Participants may go off on tangents and need to be led back to the topic. If the person strays from answering the question, the interviewer needs the ability to assess the situation and get the participant back on track.
- **Empathy.** Participants may be sharing personal situations; researchers should be empathetic. For example, if a woman starts talking about how her first child was in a neonatal intensive care unit for a few weeks and how she wishes she'd had an app to document that experience, you need to let her talk, and as she does, her emotions related to that experience will certainly come to the surface.

- **Flexibility.** Participants may take the researcher down new and fascinating paths. While this might require more time, you could hit a watershed moment for your app that helps set it apart from everything else in the App Store.

If none of your team members have these skills, you should hire a trained user researcher to conduct the interviews.

Shadowing studies are generally more complicated when it comes to team roles. As mentioned earlier in the chapter, you may be following individuals around for a full day, traveling with them to work, joining them on public transportation, and so on. Instead of three team members, you should have no more than two team members—the interviewer and the note taker—shadow a person throughout the day. In some cases you'll find that one person can effectively get the job done, and it's always best to ask the person being followed what's more comfortable.

EQUIPMENT

Your user research plan should describe what type of equipment and/or software is needed for the study. Christian Rohrer, Director of User Experience at Move Inc., includes the following checklist in his field study course:

- A schedule of the sessions
- Mobile phone numbers for participants and observers
- Participants' addresses (ideally already added to your iPhone's Address Book or in-car GPS)
- Timekeeping device (your iPhone should be sufficient)
- Forms (consent, confidentiality/NDA)
- Discussion guide (enough copies for observers)
- Data collection sheets and session debrief template
- Recording media (paper, pens, cameras, audio/video recorders, tripod)
- Power (batteries, extension cords, power strips, chargers)
- Bags and folders (to carry documents and artifacts)
- Incentives and gifts
- Business card, photo ID, company badge (if applicable)
- Allergy medicine (in case participant has pets and you're allergic)
- Water and snacks

In addition to creating the equipment checklist for your project, you may want to divvy up the responsibilities between you and your teammates. For example, if you're video recording user sessions, you may want to make one person responsible for bringing *all* of the video equipment (camera, batteries, tripod, etc.) and another responsible for everything else (video equipment alone is a big job). It can be challenging to manage everything on your own, so don't be shy about asking for help.

REPORT CONTENTS

Clearly stating how research findings will be distilled and shared is a must. Some teams may be satisfied with an informal debriefing, whereas others may require a formal presentation along with video clips. If key stakeholders or executives can't attend the research sessions, video clips can support your insights and make them more convincing. Setting report expectations ahead of time may prevent problems from arising after the study.

Recruiting

The user profile outlined in your research plan will help you determine *whom* you want to recruit for the study. Next, you'll need to decide *where* you plan to find these participants. There are several avenues you can pursue, but the most common ones include recruiting agencies, Craigslist, links on the company web site, or friends and family.

- **Recruiting specialist or agency**

  If you have the budget to hire a user research recruiter or recruiting agency, it's often worth the investment. Recruiting can take a long time (surveys, emails, calls), and chances are your team members have many other tasks on their plates. The cost for finding each participant will vary based on the agency, the participant requirements, and your geographical location, but it can typically range between $100 and $250 per participant for qualitative studies (not including the participant compensation). As mentioned earlier, compensation to participants will vary depending on their expertise and the interview duration.

- **Craigslist (or similar service)**

  Craigslist will be cheaper than an agency. Rates vary by city (e.g., in San Francisco it's $75 for an ad; in Chicago it's $25), so check your local site for rates. One of the potential downsides of using Craigslist is that some respondents may be too tech-savvy, and you may get hundreds of replies within a few hours. Screener questions (discussed in the next section) can help filter out advanced users as well as serial usability study participants.

- **Link on the company site**

  If you're planning to include your current app in the study, you may want to consider recruiting through your company web site. Large tech companies with a user focus often create participant databases to make it easier to conduct impromptu user research. One downside is that visitors tend to like the service, which may skew your data toward the positive/easy to use. Unfortunately, it can be hard to find real users for products with small audiences. If you choose this route, be sure to include some folks from alternative recruiting avenues (i.e., Craigslist or friends and family) in your sample.

- **Friends and family**

  In an ideal world, your research participants *should not* be friends and family since they are less likely to be honest about your app (assuming you are showing prototypes), and they tend to lack the diversity of your target audience. However, recruiting friends and family can reduce costs and is typically much faster than the methods described earlier.

  Also, to be clear, you still need to screen friends and family to some degree, whether it's by age, experience, or interest in your type of app. For example, if you're creating an app for mountain biking and you are the only one in your extended family who cycles, you might be able to recruit riders at your local bike shop. You might also consider joining a riding club so you can recruit cyclists to be part of the study.

Choosing a recruiting approach will depend on your goals, user profile, and budget. If possible, try to go outside your personal network; otherwise, recruiting through friends and family can be a viable option.

SCREENER

Regardless of which recruiting channel you choose, you will need to develop a participant screener. The screener is a document that contains questions to help you determine whether a prospective participant meets the criteria outlined in your user profile.

Screener questions can be posed over the telephone, included in a Craigslist post, or presented in an online survey, such as SurveyMonkey (**www.surveymonkey .com**), Wufoo (**www.wufoo.com**), or even using Forms in Google Docs (**http:// docs.google.com**). For example, for a high-level iPhone study, my colleague Michelle Reamy and I wanted to recruit parents with young kids, college students, and small businesses. We posted a link to a screener survey on Craigslist, then followed up by phone with the people who responded. Some of the online screener survey questions are shown here (notes in *italics* explain the rationale behind the question):

- How long have you owned an iPhone? Which iPhone model do you have?

  (We didn't want completely new users. They are often in the "honeymoon stage.")

- Tell us what applications you've downloaded to your iPhone.

  (Up to ten were allowed in the form; we wanted users who had downloaded and used at least a few apps.)

- What is your gender?

  (We wanted a 50/50 target mix of men and women.)

- Do you have children living at home?

  (Helped identify parents; we clarified this over the phone.)

- How old are you?

  (Enabled us to exclude minors and find a range of ages.)

- What is your job title/profession?

  (Helped identify college students and small businesses.)

- If you are selected to participate in this study, are you willing to sign an agreement stating that you'll keep all information regarding the study confidential?

  (If respondents declined, they were not invited to participate.)

- Please enter your phone number. We may have follow-up questions related to this survey.

  (This was used for the follow-up phone interview.)

After you draft your screener questions, you may want to have a pilot (test run) with one or two prospective participants. The pilot may reveal that additional questions or clarification is needed for the screening process.

NUMBER OF PARTICIPANTS

The number of participants in your study greatly depends on your research goals, the user profiles, and your budget. Traditional qualitative user research literature typically recommends ten participants for each profile,[8] although newer texts suggest you'll get diminishing returns after three to five participants.

---

8. Hugh Beyer and Karen Holtzblatt, *Contextual Design: Defining Customer-Centered Systems* (Morgan Kaufmann, 1997).

If the types of findings you are interested in are unlikely to be easily discovered, you should lean toward having a higher number of participants. However, if you're creating an iPhone app with several different target users (e.g., a photo app for bloggers, travelers, and parents), the number of participants can quickly add up. While this approach can certainly yield rich findings, it's often impractical given budget and schedule constraints. If the choice is between no research or research with fewer participants, I recommend the latter strategy.

COMPENSATION

The compensation for user research depends on a variety of factors, such as the duration of the study, the level of intrusiveness (are you in people's homes or offices?), and the participant's expertise. If you work with a recruiting agency, they can usually provide a good sense of market rates. Alternatively, you can search the [ETC] section of Craigslist and see what other researchers are offering study participants. Keep in mind that qualitative, up-front research usually provides more compensation than standard usability studies.

Facilitating Interviews

If you plan to conduct field interviews, you should create a discussion guide in advance of the session. As mentioned in the section "Questions for Research," the high-level questions in your research plan can help formulate specific interview questions.

The discussion guide's contents will vary with your study goals. For example, in some cases you may plan to interview the participant and get feedback on a paper prototype of your app. In other cases you may want to forgo a prototype and simply interview the participant. Either way, the document is simply a "guide" since the facilitator may need to change direction if something relevant comes up that was not initially outlined. That said, be sure to do a test run a few days before the study so you have enough time to make any changes needed.

Shadowing, on the other hand, does not require a discussion guide since the participants will be carrying on with their regular activities with limited interruptions. Although the sessions will be unstructured, the researcher should have a checklist for what he or she wants to closely observe and document as well as potential follow-up questions.

Regardless of the method you choose, the next sections describe some things to keep in mind while interviewing or shadowing.

ASK OPEN-ENDED QUESTIONS

Asking open-ended questions instead of yes/no questions will enable your participants to tell their stories. In most instances the journey leads to more insights than the ultimate answer. For example, if you want to get a sense of how children are using their parents' iPhones, an open-ended question can lead to a rich discussion, as shown here:

> **Question: Can you tell me about your son's first experience with the iPhone?**
>
> **Answer:** I took a picture of him and showed it to him. He loves the portability of it; looks like a camera, something you can carry around. Sometimes he'll use it when sitting on my lap at the computer. We've also used it to watch YouTube while waiting at the airport. He knows the pictures, though he doesn't know how to read yet, and the sounds. He loves looking at the weather, turning the pages. We have every city for every relative. When we drive to San Diego to see my parents, he can see the blue icon and asks, "Why isn't it going fast enough?"

Note the specificity of the question. If the question were too broad ("What does your son do with the iPhone?"), it may have been difficult for the mother to come up with an example.

LOOK FOR CONCRETE EXAMPLES

You should look for concrete examples when participants discuss their experiences in general terms. Concrete examples will clarify the situation and may lead to valuable insights. For example, a participant told me that he uses Google Maps "all the time." When asked to describe a specific situation, he replied as follows:

> **Question: Can you describe a specific situation when Google Maps was helpful?**
>
> **Answer:** My mother-in-law collapsed in Chinatown. She was able to call us, but we couldn't find her. I told her to look up and she gave me a partial name of an alley. I went to Google Maps, found the alley, and then sent the information to a 911 operator. They blocked off the whole block to get her. Now I say to my wife, "My iPhone saved your mom." She doesn't have an issue when I want to upgrade my phone. We can joke about it now.

If your participant is struggling to provide concrete examples, try to provide prompts, for example, "When was the last time you used [*app name*]?" If the app has a Recents or other history section, those may also jog the participant's memory.

PROBE WHAT'S NOT THERE

What participants don't reveal can also provide valuable insights. For example, a participant gave me a tour of the apps on her iPhone and explained what worked well, what didn't work well, and so on. Over the course of our meeting, she also mentioned several apps that weren't on her phone. When I asked what happened, I learned that she had deleted them because of various user experience issues. Here is our exchange:

> **Question: Why did you delete the Wallet app?**
>
> **Answer:** I liked the idea but it was too difficult to get started. You put in your passwords; you would have all the information in one place. Apparently it's safe. Then if you lose your card, you can call Visa directly from the app. It's a way of storing all that information. My boyfriend told me about it.
>
> **Question: And the Wiki one?**
>
> **Answer:** I didn't trust the [third-party] app because the font didn't look like the Wikipedia font.
>
> **Question: Any others?**
>
> **Answer:** The first app I downloaded was a grocery store finder. It didn't show any grocery stores near me, but there's a Whole Foods right down the road.

Although some participants may provide openings to probe into, others may deliberately withhold user experience issues. Often it's because the participants think the problem is their fault, or they want to please the interviewer and hope positive comments will have that effect. If participants paint an unnaturally rosy picture of everything, try to uncover how things could be even better for them.

Also, look for places where what participants *say* doesn't match what they *do*. For example, when I interviewed an iPhone user, she spent the first 20 minutes or so talking in glowing terms about the iPhone and iPhone apps. At the same time, I noticed that she had five different camera apps with similar names. When I asked why she had all of those apps, I learned about the problems she encountered with each one. She didn't have five apps because they were great; she was still on a quest to find *one* that met her needs.

CAPTURE RELEVANT ARTIFACTS

As you interview participants, try to capture photos, app screens, and other relevant artifacts that support your observations. For example, for the camera app example in the previous section, it would be helpful to have a screen capture that shows all of the camera apps on the participant's iPhone. You may also want to photograph the participant using the apps so you have a visual record of their context of use.

As you gather artifacts, make sure your efforts do not disturb the flow of your conversation. Participants may lose focus or feel overly self-conscious if you or your team members are constantly snapping photos and interrupting to document an artifact. Artifacts that you may want to capture during the session include

- Photo of a participant using the iPhone
- Photos of the computing environment (e.g., laptop, desktop, printer)
- Photo of the syncing setup
- Screen capture of the participant's home screen
- Screen capture of any customization the participant has done to the iPhone (e.g., background or screen saver)
- Screen captures of the apps discussed
- Artifacts created by the apps, including Twitter posts and photos

In some cases you may want to ask a participant to bring an artifact to the interview. This can be helpful if it takes time to track down the artifact or bringing it requires some advance preparation. Using a travel app as an example, you may want participants to share travel photos or other memorabilia from a recent vacation. Be sure to get written permission to take photos, video, and so forth *before* starting the session.

WRAP-UP AND DEBRIEF

At the end of each research session, give the participants an opportunity to ask questions or share any remaining comments. Next, be sure to thank them for their time and input. I often say something like *"Thanks for your help today. Your feedback will help us build better products."*

Finally, provide the participants with their incentive gift and ask them to sign a document stating that they received the incentive. This will protect you in case a participant later claims that he or she never received payment. Also, you'll need this document if you want to declare participant compensation as an expense on your taxes.

If you're conducting user interviews with colleagues, consider holding team debrief sessions immediately afterward. The debrief involves the moderator and observers sharing their observations and sometimes developing one set of team notes. It's a great time to collaboratively analyze your observations since everything is fresh in your mind and the notes don't need to be rushed.

Related Research Activities

User research can provide valuable insights, but it's not the only way to understand your users. In addition to user research, be sure to consider some of the other activities outlined in **TABLE 3.2**. Competitive research will be discussed further in Chapter 5, "Evaluating the Competition."

TABLE 3.2 Activities That May Help Define Your App

Activity	Description	App Stage
User research	Develop an understanding of your users' needs and how they are currently being met on the iPhone and other relevant platforms.	New or existing
Competitive research	Evaluate what your competitors are doing on the iPhone, as well as on other relevant platforms (Mac OS X, Android, Windows OS, BlackBerry, etc.).	New or existing
Market research	Evaluate your app's potential for a specific market.	New or existing
Literature review	Read existing research related to the app: market research, academic research, white papers, industry news, etc.	New or existing
Analytics	Evaluate how users are currently using your app. Many tools such as Flurry (www.flurry.com) can be used to show how users navigate through your app and what features are used most/least frequently.	Existing
App Store reviews	Read your app's reviews in the App Store; look for trends within the comments.	Existing
Customer support	Analyze what users are saying in your customer support forums.	Existing
Online forums	Analyze what your users are saying in relevant online forums, such as Twitter, Get Satisfaction, or Facebook groups.	Existing

Summary

Up-front user research can benefit both new and existing apps, shedding light on prospective users' context of use, perceptions, pain points, language, and customs. Using this foundation, you can make informed decisions throughout the product development process. Moreover, research can reveal new app opportunities and inspire innovative solutions.

The user research strategy depends on the type of app and its stage in the development cycle. In most cases, apps in the very early stages will benefit from observational methods, whereas apps in later stages will benefit from observational methods combined with app prototypes. As you develop and execute your research plan, keep in mind the following:

- *Some* user research is better than *no* user research. If you're seriously strapped for time, keep the study small and recruit through friends and family.
- Don't skip the user research plan! Sorting these details out in advance will save time and aggravation.
- Be empathetic and respectful toward your participants. Your sessions will be richer and the benefits greater if there is mutual respect and understanding. ■

Analyzing User Research

AFTER COMPLETING THE USER RESEARCH for your app, you will undoubtedly be armed with reams of notes, dozens of photographs, and hours upon hours of audio or video footage to sift through. The sheer quantity of these artifacts can be overwhelming, but it's a priceless resource that you may refer to for months—potentially years—to come.

The challenge is how to translate these artifacts and observations into insights that can easily be used by designers, developers, and other members of your team. This chapter provides you with step-by-step advice on how to effectively analyze your user research, with an emphasis on collaborative affinity diagramming.

You'll also learn how your findings can be used to create valuable design tools such as personas, scenarios, and user journeys. These tools will help you prioritize features and ensure that your app designs meet your users' needs. To illustrate, we'll look at case studies demonstrating how other app designers and developers used similar methods in their design process.

Share the Wealth

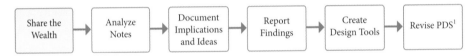

One of the first things to do after a study is gather the artifacts and post them in a place where other team members can view them. Intranets and wikis are great, but so is an actual physical space within your company such as a conference room, an office, a cubicle, even the hallway if that's your only option. You can use invisible tape on the wall, whiteboard, or foam core.

Making the artifacts visible has several benefits:

- Surrounding everyone with this content will create a shared understanding within your organization.
- It simplifies analysis since the medium makes it easy to collaboratively analyze findings.
- The physical representation can be referred to in the later design stages, as it's continually updated and refreshed.

Initially, you'll want to organize these artifacts according to participant, as shown in **FIGURE 4.1**; later on you'll look for themes across participants. As discussed in the previous chapter, artifacts may include photos, notes, screen captures, video, audio, or all of the above.

FIGURE 4.1 Participant board for iPhone field interview analysis

---

1. Product Definition Statement

Analyze Notes

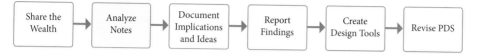

Once you've gathered your notes, start extracting observations and grouping them into themes as you uncover them.[2] Sounds simple, right? If you are working independently and have observed nearly all of the sessions, the process can go rather quickly. However, if you are working with a group and not everyone has attended the sessions, the process may take a few days. People who didn't attend may be curious about some observations or debate whether a behavior even occurred. One rule that can help alleviate this problem is that team members must have attended at least two user interviews to participate in the analysis sessions. The depth and format of your interview notes (handwritten, transcripts, verbatim notes) will influence your approach.

HANDWRITTEN NOTES

As mentioned in the previous chapter, handwritten notes are a good option if approximate user quotes are acceptable. Study participants may also be more comfortable since a notebook is less intrusive than a laptop or video camera. Unfortunately, when notes are handwritten, the person who wrote them is typically the only one who can fully decipher them. Even the note taker may have a hard time interpreting incomplete sentences and shorthand. If there isn't time to create a transcript, consider having the note taker read the notes aloud while others in the group write observations on sticky notes. Additionally, holding debrief sessions immediately after each interview is a great way for teams to collaboratively analyze and expand upon notes.

TRANSCRIPTS

Transcripts can be created from the audio or video captured during your sessions. They are helpful if your team needs precise user quotes along with timestamps. Although transcripts are the most accurate option, they can take a long time to review since they include every single word that you, the participant, and the observers said during the interview.

Transcripts can be read to a team during an analysis session, but they require some filtering on the part of the reader. In this situation, it might help to divvy up the transcripts and have team members independently analyze each one.

NOTE

Creating transcripts is a time-consuming process. Companies sometimes outsource this step to a transcription service, which costs approximately $60 for each hour of footage. Another option is to use software to help transcribe content such as InqScribe or Transcriva.

---

2. The process is commonly referred to as *affinity diagramming* and was developed in the 1960s by Japanese anthropologist Jiro Kawakita.

VERBATIM NOTES

Typed verbatim notes (also known as "approximate" transcripts) typically require less filtering since they contain valuable details and quotes without the extra noise included in a transcript.

The following paragraphs are an excerpt of notes taken during an iPhone field interview with a college student. The notes totaled five pages for a 1.5-hour interview. The participant was asked to describe how he uses the iPhone at school.

> I would have chemistry in the morning for 5 hours, Trig in afternoon, English at night. My chemistry teacher would lecture for 2 hours. I would have my periodic table open. I was in class one day and forgot my periodic table. I Googled it and found an iPhone periodic table app. I showed everyone in class and then they got it. It's free and they have a light version. A lot of people in class have an iPhone; half the class. Everybody is on the iPhone, especially on the train.
>
> I'd also use my scientific calculator. If you turn the iPhone landscape, it expands. I removed the other one [he purchased a different one for class]. Don't like a ton of apps on my phone at once. Replaced my TI-89. The other app allowed more numbers than the built-in calculator app; could do longer equations with iPhone app. I looked in the App Store under scientific calculator. Looked for graphing one. I got this one. [shows me] There was a pop quiz one day so I asked: Can I use the phone? Professor said yes but some would say no.

To see how to analyze a user interview, examine the highlights indicating the notable observations:

> I would have chemistry in the morning for 5 hours, Trig in afternoon, English at night. My chemistry teacher would lecture for 2 hours. I would have my periodic table open. I was in class one day and forgot my periodic table. I Googled it and found an iPhone periodic table app. I showed everyone in class and then they got it. It's free and they have a light version. A lot of people in class have an iPhone; half the class. Everybody is on the iPhone, especially on the train.
>
> I'd also use my scientific calculator. If you turn the iPhone landscape, it expands. I removed the other one [he purchased a different one for class]. Don't like a ton of apps on my phone at once. Replaced my TI-89. The other app allowed more numbers than the built-in calculator app; could do longer equations with iPhone app. I looked in the App Store under scientific calculator. Looked for graphing one. I got this one. [shows me]

There was a pop quiz one day so I asked: Can I use the phone? Professor said yes but some would say no.

Next, write each observation on a sticky note along with the participant's number—P1, P2, P3, and so on. If you notice any similarities, create a label and write them on different-colored sticky notes. For example, FIGURE 4.2 shows a blue sticky with the text "How people find apps." This is used to label the different ways people find iPhone apps (such as Google, searching the App Store, through friends). As you continue the analysis, you will eventually include other stickies within a high-level grouping. If an observation belongs in more than one group, create another sticky and try to cross-reference the two with a unique letter or number.

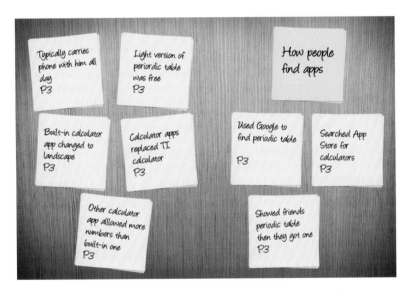

FIGURE 4.2 Affinity diagram for iPhone field interview analysis

Here are some additional tips for this type of analysis:

- Try to limit your team to four to six people.
- Minimize conversations and debates while writing up observations.
- Ensure that observations are written in concise phrases or sentences.
- If one sticky group is much larger than the others, consider splitting it or creating subheaders.
- Connect related sticky groups with lines.
- Collaboratively prioritize findings when all observations have been placed within a group.
- Provide a key if you color-code your stickies (e.g., heading versus findings versus idea).

Document Implications and Ideas

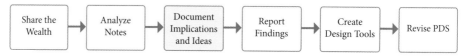

Eventually you'll have several walls and/or foam-core boards filled with clustered observations from your fieldwork. Some stickies will have only one participant number, but observations witnessed in more than one interview may have multiple participant numbers. In addition to the observations and group titles, you may want to start incorporating implications and design ideas, as shown in FIGURE 4.3.

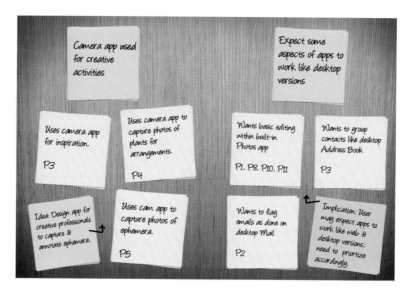

FIGURE 4.3 Affinity diagram with implications and ideas

Implications suggest best practices or design principles your team wants to follow, whereas ideas are specific features or concepts you may want to incorporate in the actual design. These should also be written on stickies, using a different color from the observations and titles. You may want to post a color key if other team members are involved in the process. At the end of the day, take photos of the groupings in case any stickies get accidentally moved or fall off the wall. Double-sided tape can help keep the stickies in place.

If you want to create electronic versions of your affinity diagrams, consider using the Stickies Dashboard widget on the Mac or lino (http://en.linoit.com), a web-based tool for organizing sticky notes. Keep in mind that these computer-based approaches typically require one person to "drive," which may make the process less collaborative. With a paper-based approach everyone can simultaneously add stickies to the affinity diagrams. Additionally, if you use a computer, your workspace will be limited by the size of your computer screen or projector image. In contrast, paper stickies can be plastered on several walls, which may make it easier to step back and see the big picture.

Report Findings

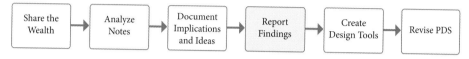

After spending time in the field and working for hours in a conference room filled with observations, implications, and design ideas, your study participants may seem like old friends. Someone on your team will mention a name and something interesting the person said and everyone will know exactly whom and what that person is talking about. Trust me, it may seem weird, but this is a wonderful stroke of serendipity.

While it may be tempting to leave the content up on the wall and move on to design, you should write up a Quick Findings report at minimum. You may be able to recite your favorite participants' quotes today, but chances are you won't even remember their names in a couple of months. Moreover, you will probably have a hard time deciphering all of your shorthand sticky notes. If you find yourself asking, "Anyone know why I wrote 'FB quiz doesn't work'?" you'll quickly understand the importance of having that Quick Findings report on hand.

In addition to clarifying all of the sticky notations, the Quick Findings report will give you an opportunity to stew on the material and brainstorm additional implications and ideas. This report also makes your findings more portable, because you can take them anywhere once you've moved from the sticky notes to electronic documents.

There are countless ways to organize your findings and make them more shareable (e.g., in a report, presentation, wiki, summary poster), as you will discover in the sections that follow.

METHODOLOGY AND GOALS

Did you shadow participants, conduct field interviews, run diary studies? A combination? Individuals who were not able to attend the sessions will want to know how you approached the research as well as the research goals.

TEAM MEMBERS

Although this information may be known throughout your organization at the time of the research, after a few months you may forget exactly who facilitated and observed the research. Identifying these individuals will make it easier to figure out whom to ask for research advice in the future and whom to include in relevant brainstorming activities.

PARTICIPANT PROFILES

Participant profiles vary based on the user research methods and goals. For example, an iPhone app study looking at overall app usage might include the following information:

- First name and photo
- Demographics (age, gender, occupation, location)
- iPhone model and date/time of purchase
- Computer setup (model, where located)
- "A day in the life" (how the participant uses the iPhone over the course of a day)
- Overall app usage
- App-specific usage
- App wish list

TABLE 4.1 shows a sample participant profile from one of our app studies (courtesy of Michelle Reamy).

FINDINGS

The format of your findings depends on your user research goals. One common approach is to summarize each finding and then include representative participant quotes and screen captures, as shown in the sidebar "Example of User Research Findings." If you captured video, consider embedding salient video clips (about 30 seconds or less) as they can be extremely beneficial for readers who were unable to attend the sessions.

If design implications or ideas were identified, these should also be included with the findings. Findings with the most significant implications are generally included in a Top Findings or Executive Summary section of your report. They may be used to generate design goals or design principles for your app.

TABLE 4.1 Sample Participant Profile

Meet Matt

When he's not playing director at a prestigious contemporary gallery in Chelsea, Matt spends his time working on his own art. The iPhone was a gift from his boss for the extra help he put in at Art Basel.

A day in the life of Matt and his iPhone

Every morning Matt grabs his phone and checks email, weather, and the surf report. He usually bikes to work, tucking the iPhone in a special pouch to protect it from condensation and sweat. At work he'll use his iPhone to check Facebook and Twitter. On this particular day, he took a photo of a great piece of art that he found really inspiring: a chrome cake on a porcelain platter. Later on he plans to look up cocktail recipes using an app so he can pick up the ingredients on his way home.

(Photograph courtesy of Michelle Reamy)

Name: Matt
Age: 34
Occupation: Gallery director
Home: Lives in an apartment in New York City with his wife
iPhone: 3G
Computer: MacBook Pro

Overall app usage

Matt calls everything on the phone an "app"—he even refers to Safari as "the web app." The first app he downloaded was a converter. He's always making calculations and converting measurements for sculptures and other artwork, so he explicitly looked for an app that could make these tasks easier. His apps are organized so the ones he uses the most are on the first page.

Specific app usage

Matt hasn't found the need to pay for many apps. Some of his favorite apps include these:

- **Tweetie.** Matt and his musician friend downloaded the app to share and track their mix ideas.
- **Public Radio.** He likes the way you can set the app to stream or search for specific stations in a location.
- **iSkateboard.** He uses this app for finding good skate parks around the city. They come and go very quickly so the app has been very handy.

Although the quality isn't great, Matt finds the camera essential: "The quality isn't really the point—it's just to remember an idea or some piece of inspiration for later." Now that he has the iPhone, he has completely changed his blogging habits: "My old blog was mostly text with a few photos. Now it's almost purely photos and that's more my style." All of his photos are on the iPhone Camera Roll. He wants the photos with him at all times in case he's looking for ideas.

App wish list

Matt would like more apps that support or augment the apps he owns: "The most awesome thing would be to actually send a music file when I post a Tweet. Honestly, I think there's more this thing can do that I don't know about. I struggle to keep up with technology. But I do love this phone."

Example of User Research Findings

When documenting specific user research findings, start with a brief summary such as the one that follows, "Setting Up an iPhone App Can Be Challenging." Next, add salient quotes from your notes along with the participant number, such as P1, P2, P3. Below the quotes you can include implications and design ideas from your analysis sessions. If you have relevant imagery or video, it can also be embedded in the document, as shown in FIGURE 4.4.

Setting Up an iPhone App Can Be Challenging

Related quotes:

- "Tried AccuWeather but took a long time to change the default. When it takes a long time, I'm gone." (P1)
- "I had the Wallet, I liked the idea, but it was too difficult to get started." (P2)
- "They [Genius app] gave you directions to go into your Settings, go to international keyboards, then add it as a Chinese keyboard." (P3)

Implication:

- Users may abandon apps if the setup process is not welcoming and easy.

Design ideas:

- Consider offering a welcome screen for first-time users.
- Consider presenting a wizard if a multistep setup process is required.

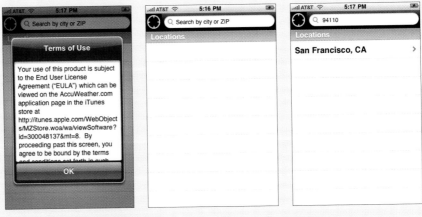

AccuWeather setup: step 1   AccuWeather setup: step 2   AccuWeather setup: step 3

FIGURE 4.4 AccuWeather setup requires three steps.

PRESENTING THE FINDINGS

If you work in a large company, chances are you will create a report, post it internally, and present the highlights of your findings in a meeting. Smaller organizations may think presentations such as these are unnecessary, especially if everyone attended most of the sessions, but these meetings can be much more than a simple recap.

In addition to sharing findings, post-research meetings are important for determining the next steps your design and development team needs to take. They also offer your team the opportunity to brainstorm about solutions to app problems and discuss new directions for the app. For example, you could hold a 90-minute meeting, dedicating the first half to presenting the findings and the second half to brainstorming. Brainstorm ideas should be transcribed so they can be incorporated into the app requirements. You may want to use large sticky pads (25 × 30 inches) since they are portable. Additional brainstorming tips are discussed in Chapter 6, "Exploring App Concepts."

Given the amount of work you've done with the affinity diagrams and the Quick Findings report, the presentation shouldn't require too much effort. In fact, the affinity diagrams and Quick Findings could be your presentation; separate Keynote slides may not be necessary.

Create Design Tools

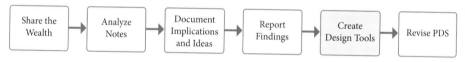

To make your research findings more readily accessible, you may want to distill the content in a variety of ways. For example, you may have gathered field data from more than ten people for your iPhone app study. It would be impractical to thumb through each profile every time you wanted to make a design decision, and it would impossible (and likely unwise) to satisfy the needs of every participant.

Over the years, user experience researchers and designers have developed a number of tools that make it easier to incorporate user research into the design process. Here I'll describe two of the most common tools, personas and scenarios, as well as a more diagrammatic approach, specifically user journeys.

PERSONAS

Personas are profiles of *archetypal* users, as opposed to profiles of actual users; they represent the needs of many users.[3] Personas allow you to keep design teams on the same page with regard to target users, and they help prevent team members from being self-referential. For example, instead of saying, *"Well, if it was me, I would use the iPhone this way,"* team members would refer to a specific persona: *"Well, Jennifer would do it this way."*

Personas are usually developed from multiple research sources, including user research, customer support, and application analytics.

Most products have more than one persona, and the appropriate number will depend on your app and your user research findings. In most cases, personas are categorized as primary, secondary, and sometimes negative (or "anti") personas:

- Primary personas are the ones whose needs you must address for the product to succeed.
- Secondary personas are important but lower priority.
- Negative personas are the ones you're clearly not addressing for business or other reasons.

Knowing your personas' needs can help with design decisions and prioritization. For example, a feature that satisfies the needs of only your secondary persona may receive a lower priority when it comes to actually implementing that feature. Personas can take a variety of formats, but they typically contain the following information:

- Name, profession, age, location
- Attitudes
- Activities
- Influencers
- Workflows
- Pain points and frustrations
- Goals

iPhone app personas may also include detailed information on the context of use, the computer and syncing setup, and the usage of web and desktop versions of iPhone applications. Organizations that already have personas for related products

---

3. See John Pruitt and Tamara Adlin, *The Persona Lifecycle: Keeping People in Mind Throughout Product Design* (Morgan Kaufmann, 2006), and Alan Cooper, *The Inmates Are Running the Asylum* (Sams, 2004).

may want to extend them with iPhone information or create new personas specifically for the iPhone app.

For example, Sonos created personas when they first designed their wireless music system. Given that the iPhone app mirrored the controller functionality, it was not necessary to create new personas. Instead, Sonos extended one of their existing personas to include iPhone-specific information. **TABLE 4.2** is an example of a persona for a college student.

TABLE 4.2 College Student Persona

"I often get caught up in my iPhone."

Every morning Marta reaches across her bed to grab her iPhone to check her email, calendar, and friends' status updates on Facebook. If she forgot to charge her iPhone overnight, she'll plug it in and let it charge while she gets ready for school.

Marta typically brings both her laptop and iPhone to campus. The laptop is stowed away in her backpack and the iPhone is tucked in her pocket. Over the course of the day, she uses the phone to listen to music, check her friends' status updates, and look up information via Safari.

Marta mostly uses the iPhone for fun, but she's been experimenting with some apps for school. She found spreadsheet and word-processing apps that work well for basic edits, but she switches to her laptop to get significant work done. Reference apps, such as the flash cards for her Chinese class, have been more valuable to her.

(Photograph courtesy of Nerea Marta)

Name: Marta, College Sophomore
Age: 19
Occupation: Sophomore at NYU majoring in psychology
Home: Shares an apartment with two other NYU students
iPhone: 3G
Computer: MacBook

Functional goals:
- Check email and AIM.
- Update status on Facebook and Foursquare.
- Listen to music.

Emotional goals:
- Stay in contact with friends and family.
- Entertain herself and friends.
- Enjoy simple and pleasing aesthetics.

Influencers:
- Friends recommend apps to her.
- Her parents pay for her monthly plan.

Frustrations:
- Many apps feel disconnected (e.g., she edits photos with Photoshop on her laptop before posting them to Facebook).

Wish list:
- She wishes she could customize the look and feel of some iPhone apps.

In addition to incorporating your personas into scenarios and user journeys, which are discussed in the next section, here are a few other ways to keep personas alive:

- Create posters and display them in your company hallway or office.
- Laminate and distribute them to team members.
- Post them on your company intranet or wiki; provide different formats for different use cases.
- Incorporate them anytime design concepts are shared.

SCENARIOS

Scenarios describe how personas may use your app to achieve their goals. In the very early stages, scenarios tend to be written at a high level without many user interface elements. Excluding these elements allows your team to brainstorm a wide variety of design directions, rather than confining yourselves to a particular solution.

As your design unfolds, the scenarios can help uncover gaps in your solutions and potential usability issues. They are also useful when demoing your working app or authoring user interface specifications. Scenario content will vary depending on the app, but it typically includes the following information:

- **Motivation**

  What prompted the persona to embark on the scenario?

- **Context**

  Where is the persona while the scenario is taking place?

  Does the context change over the course of the scenario?

  Who else is involved?

  What other devices are involved?

- **Distractions**

  What kinds of distractions or interruptions typically occur in the scenario?

  How does the persona deal with such distractions?

- **Goal**

  What is the persona's goal in the scenario?

  Is it information, an artifact, an emotion?

To illustrate, imagine that you're developing an iPhone app to help NYU students find their way around campus. It would probably make sense to include more than one persona, such as New Student, Existing Student, and Prospective Student personas. Although students are the primary personas, instructors and administrators may also use the app, and you may find it helpful to develop secondary personas for them as well. The scenarios could start off at a relatively high level, then be refined as the design develops. TABLE 4.3 shows a "need" scenario, using the College Sophomore persona. A need scenario implies that a solution has not been generated and can be used in the context of a brainstorming session.

TABLE 4.3 **Need Scenario with College Sophomore Persona**

Getting to a new classroom

It's the first day of Marta's sophomore year at NYU. She just finished eating lunch at a café on Waverly Place and is scanning her afternoon schedule in iCal, which she synced to her iPhone from her laptop the night before.

Marta notices that her 2:00 p.m. class is held in the Puck Building. Although Marta is a sophomore, she's never taken any classes at Puck. She goes to the NYU web site using Safari on her iPhone, but the site isn't formatted for the device. After several minutes of pinching and zooming, Marta finally finds the building. It's not linked to Google Maps, so she mentally notes the cross streets before exiting Safari.

Brainstorm topic:

How can an iPhone app make Marta's life easier?

(Photograph courtesy of Nerea Marta)

Name: Marta, College Sophomore

While this scenario may seem overly simple, that's what you're shooting for in the early stages. The simplicity will provide just enough of a foundation for your team to brainstorm, which is covered more in Chapter 6, "Exploring App Concepts." If everything were spelled out from the beginning, there wouldn't be any room for innovation along the way.

At the same time, having a basic scenario framework will help keep your team grounded. For example, the college student scenario highlights a potential shortcoming of the app: the inability to access the campus map directly from iCal. In addition, it unveils potential interruptions, such as bumping into a friend, and reminds the team that it's important to maintain the app's state.

Common Questions

Authoring scenarios may seem like a daunting task, but a small investment can go a long way. This section answers common questions regarding scenarios and their relation to similar tools such as use cases and user stories.

- **How many scenarios should I write?**

  The number of scenarios you write depends on the number of personas and the complexity of the app. Utility apps may need only one or two scenarios, whereas Productivity apps may benefit from a series of short scenarios that cover different goals.

Although scenarios are highly valuable, keep in mind that they are a tool for design. The scenarios should be simple and focused. Instead of trying to document every possible scenario at the beginning of your project, start out by focusing on what's most important. As you get into the design phase, you can expand with edge case scenarios as needed.

- **Are scenarios just for design?**

Other teams within your organization may also leverage your scenarios. If the scenarios are relatively comprehensive, they may provide a starting point for help documentation and for training your support team. Similarly, QA teams may find the scenarios useful when developing their test plans. Keep in mind that the goals of help and QA are quite different from those of design; a one-size-fits-all approach may not be desirable. Ideally, the teams will share their knowledge and adapt as needed.

- **What's the difference between use cases and scenarios?**

Use cases are much more concise than scenarios and may include aspects of the back end, often called the "system." They help uncover flow and usability issues in the later stages of design, but they are generally too system-oriented for early-stage brainstorming. The NYU iPhone app, for example, could be described with the following use cases:

  - User chooses building list.
  - System provides list.
  - User chooses P.
  - System shows buildings that start with P.

- **What about user "stories"?**

User stories are commonly used in the Agile software development process.[4] They tend to be more feature-oriented than scenarios since they must be broken down for the "backlog" (items planned for the next development cycle). Moreover, although the term *story* is used, user stories read more like requirements given the language and specificity. For example, here are three potential user stories for the NYU iPhone app:

  - A user can browse campus buildings by name.
  - A user can view detailed information for each building.
  - A user can get directions to each building.

---

4. Mike Cohn, *User Stories Applied for Agile Software Development* (Addison-Wesley, 2004).

USER JOURNEYS

User journeys (shown in TABLE 4.4) offer an effective way to share research findings. The design team can use them as a quick reference throughout the design process or as a communication tool when explaining design decisions to other members of your company. The journeys typically encompass the entire user experience—from app discovery to app usage along an abstract timeline—with each part kept at a very high level. User journeys may seem overly linear at first glance, but they are not meant be taken literally. It may help to view them as design requirements based on persona needs, rather than actual user flows. As you'll see in TABLE 4.4, user journeys assume some concrete understanding of the user experience. If your app's definition is still vague, even high-level groupings may be too detailed.

TABLE 4.4 illustrates the user journey created for an app that complements an existing web site for art events. The labels along the top represent the high-level goals that can be achieved with the app, and the labels along the side represent the different personas that may use the app. Having this reference helped the team prioritize features and make specific design decisions.

TABLE 4.4 User Journey for Art Events Web Site

	DISCOVER Where they learn about the app	FIND How they find events	LEARN What they need to decide to attend	ATTEND What they need to get to the event	REVIEW What they want to include in a review
All personas	App Store		Artist name, reviews, images, description	Venue name and address	
Martin *Local art enthusiast*	Our web site Artist friends Galleries	Prefers to search or browse for genre or artist of interest	Number of days before the event closes	May not need maps if attended the venue in the past	Prefers to do lengthy reviews, thus more likely to do via the web site
Katherine *Local art dabbler*	Our web site Galleries	Relies on popular lists or proximity to work/home	Days before the event closes and gallery hours	Often needs maps and directions	Occasionally does brief text reviews
Zoe *Tourist art enthusiast*	Art magazines	Often seeks out a genre or artist of interest; hotel may be located in an area with galleries	Gallery hours	Needs maps and directions	Prefers to do lengthy reviews; may write in the hotel on a laptop
Charles *Tourist art dabbler*	Guidebook Google Time Out New York	Relies on popular lists and proximity to hotel	Gallery hours	Needs maps and directions	Rarely does reviews; if anything may do thumbs up/down

Revise the Product Definition Statement

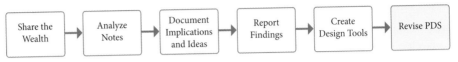

At the beginning of Part Two, we discussed how up-front user research can help refine your Product Definition Statement (the declaration of your application's main purpose and its intended audience).[5] To illustrate how this may be done, imagine that you're planning to develop an app for finding local art events. Before conducting up-front user research, your statement may look like this:

A tool for helping people find art events.

Now consider some of the problems with this statement:

- Who are the "people"? Art enthusiasts? Art students? Tourists?
- "A tool" is vague, and "find art events" seems relatively narrow and uninspiring.

After conducting your user research, perhaps you'll discover that the urban art enthusiast is your primary persona. Moreover, let's say you learned that this persona enjoys reviewing art events and sharing event information with friends on Twitter or Facebook. Your revised statement might look like this:

An app to help urban art enthusiasts find, share, and review art events.

While this may seem like a trivial exercise, you should take the time to formulate this valuable statement. Although we'll emphasize its importance in the design phase, your cross-functional team (sales, marketing, advertising) will eventually refer to this statement as they speak with investors, customers, and partners. Don't wait until after you've coded your app to come up with the Product Definition Statement.

Summary

This chapter showed you how to analyze the text, photos, and other artifacts you gathered during early-stage user research. One of the first things we recommended is to post the artifacts where other team members can readily access them, such as in the hallway, a conference room, or a dedicated cubicle. Having

---

5. iPhone Dev Center, *iPhone Human Interface Guidelines*, http://developer.apple.com/iphone/library/documentation/userexperience/conceptual/mobilehig/Introduction/Introduction.html.

the artifacts readily available will expedite affinity diagramming sessions and your subsequent Quick Findings report.

You were then introduced to a variety of ways to translate your findings into design tools that can be used throughout the app design process, specifically personas, scenarios, and user journeys. You also learned how the user research can be used to develop your Production Definition Statement, which is created in the app "idea" phase but should be revisited as the vision evolves.

Using the methods in this chapter will be helpful when you develop your own application. As you analyze your research, keep in mind the following:

- Be inclusive; make sure your core team and key stakeholders are involved.
- Share your discoveries *throughout* the process; don't wait until the end.
- Take time to document your findings so they can easily be referred to in the design phase and for future projects. ◾

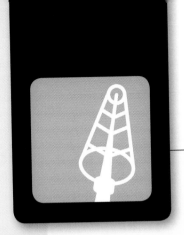

CASE STUDY 1

Windspire

CREATE WITH CONTEXT is a Silicon Valley–based consultancy doing research, innovation, and design for digital products. The firm's unique approach connects people, context, and technology to help clients create successful digital products. Create with Context offers a broad set of services to organizations around the world, including making existing products easier to use, defining next-generation products, and entering new markets. Create with Context provides services across web, mobile, consumer electronics, and desktop environments to emerging technology start-ups, government agencies, and Fortune 500 companies.

FIGURE CS1.1 Early sketch of the Windspire iPhone app

Can you tell me more about the Windspire products?

When most people think of wind turbines, they imagine the large ones found along rural highways. But the Windspire is completely different—it's small enough to fit in your backyard (30 feet tall but quite narrow) and makes little noise. More important, you don't need a lot of wind for the Windspire to work. The 1.2-kilowatt turbines can operate in areas with a minimum average speed of ten miles per hour.

How did you approach the project?

Mariah Power, the company that created Windspire, wanted to create more awareness around the Windspire and the potential for people to obtain them. Customers were often uncertain about whether they could benefit from a turbine and would ask, "Do I have enough wind to power a Windspire?" To better understand their customers' needs, we recommended ethnographic-style interviews in three regions: the San Francisco Bay Area, rural Kansas, and Washington, DC.

What did you learn from the research?

Through these ethnographic-style interviews we discovered two distinct user groups: the Green tribe and the Easy Eco tribe. The Green tribe wants to leave the world in a better place—they monitor their electric bills, drive hybrid cars, reuse plastic bags. In contrast, the Easy Eco tribe makes environmentally friendly decisions because they want to fit in—they would be embarrassed to forgo recycling or drive an SUV.

What happened after the user research?

We started brainstorming solutions for these two user groups. Helping users determine the cost of the turbines was easy to accomplish on the web site, but measuring the wind speed was impossible. That's when we came

FIGURE CS1.2 Instructions before the usability study

FIGURE CS1.3 Final Windspire app design (capturing wind)

up with the app idea. Have you seen the Zippo app? You can blow on it to put out the "flame." If the Zippo app can detect the user's breath, we thought, "Maybe we can create an iPhone app to measure wind."

What was the outcome of your technical investigation?

We discovered that it would be possible to use the phone's microphone to capture wind noise. After filtering out ambient sound, an algorithm could convert the wind noise into a decibel rating that corresponds to wind speed. Once we knew this was possible, we started sketching our ideas and building prototypes.

Were you able to test your early designs with prospective users?

Absolutely—we conducted two rounds of user testing. The first was with a paper prototype; the second was with static images on the iPhone [see FIGURES CS1.1–CS1.2]. One of the main findings from the first round of testing was

that the copy didn't speak to the Easy Eco tribe—we didn't have any concrete examples of the benefits. Another significant problem was related to how participants were holding the iPhone—many were covering the microphone and pointing it in the wrong direction.

How did these findings impact the design?

To address the copy issue, we refined the messaging to show how the wind turbine could help people save money and protect the environment. For example, one of the benefit statements says, "Installing Windspire will help reduce your home's carbon emissions." In the case of the app's microphone and orientation, we included an illustration with text showing how and where to point the app.

What happened when you tested the app the second time?

Our efforts at fine-tuning the messaging paid off—in the second round of testing, the participants had a better understanding of the wind turbine benefits. Moreover, the new infographic solved the microphone and orientation problems [see FIGURE CS1.3].

How have users responded to the app?

Feedback has been very positive, and we've been excited to see that it has generated a lot of buzz in the media around wind energy. People all around the planet have measured the wind in their backyards, at local parks, and at their workplaces and have left their marks on the map for others to see. And the app has been mentioned in the media, including the *New York Times*, *Fast Company*, CNET News, and Reuters. ■

(Windspire icon and application screenshots courtesy of Create with Context)

CASE STUDY 2
Aardvark Mobile

AARDVARK is a new kind of tool that lets you tap into the knowledge and experience of friends and friends of friends. Send Aardvark a question (from iPhone, http://vark.com, IM, email, or Twitter) and Aardvark will discover the perfect person to answer in minutes. Rob Spiro is the cofounder of Aardvark, where he leads user research and product design.

What inspired Aardvark to build an iPhone app?

We launched Aardvark over Instant Messenger in March 2009, and almost immediately users were asking for a way to use Aardvark on the go. This made sense since Aardvark is extremely useful for local recommendations (Can anyone recommend a coffee shop near the train station?), suggestions for activities (What's a great way to spend a few hours before dinner?), second opinions (Should I really buy this GPS device?), and more. [A few key app screens are shown in **FIGURES CS2.1–CS2.3**.]

How did you approach the project?

The first step in our process was to validate the concept. We had a lot of users requesting an iPhone app, but would they really download and use it? What type of Aardvark iPhone app would meet our users' needs but wouldn't compete head-on with formidable and entrenched players? To answer these questions we ran a series of interviews with both existing Aardvark users and nonusers whom we recruited via Craigslist. We asked them to walk us through their typical iPhone app usage, watched them browse through the App Store, and showed them a number of splash screens for a potential Aardvark app.

What was the outcome of the user studies?

Ultimately we were convinced that there was, in fact, a manifestation of the concept that would make a successful app. People were responding positively to a subset of the splash screens, and those reactions made sense given the usage patterns that we observed.

Our design team then came up with a series of mock-ups illustrating the concept in more detail. We were able to get the mock-ups directly onto the phone by using a free tool called LiveView. We then brought in another group of

FIGURE CS2.1 The Answer screen shows questions users can answer on Aardvark.

users to react to these mock-ups, using a usability-testing method called talk-aloud protocol, which encourages people to verbalize the actions they're taking.

At this point we started writing code to build a rough first draft of the app. The first draft had very limited functionality since we wanted to release something quickly and add secondary features later. We released this app to a group of ten users, all employees of Aardvark, using the iPhone's Ad Hoc Distribution method.

We then began a process of collecting feedback, running usability tests, refining the app, and releasing a new version via Ad Hoc Distribution. Each time we released a new version we increased the size of the test group, ultimately reaching the 100-user limit. We had in-depth email exchanges and phone calls with each and every tester to delve into their feedback. With this large sample, we were able to identify patterns that signified problems or opportunities, then react quickly. We also quantitatively tracked usage with software from Flurry.

 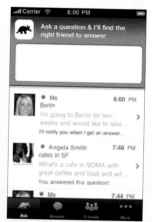

FIGURE CS2.2 Aardvark sends a push notification when users' questions are answered.

FIGURE CS2.3 The Ask screen shows the user's previous questions and answers on Aardvark.

How did the research impact your initial designs?

At each stage our user research fundamentally altered the app design. Our first interview series helped us validate the initial concept and confirmed that the core functionality should be asking a question and reading an answer. Subsequent usability tests taught us that the asking screen and the history screen should be combined (initially they were separate), that we needed an answering experience to allow for a more passive engagement (initially there was no answering experience), that people wanted to see a list of their friends using the app, and so on, right down to the position of the buttons and the shape of the icons.

How have your users responded to the app?

The response has been extremely positive. We built a feedback form directly into the app, and since launch we've received thousands of comments and suggestions. We've also benefited immensely from tracking usage patterns via Flurry, which helped uncover opportunities to improve the app. Since launching the app, we've released two updates, including new features, interface tweaks, and bug fixes that weren't surfaced by our initial test group. We are hard at work on our next update now, continuously iterating and improving the app design. ■

Evaluating the Competition

UNDERSTANDING USER NEEDS is critical, but there will be gaps in your knowledge if your up-front research stops there. You must also understand how your user needs are currently being met in the marketplace. An in-depth competitive user experience (UX) analysis can provide a holistic view of the competitive landscape, which you can then reference throughout the app design process.

This chapter introduces a variety of ways—two-by-two diagrams, heuristic evaluations, competitive benchmarking—to conduct competitive user experience analyses and explains how your findings can help shape your Product Definition Statement, which is outlined in Apple's *Human Interface Guidelines*.

Benefits

Competitive UX analyses can help your team uncover best practices as well as approaches to avoid when designing your app. These analyses can assess how competitors are meeting the user needs identified in your up-front user research and uncover market opportunities. In some cases a variation of the analysis may also be used when pitching your app to investors.

BEST PRACTICES

Best practices—aspects of the design that work well—can encompass almost any aspect of the user experience, including flows, screen layout, controls, and terminology. For example, imagine that you need to design the registration experience for your iPhone app. After conducting a competitive analysis, you may determine that users are more likely to complete registration when presented with a welcome screen. Thus, your best practice may state, "Include welcome screen with basic app and registration information," along with the rationale and representative examples. Keep in mind that iPhone app design is relatively new and is evolving each day. Some best practices you identify will have staying power; others may eventually need to be updated or replaced.

WHAT TO AVOID

Understanding what your competitors are doing wrong can also lead to insights about what you should do with your own app. Let's say you're developing an iPhone app that works with an existing web site. After evaluating the competition, you discover that none of those apps allow users to access "favorites" saved via the web site. As a result, users must duplicate their efforts—save the item once on the web, then again via the app. This pitfall can be translated into a best practice: "Ensure that web and iPhone favorites are synced."

NEEDS ALIGNMENT

Although best practices for flows and user interface elements are important, they are meaningless if the overall app does not meet user needs. Competitive UX analyses can help assess where the competition has succeeded in this regard and where they fall short. For example, your user research may indicate that the primary users of "to-do" apps must have the ability to sync their "to-do" items with their desktop "to-do" list. If none of your competitors enable users to achieve this goal, you would have identified a gap in the landscape as well as an opportunity for your app to fill that gap.

INSPIRATION

UX competitive reviews tend to focus on strengths and weaknesses in usability terms, but there are many observations that are hard to categorize—they have an intangible quality that makes them distinctive or attractive. These things could be identified as "strengths," but they are much more: They are inspiration; they are what gets people excited about design. For example, when my colleague interviewed a college student about her favorite iPhone app, Fluid, she gleefully described the experience of touching the screen and watching it respond. Does this fit into a specific usability category? Not exactly. So while you should be thinking about user needs and usability, you should also be noticing the subtle things that don't have a clear definition or category. Donald Norman delves into this subject in his book *Emotional Design*.[1]

Apps to Include

As you prepare your list of apps to analyze, consider consulting with your friends, perusing relevant categories in the App Store, and reading app reviews of competitive or similar apps. It may be tempting to focus exclusively on your top competitors, but that's not necessarily the most effective strategy. If your top competitors have nearly identical user experiences, you may not learn anything significant after evaluating the first one. Instead, you may find it valuable to expand your evaluation to include emerging competitors with distinct user experiences and noteworthy apps in related domains.

NOTE

While it's valuable to focus on the iPhone space, consider branching out to other platforms—web, desktop, other mobile solutions—especially when there are few competing iPhone apps. In addition, you may want to include consumer products with little or no software. For example, when designing a whiteboard app, it would make sense to review ordinary office whiteboards, pens, erasers, and so on.

Methods

In this section we'll look at a variety of competitive UX analysis methods, including

- Needs alignment charts
- Two-by-two diagrams
- Heuristic evaluations
- Competitive benchmarking

NEEDS ALIGNMENT CHARTS

Needs alignment charts are an effective way to see how your competitors are currently meeting user needs. Places where needs are met can be indicated with

---

1. Donald Norman, *Emotional Design: Why We Love (or Hate) Everyday Things* (Basic Books, 2003).

yes/no values, scores, check marks, or brief descriptions[2] (**TABLES 5.1–5.2**). Given their brevity and reliance on text, the charts are less useful when formulating best practices or seeking design inspiration.

TABLE 5.1 A Sample Needs Alignment Chart with Check Marks

Needs	Urbanspoon (1.07)	Yelp (1.10)
Find restaurants near me	√	√
Bookmark restaurant		√
Call restaurant	√	√
Map restaurant	√	√
Get directions		√
Rate restaurant	√	√
Review restaurant	√	√

TABLE 5.2 A Sample Needs Alignment Chart with Brief Descriptions

Needs	Urbanspoon (1.07)	Yelp (1.10)
Find restaurants near me	Shows ~50 restaurants; list is top-heavy on UI elements	Shows only ten restaurants; categories take up most of the screen
Bookmark restaurant		Available from the restaurant screen
Call restaurant	Must confirm before call made	Goes directly to call
Map restaurant	Must leave the app to go to Google	Interactive map; user can stay in context
Get directions		Available from the restaurant screen
Rate restaurant	Thumbs up/down	Five-star rating system
Review restaurant	Can write on the phone and share via Facebook and Twitter	Can draft on the phone and finish on the web site; also has "quick tips"—short reviews

---

2. Dan Brown, *Communicating Design* (New Riders, 2007), Chapter 5.

TWO-BY-TWO DIAGRAMS

Two-by-two diagrams are an easy way to illustrate the overall app landscape and identify high-level opportunities. As indicated by the name, these diagrams focus on two defining aspects of your app. The criteria will vary depending on the domain and your app strategy. For example, FIGURE 5.1 shows a two-by-two diagram created for the Foodspotting service, which includes a web site and an iPhone app. One axis indicates how food is presented in the competitive landscape—verbal versus visual—and the other indicates to what degree the service is focused on food. These axes were chosen since they effectively illustrate how Foodspotting can stand out from the competition.

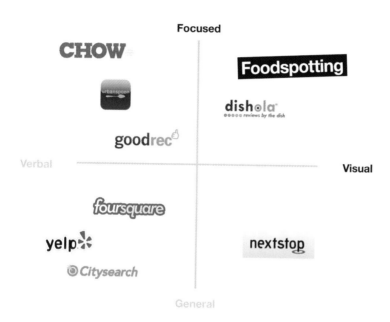

FIGURE 5.1 Two-by-two diagram for Foodspotting *(Courtesy of Alexa Andrzejewski)*

HEURISTIC EVALUATIONS

Heuristic evaluations involve inspecting a user interface and judging its compliance with recognized usability principles, known as *heuristics*.[3] Over the years, practitioners and researchers have adapted the method for different industries and platforms.[4] One common alteration is to walk through the interface with user

---

3. Jakob Nielsen, "Ten Usability Heuristics," www.useit.com/papers/heuristic/heuristic_list.html.
4. Enrico Bertini, Silvia Gabrielli, and Stephen Kimani, "Appropriating and Assessing Heuristics for Mobile Computing," *Proceedings of the Working Conference on Advanced Visual Interfaces* (ACM, 2006), http://portal.acm.org/citation.cfm?id=1133291.

scenarios, instead of systematically going through the user interface screen by screen.[5] Aspects of heuristic evaluation we'll examine here include

- Potential heuristics
- Use of scenarios
- Location of the evaluation (laboratory versus field)
- Capturing and documenting findings

Heuristics

The heuristics you choose can be based on established lists, such as Jakob Nielsen's heuristics or Bruce Tognazzini's "First Principles of Interaction Design."[6] However, in most cases you'll want to adapt and expand these more generic classics to include specific areas of interest for your app. For example, location-based apps may have their own heuristics (e.g., "Users can always locate their current position"), and content creation apps may have heuristics for topics such as autosaving content. At a minimum you'll want to adapt the classic heuristics for the iPhone, removing web and desktop references. Nielsen's severity ranking scale and iPhone-adapted heuristics are included in **TABLE 5.3** and **FIGURE 5.2**.

One of the major weaknesses of heuristics is the emphasis on usability problems. Understanding what your competitors are doing wrong is valuable, but there are also best practices that you'll want to emulate. Moreover, you will undoubtedly be inspired by many of the innovative design solutions in the iPhone space. As a result, you should stray from the heuristics from time to time. They're an excellent starting point, but they can be limiting if you're trying to match every observation to a specific heuristic. If something is interesting to you—good or bad—and there isn't a label, create your own!

TABLE 5.3 Nielsen Severity Ranking Scale[7]

Rating	Description
0	I don't agree that this is a usability problem at all.
1	Cosmetic problem only. Need not be fixed unless extra time is available.
2	Minor usability problem. Fixing this should be given low priority.
3	Major usability problem. Important to fix, so should be given high priority.
4	Usability catastrophe. Imperative to fix this before product can be released.

---

5. Shirlina Po et al., "Heuristic Evaluation and Mobile Usability: Bridging the Realism Gap," *Mobile Human-Computer Interaction* (ACM, 2004), www.springerlink.com/content/yven5m13vf437y1u/.
6. Bruce Tognazzini, "First Principles of Interaction Design," www.asktog.com/basics/firstPrinciples.html.
7. Jakob Nielsen, "Severity Ratings for Usability Problems," www.useit.com/papers/heuristic/severityrating.html.

1. Visibility of app status

The app should always keep users informed about what is going on, through appropriate feedback.

Shazam provides feedback as it analyzes audio.

2. Match between app and the real world

The app should sense the user's environment and adapt the information display accordingly.

The compass changes the map orientation as needed.

3. User control and freedom

Users often choose app functions by mistake and need a clearly marked "emergency exit."

"Cancel" and "x" buttons are common iPhone controls.

4. Error prevention

Eliminate error-prone conditions or check for them and present users with a recovery option.

Spell check has an option to reject its recommendation.

5. Consistency and standards

Users should not have to wonder whether different words, situations, or actions mean the same thing.

Kindle uses standard controls for bookmarking and showing progress.

6. Recognition rather than recall

Minimize the user's memory load by making objects, actions, and options visible.

Yelp's Recents tab stores businesses recently viewed.

7. Flexibility and efficiency of use

Accelerators can help expedite tasks and reduce typing.

Urbanspoon provides suggestions as a user enters a query.

8. Aesthetic and minimalist design

Screens should not contain information that is irrelevant or rarely needed.

Photo controls are hidden when not in use.

9. Help users recognize, diagnose, and recover from errors

Error messages should be expressed in plain language that precisely indicates the problem and the solution.

Epicurious displays a message when users are offline.

10. Help and documentation

Help should be contextual, concise, and specific.

Ocarina provides contextual help upon start-up; users can also access tutorials while using the app.

FIGURE 5.2 Nielsen's ten usability heuristics adapted for the iPhone

Scenarios

Depending on the evaluation goals, you can walk through the entire app or focus on a small set of scenarios. When embarking on a new app design, I recommend evaluating as much of the competitors' designs as possible. If time is limited, focus on the scenarios that enable users to achieve their primary goals and postpone scenarios associated with secondary goals. Here are potential differences between these goals, using Urbanspoon as an example.

Primary goals:

- Find a restaurant.
- Get directions to the restaurant.

Secondary goals:

- Review a restaurant.
- Add/edit restaurant information.

Apps that are connected to web sites or desktop applications should not be considered in isolation, especially when some level of syncing is involved. For example, Yelp enables users to draft reviews on their iPhone and then complete the reviews on the Yelp site. Of course, it's not necessary to review the entire Yelp web site, but it would be important to provide a scenario that includes completing the draft started on the iPhone app.

Laboratory versus Field

Heuristic evaluations can take place in the lab or in the field—the decision should be based on user behavior, the type of app, and the dependency on context to generate the insights needed.[8] For example, if you're evaluating an app that is largely driven by location-based data, such as Yelp or Foursquare, you should be out in the field to fully evaluate the user experience. However, if the app has less demanding contextual dependencies, you may be able to simulate the context in the lab. If you take a simulation approach, some questions to consider include the following:

- **Environment**

    What is the environment like where the app is used—is it dark, noisy, crowded? Think of creative ways to simulate this environment in the lab.

---

8. Christian Monrad Nielsen et al., "It's Worth the Hassle! The Added Value of Evaluating the Usability of Mobile Systems in the Field," *Proceedings of the 4th Nordic Conference on Human-Computer Interaction: Changing Roles* (ACM, 2006), www.usabilityprofessionals.org/upa_publications/jus/2005_november/mobile.html; Anne Kaikkonen et al., "Usability Testing of Mobile Applications: A Comparison between Laboratory and Field Testing," *Journal of Usability Studies* 1 (November 2005).

- **Concurrent activities**

  What other activities occur concurrently? If the user watches TV, sit back and relax. But if the user is typically running or walking, you may need to get moving!

- **Entities**

  What other people, devices, or objects are involved when the app is in use? Apps used in pairs (e.g., games or messaging) will require help from your colleagues.

- **Time**

  Is the app used during a certain time of day or season? If your app is influenced by these factors, schedule your heuristic evaluation accordingly.

- **Network**

  Does the app require an Internet connection? Consider trying the app in the company elevator or basement, or switch to Airplane Mode and see how the app behaves. Also, you may want to test the app without WiFi (with only a cell connection), or with only WiFi on but a slow WiFi connection.

- **User data**

  Does one need existing data to fully evaluate the app? You may need to create a user account and pre-populate it with content before getting started.

Capturing Findings

If the heuristic evaluations are conducted out in the field, take shorthand notes and expand upon them later. Regardless of whether you're in the lab or field, be sure to take copious screenshots along the way. When you return to your office, consider posting the screenshots on foam boards, then adding sticky notes with your observations, as shown in **FIGURE 5.3**. After going through each competitor, start looking for themes across competitors. Placing similar screens side by side can help illuminate differences. For example, **FIGURE 5.4** includes heuristics as well as interesting terminology and navigation differences; Yelp uses the term *Nearby* whereas Urbanspoon uses *Near Me*.

Documenting Your Findings

Depending on your company's needs, foam boards covered with screenshots and observations may be sufficient documentation for your team. In the past, my teammates and I have kept these types of boards in our "war room" and referred to them over the course of a particular project. Alternatively, you can create slides with findings and recommendations; a few examples can be found on Ginsburg

FIGURE 5.3 The Yelp iPhone app search form and results with relevant heuristics: "Flexibility & efficiency of use" and "Recognition rather than recall"

FIGURE 5.4 Side-by-side comparison of the Yelp and Urbanspoon Nearby/Near Me views. In this particular case, both designs have some weaknesses—too many categories and too cluttered—thus the insight might be "Prioritize the display of business information" (as opposed to categories and UI debris).

Design's Slideshare page.[9] And if you really need a formal document, you can use the same outline included in the slides, with a more fully developed narrative. Your outline might contain the following information:

- Executive summary
- Methodology
- Apps included
- Scenarios included
- Findings with annotated screens
- Best practices

COMPETITIVE USABILITY BENCHMARKING

Although heuristic evaluations will provide rich insights, your company may want to supplement these qualitative findings with quantitative data. One widely used method is competitive usability benchmarking, which involves quantitatively measuring how well users perform certain tasks with your competitors' apps. Metrics typically logged include

- Number of errors
- Task completion time
- Whether the task was successfully completed

---

9. Ginsburg Design on Slideshare, www.slideshare.net/ginsburgdesign/.

Benchmarking studies focus more on the metrics and less on the understanding of why there are problems; this type of controlled focus is needed in order to generate comparable results.

Benefits

Benchmark findings will help you assess where your competitors are failing in the user experience and may suggest ways to differentiate your app. For example, imagine that you're creating an app for finding local restaurants and you've decided to conduct a benchmarking study that would include Yelp and Urbanspoon. If you discovered that only a small percentage of users are able to successfully create a new account on the iPhone, this may be an area where you could differentiate your user experience. Additionally, you could use this metric to establish goals for your app. If the success rate for your competitors' sign-up was 50 percent, perhaps you would establish a goal of 60 or 70 percent for your app.

Protocol

In traditional usability studies, the facilitator asks participants to think aloud as they proceed through a series of tasks. This enables the facilitator to understand the participants' cognitive processes and whether the interface supports their way of thinking. In the case of benchmarking studies, facilitators tend to stay in the background, interrupting only to start and stop tasks. One of the main reasons is that benchmarking is focused on measurement and the "thinking aloud" protocol prolongs task completion times, making it difficult to compare results across participants. Keep in mind that the benchmarking numbers won't necessarily tell you the *why* behind completion rates. Therefore, you may want to follow the benchmarking session with an interview to probe into specific interactions with the app.

NOTE

The "thinking aloud" protocol and other usability-testing details will be discussed in Chapter 8, "Usability-Testing App Concepts."

Capturing Data

How you capture benchmarking data depends on your needs. Simply put, the more data you need, the more sophisticated the setup.[10] Here are three possible configurations:

- **Low-tech**

  With this option, the facilitator manually notes errors, completion times, and whether the scenarios were successfully completed. This can be accomplished in the lab with relative ease but can be more challenging in the field.

---

10. Antti Oulasvirta and Tuomo Nyyssönen, "Flexible Hardware Configurations for Studying Mobile Usability," *Journal of Usability Studies* 4 (February 2009), www.usabilityprofessionals.org/upa_publications/jus/2009february/oulasvirta1.html.

- **Logging software**

  Another option is to use logging software combined with observation.[11] This reduces the burden on the facilitator and generates more accurate start and end times.

- **Audio and video**

  Finally, you can capture audio and video of the sessions. Video setups can range from one camera on the phone to multiple cameras that capture the participant's face and environment. More complex setups provide facilitators with a view into the participant's screen.

Other Setup Tips

Additional tips on the number of participants, apps, and scenarios are discussed in this section.

- **Number of participants**

  The number of participants is highly correlated to the degree of confidence you can have in your results. Statistical sampling best practices tell us that 30 observations is a good rule of thumb for obtaining precise results, but you may need to adapt this number depending on your study goals. You can recruit participants using the profile identified in your up-front user research, as discussed in Chapter 3, "Introduction to User Research."

- **Number of apps**

  Given the amount of time required for capture and analysis, you may want to focus on two apps. But if you have the resources, you can certainly benchmark additional apps.

- **Number of scenarios**

  The benchmark study should cover the scenarios that enable users to achieve their primary goals. However, if these take more than one hour, you'll want to prioritize accordingly.

- **Laboratory versus field**

  As with the heuristic evaluations and other user research, the context should be determined by the type of app. Location-based apps should be tested in the field, but testing of apps with less stringent contextual dependencies can take place in the lab.[12]

---

11. Jurgen Kawalek, Annegret Stark, and Marcel Riebeck, "A New Approach to Analyse Human-Mobile Computer Interaction," *Journal of Usability Studies* 3 (February 2008), www.usabilityprofessionals.org/upa_publications/jus/2008february/kawalek.html.
12. Kaikkonen et al., "Usability Testing of Mobile Applications."

Analyzing and Presenting Data

Your data analysis approach will be influenced by the benchmark goals and data-capturing technique. With low-tech data capture—manually logged data—you could create simple tables (TABLES 5.4–5.5). If you use logging software, most products provide built-in analysis and charting tools.

Additionally, if the sessions were recorded, you may want to analyze the video. However, keep in mind that video analysis is labor-intensive. If you have solid notes, video can be used for reference or to supplement your report.

TABLE 5.4 **Comparing Scenario Completion Rates Alongside Your Company's Goals**

	Competitor A	Competitor B	Our Goal
Scenario 1	50%	55%	60%
Scenario 2	40%	60%	65%
Scenario 3	45%	55%	60%

TABLE 5.5 **Comparing Number of Errors Alongside Your Company's Goals**

	Competitor A	Competitor B	Our Goal
Scenario 1	3	2	1
Scenario 2	4	5	2
Scenario 3	2	1	0

Choosing a Method

As you consider which method to use, it's important to evaluate your competitive analysis goals. Are you interested in formulating best practices? Do you want an overview of how your competitors are meeting users' needs? Are you seeking inspiration? In many cases combining methods is the most effective strategy. Strengths and weaknesses of alternative methods are summarized in TABLE 5.6.

TABLE 5.6 Summary of Competitive Analysis Methods

Method	Strengths	Weaknesses
Needs alignment charts	Good for assessing where competitors are meeting user needs	No best practices or inspiration
Two-by-two diagrams	Good way to illustrate how the app fits into the overall competitive landscape	No best practices or inspiration Attributes highly subjective
Heuristic evaluations	Fast and inexpensive Good for determining best practices and finding inspiration	Dependent on reviewer's expertise and heuristics used
Competitive benchmarking	Good for gathering quantitative data	Time-consuming and expensive No understanding of *why* behind behaviors unless follow-up interview is included

Impact on the Product Definition Statement

In the previous chapter we discussed how up-front user research can help refine your Product Definition Statement—the declaration of your application's main purpose and its intended audience. An in-depth analysis of your competitors may also impact your app purpose and audience. To illustrate, let's revisit the Product Definition Statement from Chapter 4, "Analyzing User Research":

> *An app to help urban art enthusiasts find, share, and review art events.*

As a result of your competitive analysis, perhaps you'll discover that there are ten other apps that claim to provide the same exact service. How will your app be different? Imagine that your competitive research revealed that only one app is focused on outdoor art—graffiti, sculpture, murals. If you choose to focus on this type of art, your revised statement might look like this one:

> *An app to help urban art enthusiasts find, share, and review outdoor art.*

Additionally, let's say that you conducted a heuristic evaluation of potential competitors and identified common pain points in these apps. You may decide that overcoming key pain points (such as those related to primary goals) could be an effective way to distinguish your app. For example, users may be more likely to choose your app if it was easier to geo-tag outdoor art; thus you may further refine your Product Definition Statement:

> *An easy way for urban art enthusiasts to geo-tag, review, and share outdoor art.*

Summary

This chapter discussed how competitive UX analyses can provide a holistic view of the competitive landscape, which you can then reference throughout the app design process. In particular, these analyses can help you formulate best practices, identify opportunities, and provide inspiration.

We introduced a variety of competitive analysis methods—needs alignment charts, two-by-two diagrams, heuristic evaluations, and competitive benchmarking—which can be combined and adapted to meet your app needs. Finally, we explained how your findings can help shape your Product Definition Statement, the declaration of your application's main purpose and its intended audience.

Competitive analyses are beneficial for both new and existing apps. As you embark on competitive analysis for your own app, remember the following:

- Cast a wide net when selecting competitors to evaluate (e.g., other platforms and related domains).
- Develop your own heuristics to cover specific areas of interest for your app.
- Post your findings in your company hallway or team war room so everyone can easily refer to them during the design process. ▪

Concept poster; see page 123

Concept screen; see page 124

Design comic; see page 127

Paper prototype; see page 143

Video prototype; see page 153

Usability testing; see page 164

PART THREE

Developing Your App Concept

After conducting your user research and competitive analysis, you may be eager to start coding your app. While this approach may be effective in certain cases (if you are building a very basic Utility-style application, for example), most apps can benefit from sketching and prototyping *before* coding.

Sketching and prototyping give you an opportunity to think through some of your design choices before you implement them in Xcode or start laying out each element in Interface Builder. We'll discuss the pros and cons of various methods in the following chapters:

- Chapter 6, "Exploring App Concepts," introduces a variety of sketching approaches, such as storyboards and concept diagrams.
- Chapter 7, "Prototyping App Concepts," explains how to bring your sketches to life by prototyping the app on paper, electronically, or in video.
- Chapter 8, "Usability-Testing App Concepts," discusses how to user-test your app and how to incorporate your findings into your app before you submit it to the App Store for approval.

Although these topics are introduced in a linear fashion, the overall process is iterative, so you may find yourself going back and forth among these three activities as your application concept evolves.

Exploring App Concepts

ARMED WITH YOUR RESEARCH FINDINGS (user needs, scenarios, competitive analyses), you will be well equipped to start brainstorming and sketching app concepts. In fact, you probably started sketching concepts when you first thought about building an app. At this stage you'll want to expand upon these initial concepts and start exploring additional ones.

This chapter starts out by discussing how to create a design-friendly environment and how to hold effective brainstorming sessions. We'll then spend the remainder of the chapter discussing various ways to illustrate and communicate your early explorations.

Additionally, this chapter includes case studies on the Foodspotting, Not For Tourists, and MUSE apps. Here you'll find insights into how the application design teams used user experience methods to conceptualize their applications.

Creating a Design-Friendly Environment

Before getting started, spend some time creating a design-friendly work environment. If your office is anything like my previous ones, you're probably surrounded by a computer screen, some combination of half- or full-sized cubicle walls, and—for the lucky ones—a window. Although quarters may be tight, lobby for a dedicated physical space for your project, such as a conference room, one large wall (**FIGURE 6.1**), or a corner in a common room. In this space you can post personas, competitive analyses, and designs in progress. Having these artifacts in an open space will enable your team to step back and look at designs together. Ideas will flow more freely and collaboration will become more organic. Even colleagues not directly involved in design can see your work as it develops. If you have remote team members, you can send them photos when significant changes are made and follow up with electronic versions to keep everyone on the same page.

FIGURE 6.1 Designer sketching at the Good Design Faster workshop run by Adaptive Path in April 2009 *(Courtesy of Sara Summers, photographer, www.uxarray.com)*

Here is a list of some supplies you may want to purchase for brainstorming and day-to-day design:

- **Whiteboard and camera**

    Consider getting a portable whiteboard for impromptu brainstorming. Having a portable whiteboard will give you more flexibility since it can be moved from room to room. Make sure you have your iPhone or other camera available for capturing whiteboard sketches.

- **Foam core**

  Use this to tack or tape research findings and designs. Extra-large boards can be ordered from office supply or art stores.

- **Easel Post-its**

  Easel Post-its (20 × 23) make it easier to rearrange items and save them for later during collaborative brainstorming and sketching.

- **Sketchbooks**

  Experiment with different sizes and textures. I have about three different sizes: 9 × 12, 6 × 8, and tiny ones at 3 × 4 that I carry with me at all times. You never know when inspiration may strike! Be sure these don't have horizontal lines—they get in the way—though grids can work well for some purposes.

- **Pencils and markers**

  Again, I recommend that you experiment with different point sizes and colors. If you're not up for experimentation, you might want to use Leah Buley's list[1] as a starting point; she's a designer at Adaptive Path.

- **Odds and ends**

  Reusable tape, drafting dots, thumbtacks, magnets (for magnetic white-boards), rulers, and lots of colorful Post-its in varying sizes are useful. Post-its can be used to organize concepts, develop information hierarchies, and more. If you want to get even more creative, I suggest you read about IDEO's famous Tech Box that contains everything from smart fabrics to clever toys.[2]

- **Snacks**

  Sweet and savory snacks will come in handy during afternoon brainstorming sessions. For morning sessions, you may want to provide breakfast.

Effective Brainstorming

To kick off your app concept explorations, consider holding a group brainstorming session. While brainstorming seems easy enough on the surface, I've seen many attempts fail over the years. The reasons differ—bad timing, no structure, wrong people—but they all leave team members thinking the same thing: What a waste of time! If one session fails, teams will be reluctant to hold future sessions. To avoid this outcome, try some of the brainstorming advice that follows.

---

1. Leah Buley, "Our Favorite Tools for Sketching," www.adaptivepath.com/ideas/essays/archives/001072.php (April 2009).
2. IDEO, "Tech Box for IDEO," www.ideo.com/work/item/tech-box/ (1999).

SET ASIDE ENOUGH TIME

One of the biggest mistakes is not allocating enough time for brainstorming. If you are focusing on one feature, an hour may be sufficient, but more time is needed when brainstorming concepts for an entire product. At the same time, participants can lose steam if the sessions are too long. Consider carving out two to three hours with two 10-minute breaks.

ESTABLISH GOALS

Establishing your brainstorming goals is critical: Are you brainstorming overall app concepts or focusing on a specific aspect of your app? Are you interested in developing completely new ideas, building upon previous ones, or both? Whatever you decide, communicating these goals will help set expectations and ensure that everyone is on the same page.

BE INCLUSIVE

You can (and should) brainstorm on your own, but collaborative sessions may generate new ideas and perspectives. If you work alone, consider bringing in former colleagues or tapping into your professional networks. Alternatively, if you work within a company, try to include three to eight team members with different expertise. In addition to engineering, design, and product management, you may want to invite individuals from teams such as sales and customer support.

HAVE AN AGENDA

When I think back to successful brainstorming sessions, images of my team members rapidly scribbling on whiteboards or large Post-its come to mind. They were energized by their colleagues' enthusiasm and the excitement in the room. But how did they get there? Successful brainstorming may look chaotic when in full swing, but most sessions start with some level of structure.

When conducting brainstorming after user research, I usually provide participants with copies of the personas and their needs. If we have a large group, we may break up into teams of three or four people and brainstorm ways to address these needs. For example, in the case of an app for finding art events, one team may brainstorm solutions for the local art enthusiast, while another team brainstorms solutions for the tourist art enthusiast. In addition to providing participants with a problem statement, it's important to articulate the desired outcome.

Some brainstorming organizers are simply looking for bullet points, whereas others may want sketches and storyboards. If you are seeking sketches—which I recommend—be sure to have the appropriate supplies on hand.

PROVIDE INSPIRATION

As mentioned earlier, you'll want to share findings from your up-front user and competitive research, including your refined Product Definition Statement. In addition, consider providing other app-related objects or experiences for inspiration. The possibilities are endless—you just need to decide what works well for your particular app.

For example, let's say you are developing a photo-editing app. You might ask brainstorming participants to bring their own snapshots. Having their own photos nearby will make the brainstorming more meaningful to them. Also, keep in mind that brainstorming doesn't have to start in a cramped conference room with a blank whiteboard. If you are developing an app to identify plants, you might take your team on a nature hike and schedule a session in a picnic area. Providing hands-on experience in the real world will enable everyone to think more like users.

LAY GROUND RULES

Consider laying ground rules before the brainstorming begins. Bob Sutton is well known for the ones listed here[3] (IDEO has an expanded version[4]):

- **Don't allow criticism**

  Criticism may be directed at the idea itself or its feasibility. For example, some team members may dismiss ideas that seem too challenging to implement.

- **Encourage wild ideas**

  Although it may be clear to everyone that certain ideas are unlikely to happen, those same ideas might also inspire other creative directions, so keep an open mind!

- **Go for quantity**

  Brainstorming should elicit as many ideas as possible (**FIGURE 6.2**). If you spend the entire time polishing one or two, many promising ideas will be left undiscovered. Also, try to aim for *divergent* ideas—you'll limit the possibilities if you merely reorder tabs or change labels.

- **Combine and/or improve on others' ideas**

  It would be great if one person put forth a fully formed idea, but most ideas are nuggets that can benefit from further brainstorming. Additionally,

---

3. Robert Sutton, "Brainstorming in the *Wall Street Journal*," http://bobsutton.typepad.com/my_weblog/2006/06/brainstorming_i.html (June 2006).
4. Linda Tischler, "Seven Secrets to Good Brainstorming," Fast Company (March 2001), www.fastcompany.com/articles/2001/03/kelley.html.

rough ideas can be improved when combined with other ideas. Over the course of the brainstorming, it's helpful if an experienced facilitator looks for these connections and communicates them to the group.

CAPTURING IDEAS

TIP

If some team members can't attend, ask them to submit ideas in advance so the documenter can add them during brainstorming.

As brainstorming participants voice their ideas, a facilitator should manage the discussion while someone else writes the ideas on a whiteboard, easel Post-its, or roll paper. Remember, all ideas should be given consideration, so the documenter should not be discarding ideas along the way. Some ideas may not be feasible in the near term but could become viable down the road.

FIGURE 6.2 Brainstorming session held at the Interaction Design Pilot Year at the Danish Design School and Copenhagen Institute of Interaction Design, Fall 2008 *(Courtesy of Ujjval Panchal, photographer)*

SELECT PROMISING IDEAS

As you wind down your brainstorming session, start thinking about next steps: What ideas should we pursue? What should we defer for later? One popular way to simplify this process is to ask participants to identify the most promising solutions with "dot voting."[5] Give participants a handful of dots and ask them to place one next to each idea they think the company should pursue. Their recommendations should be based on the user needs identified in your up-front research as well as the company goals. Ideas with the most dots get prioritized for further development; the remaining ones can be documented for future reference.

Sketching Your Concepts

After your brainstorming session, you will have several potential directions for your app, along with partially completed sketches. Next, you should spend some time expanding upon these ideas. While you may be tempted to abandon your early sketches and reach for tools such as Adobe Fireworks or OmniGraffle (which will be useful later on), try to resist the temptation. This section discusses the benefits of starting with hand-drawn sketches (**FIGURE 6.3**) and introduces a variety of sketching techniques.

FIGURE 6.3 Developer sketching at iPhone Dev Camp, Silicon Valley, 2008
(Courtesy of George Chen)

---

5. Joyce Wykoff, "Group Brainstorming: Dot Voting with a Difference," www.innovationtools.com/ Articles/ArticleDetails.asp?a=141 (June 2004).

CHARACTERISTICS

The term *sketch* means different things to different people. In this book I refer to both the exercise that helps designers think through an idea and the resulting artifact that communicates the idea. Sketches in this context tend to have these qualities:[6]

- **Minimal detail**

  They may exclude items that are not central to the design; for example, some app sketches may omit the battery and status indicators.

- **Limited refinement**

  Screen contents may not be pixel perfect and may have a "rough" quality. Eschew visual treatment; focus on key tasks, features, and workflow.

- **Ambiguity**

  Sketches do not have to include the entire user experience or be fully worked out. Ambiguous sketches invite others to contribute their vision and collaboratively work through designs.

BENEFITS

Some benefits of starting with hand-drawn sketches include the ability to think big, the ability to break down boundaries, and improved collaboration among your team members.

Thinking Big

The goal of most sketching software programs—with the exception of low-fidelity tools like Balsamiq[7]—is to help you achieve perfection. They contain rulers, guides, alignment widgets, and other gadgets to help in this effort. Regardless of your good intentions, you may get dragged into pixel-pushing mode when working with this type of software. In the early exploration stage, the last thing you want to do is spend unnecessary time polishing designs. Your time should be spent thinking holistically, cracking open the overall concepts.

No Boundaries

Nearly all of the popular sketching software programs have iPhone design templates. These templates are particularly helpful when creating screens that contain standard controls. In most cases, however, your app will contain both standard and custom controls. If you're working with hand-drawn sketches, you can quickly add the custom items. With software templates, you may spend extra time hunting for the perfect icon or widget, or end up choosing something that's less than ideal.

---

6. Bill Buxton, *Sketching User Experiences* (Morgan Kaufmann, 2007).
7. Balsamiq, www.balsamiq.com/.

Collaborative

Another benefit of hand-drawn sketches is their collaborative quality. As discussed in Bill Buxton's *Sketching User Experiences*, sketches are social objects. They invite others to comment on them since they appear less finished, more open to criticism. For example, if you approach a colleague with a notebook sketch, it will be obvious that the design is a work in progress. In contrast, a highly polished Adobe Photoshop sketch may appear ready for coding, even if you intend to iterate on the design for two more weeks. Colleagues may be reluctant to suggest significant changes since they may seem like a burden.

BUT I CAN'T DRAW

Getting into sketching may seem challenging given that many people are accustomed to drawing with software. And, yes, sketching can be intimidating when looking at the work of experienced designers—their sketches can technically be described as rough and ambiguous but they are still somehow beautiful. Aesthetically pleasing sketches are a nice bonus, but your sketches don't have to be works of art since they are primarily a thinking and collaboration tool. If you are still uneasy, consider taking a drawing class at your local college or reading up on the subject (and practicing!).[8] Alternatively, you may want to start with tracing or stencils (**FIGURE 6.4**), then slowly add your own design elements. Once you figure out what works well for you, it will be hard to leave sketching out of your process. If you're still not comfortable with sketching, you may want to hire a sketch artist to help illustrate early design concepts.

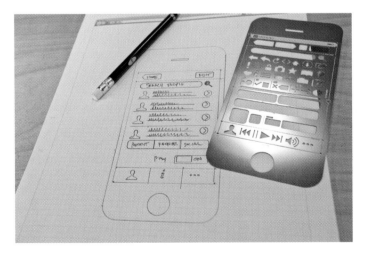

FIGURE 6.4 iPhone Stencil Kit by Design Commission
(Courtesy of Design Commission, www.designcommission.com)[9]

---

8. Dan Roam, *Back of the Napkin* (Portfolio Hardcover, 2008).
9. iPhone Stencil Kit, www.designcommission.com/shop/iphone-stencil-kit/.

SKETCHING TIPS

Regardless of your skill level, consider these tips as you delve into your app sketches:

- **Start simple**

  Having too many drawing tools at your disposal may overcomplicate your solutions as well as your process. When you begin sketching, consider limiting your toolkit to black Sharpies and unlined white paper (**FIGURE 6.5**). As you get comfortable with sketching, start to bring in additional tools for highlighting and shading.

- **Draw *almost* to scale**

  Fluidity and openness are important, but creating iPhone sketches at 8 × 10 may be challenging to scale back later. Having said that, trying to precisely fit the contents into the actual iPhone dimensions of 320 × 480 pixels (640 × 960 for iPhone 4) is not necessary in the early stages. Thus, I recommend drawing *almost* to scale—index cards are a good starting point. If you want to draw closer to scale, consider trying some of the iPhone notepads on the market.[10]

FIGURE 6.5 Designer working on iPhone app sketches at the Good Design Faster workshop run by Adaptive Path in April 2009 *(Courtesy of Sara Summers, photographer, www.uxarray.com)*

---

10. See, for example, Notepod, http://notepod.net/, and App Sketchbook, http://appsketchbook.com/.

- **Consider all of the senses**

  In contrast to other platforms, iPhone apps have a wide range of senses at the designer's disposal: sight, sound, touch. While it's tricky to make your paper sketches buzz and vibrate, you can start off by indicating swipe motions with arrows and sounds with annotations. Don't wait to think about these things until later.

TYPES OF SKETCHES

There are countless ways to sketch your app concepts. The approach you choose will largely depend on the app and your design goals. Be sure to tie these diagrams into your app personas and scenarios, as discussed in Chapter 4, "Analyzing User Research." Sketching approaches discussed in this section include

- Diagrams
- Posters
- App screens
- Storyboards
- Comics

Concept Diagrams

Starting with screen sketches may seem like the natural first step, but certain apps may warrant a more abstract approach—concept diagrams. In some cases the complexity of the app requires an abstract representation to distill the idea. Other times, screen sketches may simply be too limited—they won't capture all of the people, objects, devices, and so on. This section introduces you to concept diagrams for apps that are part of a larger system, apps with multiple objects, and apps with multiple users.

Part of a larger system. Many apps are part of a larger system that provides similar content or services via the web, desktop, or even print. When designing an app for one of these services, it's important to consider the entire system and the relationships between its various components. Concept diagrams can provide a holistic view of such systems and may include

- Connections between the components
- Paths users will take between components
- Notable differences between components

Multiple objects. Apps are increasingly interacting with real-world objects such as televisions, printers, and speakers. Some apps "push" content to the object, while others offer fine-grained control over the objects. For example, Sonos created an iPhone app to enable users to control speakers throughout their home, and the Zipcar app allows users to reserve, locate, and unlock cars. Given that a large part of these experiences take place outside the device, your sketches will fall short if they rely exclusively on iPhone screens. Consider including the following in these diagrams:

- Physical proximity of objects
- Orientation of objects
- Data exchanged
- Gestures and feedback mechanisms

Multiple users. A large number of iPhone apps for messaging, social networking, and gaming involve multiple users. Side-by-side screen designs (e.g., User A sitting next to User B) can illustrate basic interactions between users. However, when the app is relatively complex, it may help to start with a concept diagram. Consider including the following in your diagram:

- Roles of users
- Physical proximity of users
- Orientation of users in relation to each other and their iPhones
- Data exchanged (e.g., messages)
- Experience evoked (e.g., flirting)
- Gestures and feedback mechanisms

Concept Posters

Concept posters are a powerful way to illustrate your app vision without getting into the design details. As you formulate your app concept, they can be an effective tool for gathering feedback from stakeholders and prospective users. In the later design phases, the poster can be displayed in your war room and used to guide design decisions. Alexa Andrzejewski, the founder of Foodspotting, developed a concept poster template, which includes the following:

- **App name and tagline**
  The tagline should explain what your app is about in a few words.
- **Pitch**
  The pitch should convey whom the app is for, what problem it solves, and how it's different from existing apps. It may also incorporate elements of your Product Definition Statement.
- **Characteristics**
  These are the qualities that make your app unique and interesting.

- **Inspiration**

  This section should capture influences and inspirations for your app, which may include products or services uncovered in your research. If you have a relatively new concept, references to familiar products may help communicate your ideas.

- **Experience sketches**

  These are simple representations of the experience your app will provide. Previous research and ideation activities—user research, competitive research, brainstorming—will be valuable references as you create these sketches.

FIGURE 6.6 shows a concept poster that Alexa Andrzejewski created for her company, Foodspotting, Inc. According to Alexa, the simple stick figures she used to illustrate how to "Discover new foods" and "Build your personal food passport" were enough to get people excited about the experience and drove many of the design decisions down the road. In addition to sharing the concept poster with stakeholders, Alexa used the poster to elicit feedback from prospective users.

FIGURE 6.6 Concept poster created by Alexa Andrzejewski *(Courtesy of Alexa Andrzejewski, founder, foodspotting.com)*

Concept Screens

Concept screen sketches are another effective way to explore alternative directions without getting into design details. With this approach, the designer may illustrate one aspect of the user experience, while explaining other elements in written annotations or verbally. Adaptive Path used this strategy when developing iPhone app concepts for Smart.fm, a learning tool. Instead of sketching the entire user experience, they initially focused on Smart.fm's reward system, the way users measure their progress. For example, one concept called "Your World" uses the change of seasons as a metaphor for progress, and another, called "Scratch-off," uses scratch-off cards to show progress (**FIGURES 6.7–6.8**). Aspects of these sketches that work well include the hand gestures, simple screen contents, and concise annotations. Additional explorations and information on this project can be found online.[11]

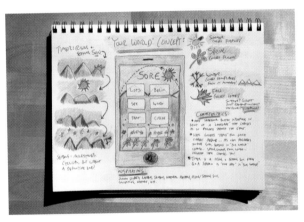

FIGURE 6.7 Your World concept for the Smart.fm iPhone app *(Courtesy of Dane Petersen)*

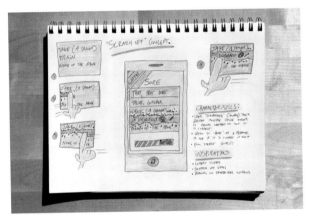

FIGURE 6.8 "Scratch-off" concept for the Smart.fm iPhone app *(Courtesy of Dane Petersen)*

Screen sketches can also be used to explore alternative interaction models for a particular concept. **FIGURE 6.9** illustrates how Cultured Code used sketches to help determine whether to include a tab bar or a list view for their Things iPhone app. The company has an impressive gallery of sketches that can be found online.[12]

Storyboards

Storyboards contain a series of illustrations or images displayed in sequence (**FIGURES 6.10–6.11**). They were originally created for pre-visualizing motion pictures but have been adapted for other interactive media such as web and mobile design.

---

11. Adaptive Path smart.fm Blog, www.adaptivepath.com/blog/category/smartfm/.
12. "Designing the UI of Things for iPhone," http://culturedcode.com/things/iphone/makingof/.

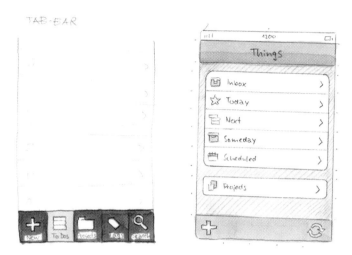

FIGURE 6.9 Alternative interaction models explored for the Things iPhone app
(Courtesy of Cultured Code)

With user-centered design, the "story" behind the storyboard is typically one of the scenarios from up-front user research. Each illustration in the sequence represents an action the user must take to reach the scenario goal. Storyboards may include arrows or instructions to indicate movement as well as annotations. In addition to communicating concepts, storyboards are an effective way to uncover potential user experience issues. As you walk through the sequence, you may discover missing elements or parts that can be more streamlined.

FIGURE 6.10 Storyboard for a project management app
(Courtesy of Daniel H. Chang)

FIGURE 6.11 Storyboard for a children's game app
(Courtesy of Jaehi Jung)

You can create your storyboards in a large sketchbook (at least 8 × 12 inches). Another option is to use a storyboard template like the one included in the book *Drawing Ideas: A Field Guide for Visual Thinking*,[13] by Mark Baskinger, an associate professor in the School of Design at Carnegie Mellon University.

Comics

NOTE

To learn more about creating comics, read Scott McCloud's classic *Understanding Comics*[14] or Kevin Cheng's book *See What I Mean*.[15]

Storyboards tend to focus on what users will see on their iPhone when interacting with your app. In contrast, comics can incorporate users, their environment, the screen, and the device itself. This holistic view is particularly valuable for apps where context is a defining aspect of the user experience. For example, if you were designing an augmented reality iPhone app, comics could be used to capture the relationships between the user, the device, and the points of interest highlighted in the app. Moreover, comics can communicate the human emotions evoked when using a particular app: delight, frustration, freedom.

Creating recognizable scenes and convincing characters may be a significant undertaking for many designers. In recent years, a number of web sites and tools have emerged to help designers create their own comics. The web site Pixton, for example, has template themes and a library of comic elements to jump-start the process. **FIGURE 6.12** shows an iPhone app comic created with Pixton's online tools. Another alternative is to combine photographs with sketches and dialogue. Whether you choose the template route, the photo route, or create your own, consider the tips listed here:

- Start with your primary scenario.
- Use your personas as characters (though not in the same scenario!).
- Include approximately six to ten panels for each scenario.

ADDITIONAL SKETCHING EXAMPLES

TIP

If you need some help adding gestures to your sketches, try the stencils created by Rachel Glaves.[16]

This section includes a few additional sketching examples (**FIGURES 6.13–6.14**). Aspects that work particularly well in these sketches include the hand gestures and their explorative quality—these are clearly "thinking" as opposed to presentation sketches. "Thinking" sketches are rough in appearance; they explore what's possible and may include many unanswered questions. Presentation sketches are more polished and less ambiguous.

13. *Drawing Ideas*, www.drawingideasbook.com/.
14. Scott McCloud, *Understanding Comics: The Invisible Art* (Harper Paperbacks, 1994).
15. Kevin Cheng, *See What I Mean: How to Use Comics to Communicate Ideas* (Rosenfeld Media, 2009).
16. Kicker Studio Touchscreen Stencils, www.kickerstudio.com/blog/2008/12/touchscreen-stencils/.

FIGURE 6.12 Augmented reality app comic created with Pixton *(Copyright © 2009, Pixton Comics, Inc.)*

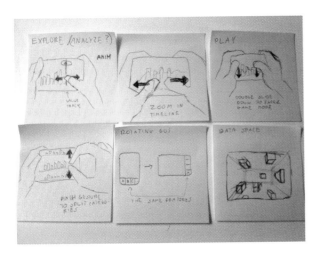

FIGURE 6.13 Sketches exploring gestures for a personal finance iPhone app *(Courtesy of Marcin Ignac)*

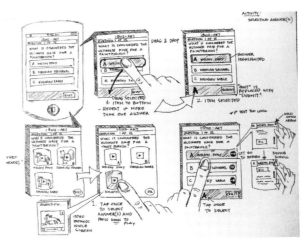

FIGURE 6.14 Sketches exploring an answer selection for a quiz iPhone app *(Courtesy of Jason de Runa)*

Common Questions

As you consider which sketching approach is right for your app, you may have some questions about the level of effort and the relationship of the sketches to other design deliverables. Answers to these questions and others are covered in this section.

WHAT IF I'M WORKING ON AN APP WITH FEW VISUALS TO SKETCH?

Certain immersive apps may not be well suited to the sketching approaches described. For example, storyboarding a musical instrument with pen and paper is missing its defining element—sound! That said, other parts of your app may benefit from visual representations, such as the first-time user experience, settings, and tutorials. Sketching these elements can be effective for almost any type of app. Alternatively, you may find that these elements are too interwoven into the overall app experience. In this case you may want to jump right into prototyping, which will be discussed in the following chapter.

WHEN SHOULD I CREATE FLOWCHARTS?

Flows are an incredibly important part of the iPhone app design process, but I recommend starting with one of the sketching approaches introduced in this chapter. Once you have explored alternative directions and narrowed down your options—we'll discuss the narrowing part in the next chapter—move on to flowcharts. If you begin with flowcharting software, you may get into edge case resolution mode as you branch every possible outcome. Don't get me wrong; solving edge cases is critical, but not in the concept stage.

HOW MUCH OF MY DESIGN TIME SHOULD BE DEVOTED TO CONCEPT DEVELOPMENT?

Every project is different, but try to allocate at least 20 percent of your overall design time to concept explorations. Having a solid concept will help make the rest of the design process go smoothly.

Summary

Concept exploration is perhaps the most liberating design phase—everybody's creative juices are flowing, there's excitement in the air, the possibilities are endless. However, designers often skip this process and run with the first good idea. While this may lead to success, it also runs the risk of missing out on something more thoughtful, innovative, and inspired.

This chapter discussed how to approach this important concept exploration phase. Specifically, we provided brainstorming tips and looked at alternative sketching techniques—diagrams, posters, screens, storyboards, and comics. As you start exploring concepts for your own app, remember the following:

- Creating a design-friendly space encourages informal collaboration.
- Team brainstorming is an effective way to jump-start concept development.
- Hand-drawn sketches allow you to think big. Instead of perfecting just one design, you can focus on developing several innovative solutions.

Whatever brainstorming and sketching approach you choose, the investment will be well worth your time. The next two chapters—Chapter 7, "Prototyping App Concepts," and Chapter 8, "Usability-Testing App Concepts"—will discuss how to prototype and evaluate your app concepts. ■

CASE STUDY 3
Foodspotting

FOODSPOTTING is a visual local guide that lets you find dishes instead of just restaurants. This web and mobile app is powered by Foodspotters, who earn points and recognition for sharing foods they've spotted while enabling Foodseekers to find whatever they're craving and see what's good at any restaurant. Foodspotting was founded by Alexa Andrzejewski, formerly a user experience designer from Adaptive Path, and Ted Grubb, a Rails engineer behind Get Satisfaction.

FIGURE CS3.1 Foodspotting start screen before usability research

FIGURE CS3.2 Foodspotting start screen after usability research

What inspired you to start Foodspotting?

When I visited Japan and Korea a year ago, I discovered dishes I'd never heard of before, from okonomiyaki to tteokbokki. Upon returning to San Francisco, I mined sites like Yelp and Chowhound in search of these dishes, only to find the local guides too broad and the discussion boards too unstructured. As I shared my frustration, I quickly found I was not alone.

How did you approach the project?

After the ideas had percolated in my head and in note-books for a few weeks, I knew I needed to both vet the idea with potential users and attract cofounders and teammates to make it real. To make the ideas tangible, I created a concept poster—a tool that I'd developed for a previous mobile project at Adaptive Path. By showing this poster to potential users, I was able to see which aspects of the Foodspotting experience were most compelling to people and which were interesting but not essential.

How did you proceed after your initial research?

I began the design phase not in front of my computer, but out at restaurants with friends, with a pocket-sized Mole-skine in hand. As we looked at the menu together, I was able to ask relevant questions, like "What do you think about when deciding what to order? What do you wish you knew?" I'd sketch up an interface idea on the spot and refine it through discussion over dinner. The ideas that emerged in the real-world context of use were almost always more interesting and relevant than the ones that I'd come up with sitting at home. Not to mention it was a great excuse to eat out with friends and try new places.

Were you able to user-test your early designs?

To test my early designs on potential users, I printed them on card stock and cut them out [**FIGURE CS3.1**]. I carried this pocket-sized deck of cards in my pocket, and whenever someone was interested, I would pull them out and ask both high-level questions like "Who does this app seem to be for? What makes it different from other food apps?" and detailed questions like "How would you look up a certain restaurant?" Although I was able to get quality feedback, it was tedious to manage more than ten screens, so I quickly looked for an on-device option.

Making an iPhone-friendly web site is not quite as obvious as it might seem. While I was able to use JavaScript code from WebKit[1] and HTML image maps to make my first prototype, I eventually found a Fireworks prototyping tutorial from UNITiD[2] that did all of the JavaScript and image mapping for me. Of course, when I was pressed for time, I could always export my designs as 320 × 480 JPEGs and simply add them to the Photo Albums on my iPhone.

How did your initial designs evolve?

About halfway through the design phase, I was sharing the concepts with Megan Casey, the founder of Squidoo,[3] when she expressed what I thought was the obvious: "What if your app really highlighted food photos and took advantage of all those people taking pictures of their food all the time?" While my initial thought was "Of course! That's the whole point," this feedback was the knock in the head that made me realize: Sure, that may have been my intent all along, but it's clearly not coming across to users in the designs!

Foodspotting felt like every other local guide, not the "tantalizing collection of the best foods and where to find them"—the words of my original pitch. Reframing

FIGURE CS3.3 Foodspotting start screen version 1.3.2

the problem as "designing an app that highlights food photos," I was able to completely revamp the designs, producing a beautiful interface concept that spoke this power much more clearly. [FIGURE CS3.2 shows the app design after these changes.]

How have users responded to the app?

We launched the Foodspotting web site in January 2010 and the iPhone app [FIGURE CS3.3] at South by Southwest in March 2010, where we introduced it through a Street Food Scavenger Hunt and demoed its capabilities at a Tech Cocktail event. When people heard about the app, they said, "I've been doing this already! Finally a place for me." By giving this activity an identity and rewarding people for doing it, we've been able to attract over 20,000 food sightings in less than three months since launching. ■

---

1. WebKit, http://webkit.org/.
2. UNITiD Interaction Action, "Prototyping for the iPhone using Fireworks," http://unitid.nl/2009/04/prototyping-for-the-iphone-using-fireworks-cs3/.
3. Squidoo, www.squidoo.com/.

CASE STUDY 4
Not For Tourists

NOT FOR TOURISTS is the ultimate guide for the savvy city dweller. Whether you've lived in your neighborhood for 55 years or 55 minutes, NFT will help you navigate and explore the city like a local. The *Not For Tourists* black book guides started in 2000. The companion series of iPhone apps launched in June 2009.

Tuft and Co. is a digital studio that creates innovative and engaging human-centered experiences for forward-thinking companies. Their passion is for digital pursuits and the people who use them, embodied by their work with rich Internet and mobile applications, customer-focused web sites, and user experience strategy and consulting.

How did NFT and Tuft and Co. get connected?

We had heard through the grapevine that NFT was casting about for a partner in developing an iPhone app. As a studio, we were already fans of the brand, so in the end we approached them about the project. What developed was an ideal partnership between the two companies to bring the NFT iPhone guides from concept to reality.

What inspired Not For Tourists to build an iPhone app?

The core NFT audience is fairly tech-savvy and "plugged in." In addition to the books, NFT customers can access their web site and a mobile-accessible site (WAP). With the proliferation of smartphones, especially the iPhone, many people started asking about a companion iPhone app. NFT realized they had a unique value proposition since their books are compact and built for on the go— great qualities for an iPhone app. We tried to capture that on-the-go ethos with features such as geolocation and embedded maps, which let you use the app anywhere (e.g., plane, train, or subway).

How did you approach the project?

At Tuft and Co. we try to design the user experience holistically. Our first step is always user research. We interviewed NFT editors as well as people currently using the books. From there, we developed a series of core user personas and scenarios which helped focus everyone on the key interactions and functionality of the app. As we update the app, we often refer back to these original personas, in addition to current user feedback.

How did you proceed after your initial research?

We began by sketching app designs and creating a paper prototype. We had hundreds of sketches on the wall, each representing a different scenario or interaction point,

FIGURE CS4.1 Early flow and sketches

screen by screen [see FIGURE CS4.1 for an example]. The walls are the perfect platform for brainstorming and envisioning the information flows and how a person interacts with the application. We often burn through dozens of paper prototypes before committing to anything on-screen.

From the paper prototype, we created static screens with initial design elements and put those into an iPhone album. This gave us a better sense of how it would feel to use the app and helped us make many important decisions—how someone would interact with the maps, what features were useful, which ones were distracting. This prototype was also the jumping-off point for technical development.

FIGURE CS4.2 Screens from Not For Tourists Manhattan 1.0

Were you able to user-test your early designs?

We conducted two different studies with the NFT app—a "man on the street" study and an internal beta study. For the "man on the street" study we wanted to get a sense for how the app would be used in the user's natural environment. We followed participants with a video camera as they used the app and asked them questions about their experience.

For the internal beta study we recruited people from NFT and Tuft and Co. who were not involved in the design process. They were given a list of tasks to complete with the app (they installed it via Ad Hoc Distribution) as well as a simple questionnaire which was returned via email. We ended up with fewer high-level insights, but it led to some significant UI improvements and some bug fixes.

How did the user testing impact your designs?

We found that users preferred lists over navigating by map and that functionality such as accessing maps at will—not being tied to having a cellular or WiFi

connection—was very important to our users. As a result we decided to bundle the app content within the app; an Internet connection is required only for occasional updates.

What is the biggest lesson you learned while designing and developing this app?

That an app is never really "done." It's common to continually push updates to our apps, because of a new feature, a content or functionality update, or a change in the software platform. Our partnership with NFT has been fantastic in that we are all able to keep the conversation going, to keep brainstorming on how the app could be improved. Unless you are specifically putting out a one-off app, it's important to remember that an app is dependent on a continual development life cycle and to plan accordingly. [FIGURE CS4.2 shows the final screens for version 1.0.] ■

(Not For Tourists icon and application screenshots courtesy of Tuft & Co.)

CASE STUDY 5

MUSE

MARGEIGH NOVOTNY is vice president of strategy and experience at MOTO Development Group, where she leads a cross-disciplinary team of design and technology professionals who develop next-generation product/service platforms for entrepreneurs and Fortune 100 companies.

How does MUSE work?

MUSE is an interface that visualizes your music library as a grid of dots; each dot is a track, and all tracks are playing. Tracks are organized into "columns" which reflect master genres such as classical, jazz, R&B, rock, alt, and so on. The tracks that I listen to most frequently rise to the top of the column (warmer-colored dots), and those I listen to less frequently float to the bottom of the column (cooler-colored dots).

As the user drags a finger across the grid, the dots "play," and the effect is like manually tuning a radio from station to station. The result is that users immediately understand the connection between touching the dots (tracks) and controlling the music. [FIGURE CS5.1 illustrates the different ways users may select tracks and create playlists—poking around, dragging around, selecting by gesture.]

What inspired you to create MUSE?

MUSE was born out of a desire for a more right-brain tool for navigating music libraries and creating playlists. Current methods for creating playlists are left-brain and laborious. The goal was to create something that didn't require reading or scrolling—a more intuitive interface that would allow users to just listen and feel music—and then use

Selecting by ear: poking around

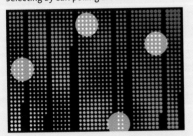

Selecting by ear: dragging around

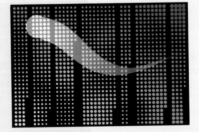

Selecting by gesture: creating a playlist (including songs from classical and jazz)

classical   jazz

FIGURE CS5.1 Interaction concepts for selecting tracks on MUSE

those results as the basis for a playlist. This interface was inspired by the beauty of flipping around an old-fashioned radio dial where songs hooked you by emotion, with the promise that the feeling would continue on that station. That's the experience I wanted to re-create.

What is design pliability, and how does it come into play with MUSE?

Maybe the best way to explain pliability is by reference to the architect Louis Kahn. Kahn is famous for asking building materials what they want to be as a way of getting to forms that reflect the nature and affordances of the material:

> . . . and you say to Brick, "What do you want Brick?" And Brick says to you "I like an Arch."

That's the basic message of design pliability:[1] to let the content and medium drive the form of the interface. Take Google Maps; there are Google Maps interfaces controlled by a mouse, a D-pad, and a touchscreen, and the level of effort required to accomplish the same task varies a lot (i.e., some interfaces for exploring Google Maps content are just more "pliable" than others). Pliability means the extent to which the hardware or software interface enables an easier, more fluid and intuitive approach to navigation—so that up means up, for example. In a pliable interface, the linkage between eye and hand, or between action and response, is essentially seamless. Hardware/ software interfaces are not all created equal, but in every case you want the interaction to be as effortless as possible by optimizing the interface for the specifics of the platform and the content.

MUSE is designed to encourage navigation by ear and as such provides a pliable interface for interacting with

FIGURE CS5.2 Final MUSE design

music. It's a way to prioritize your senses of touch and hearing over a reliance on song titles and album covers. It gives the users random access to all the music they have, in a way that lets them hear what they're choosing as they slide their finger across the interface.

How did the design evolve from the initial concept?

We started with a very basic visualization, a grid of pixels or clusters of objects. Gradually, the visualization evolved from a banal grid into a much more interesting aesthetic inspired by the ideas of optical art—abstract two-dimensional images that create the illusion of texture or depth. Op art is very minimalist, but it's evocative, and functionally it provides clear feedback to show where your finger is at any given point by magnifying an area of the grid. The switch to op art made the interface much more engaging, because as you drag your finger across the grid it creates a contour that looks magnified. The function of the app remained the same, but this visual expression moved the user experience in a new direction. [FIGURE CS5.2 shows the final app design.] ∎

---

1. Jonas Lowgren, "Pliability as an Experiential Quality," *Artifact* (2006).

(MUSE icon, images, and application screenshots courtesy of MOTO Development Group)

Prototyping App Concepts

THE WORD PROTOTYPE comes from the Greek *protos*, which means "first," and *typos*, which means "impression." In the 1600s prototyping was used to describe the first impression from a printing press. Over time, its meaning has evolved to include the early forms of many things: automobiles, retail stores, home appliances. Perspectives on prototyping often differ depending on whom you ask—designer, developer, researcher. Regardless of the industry or discipline, I find it instructive to refer to Bill Moggridge's definition from *Designing Interactions*:[1]

> *A representation of a design, made before the final solution exists.*

This chapter looks at various iPhone prototyping approaches—paper, software, and video—and suggests how to choose the best approach for your app.

This chapter also includes case studies on prototyping at Dan4, Inc., and on the What's Shakin' iPhone app. Here you'll find insights into how the application design teams used prototyping to conceptualize their applications.

---

1. Bill Moggridge, *Designing Interactions* (MIT Press, 2007).

Why Prototype?

Prototypes can help you solve design problems, evaluate designs, and communicate design ideas. These up-front activities can also expedite the development process, saving valuable time and money.

> *The most common estimate is that it's 100 times cheaper to make a change before any code has been written than it is to wait until after the implementation is complete.*
>
> —*Jakob Nielsen*[2]

SOLVE DESIGN PROBLEMS

Prototypes can be an efficient way to work through design problems before getting deep into coding. They can help address everything from higher-level conceptual issues to lower-level interactions. For example, imagine that you're creating a messaging app that will display a transition when users move messages from one folder to another: What is the optimal speed of the transition? What is the best form for the visual feedback? How do these two elements work together? Storyboards with directional arrows could illustrate the general concept, but an interactive prototype would be more effective at fine-tuning the solution.

EVALUATE DESIGN IDEAS

Prototypes are often used to evaluate design ideas—concepts, flows, and interactions—before investing development time. Evaluators may include the designer, design colleagues, and, of course, end users. Internal reviews can take a critique format or employ user-centered design methodologies such as heuristic evaluation, as discussed in Chapter 5, "Evaluating the Competition." Although internal reviews are tremendously valuable, they are no replacement for usability testing, which will be discussed in Chapter 8, "Usability-Testing App Concepts."

COMMUNICATE DESIGN IDEAS

Often prototypes are the only way to effectively communicate your app idea. In particular, apps that interact with the "real world"—location-aware apps, bar-code-scanning apps, voice recorders—must go beyond static screen designs to truly tell their stories. They need context: the people, places, and objects that are an integral part of the app.[3] Similarly, immersive apps such as musical

---

2. Jakob Nielsen, "Paper Prototyping: Getting User Data Before You Code," www.useit.com/alertbox/20030414.html.
3. Marion Buchenau and Jane Fulton Suri, "Experience Prototyping," *Proceedings of the 3rd Conference on Designing Interactive Systems: Processes, Practices, Methods, and Techniques* (ACM, 2000).

instruments and games are considerably less compelling when presented in a static sketch format. Prototypes will take your app off the page and into a format that feels closer to the real thing. These may be presented within your company, shared with investors, or used to elicit feedback from users.

Common Questions

This section provides answers to common questions with regard to prototyping.

HOW MANY VARIATIONS SHOULD I PROTOTYPE?

Ideally, you should try to prototype a few divergent directions in the early design stages. As the design progresses, teams tend to get attached to one direction so it may be challenging to change course. Be sure to choose your prototype medium wisely—lower-fidelity options like paper make it easy to explore multiple directions, whereas some higher-fidelity tools tend to encourage incremental or superficial design changes.

HOW MUCH OF THE APP SHOULD I PROTOTYPE?

The scope of your prototype will depend on the design stage and your goals. At the onset of your project, it's beneficial to take a holistic approach to the prototype. This doesn't mean you must prototype every single screen and interaction, but you'll want to cover the primary scenarios identified in your up-front user research. In the middle to later design stages, you may return to prototyping to help resolve a particular flow or interaction issue. If you are creating a slideshow app, for example, you may want to fine-tune the transitions via a prototype.

WHAT IF THE DESIGNS AREN'T COMPLETELY WORKED OUT?

You don't have to wait until every aspect of the interface is completely worked out. It's fine to use *Wizard of Oz*[4] techniques to demonstrate certain aspects of the app. *Wizard of Oz* techniques require a human to simulate app interactions. For example, let's say a usability participant wants to search restaurant listings on your app but you haven't coded search yet. With a *Wizard of Oz* approach, you could ask the participant to wait a moment while the app "processes" the request. In the meantime, you or one of your colleagues could search for the information and provide the results on the fly. In addition to uncovering usability issues, this approach could help you refine requirements before coding begins.

---

4. "Wizard of Oz Experiment," http://en.wikipedia.org/wiki/Wizard_of_Oz_experiment.

NOTE

The Lorem Ipsum web site (www.lipsum.com) has a generator to easily create filler text. The site also provides history on the origins of this practice.

WHAT IF MY SUPPORT CONTENT ISN'T FINALIZED?

Jared Spool recommends "Incredibly Intelligent Help"[5] to simulate a help system. Essentially, when users tap on help, the human "computer" responds to their questions. This approach provides a relatively seamless experience and can also identify areas of the interface that need design improvements or support content. On the other hand, be conservative with *greeking*, the practice of including *lorem ipsum* and other filler text instead of real text. If the text is central to the user experience, include draft copy and then iterate based on user feedback.

WHAT IS THE APPROPRIATE LEVEL OF FIDELITY?

The fidelity of your prototype should match the design challenge at hand as well as the stage in the design process. For example, paper prototypes (**FIGURE 7.1**) can typically uncover most flow and terminology issues but are less successful when it comes to low-level interaction issues. This doesn't mean that paper prototypes should always be your starting point. As discussed later in the chapter, some apps may require a higher-fidelity prototype earlier on.

If you plan to present to company executives or investors, you should assess their comfort level with low- versus high-fidelity prototypes. Some individuals may view low-fidelity prototypes in a negative light since they can be "rough" in appearance. That said, if you want to convince them otherwise, consider how Jane Fulton Suri, a partner and creative director at IDEO, assesses whether a prototype is effective: "If it is [a good experience], people get so involved in the experience that they forget about the limitations of the prototype."

FIGURE 7.1 Paper prototype for a gaming app *(Courtesy of Dennis Paiz-Ramirez, photographer)*

---

5. Quoted in Carolyn Snyder, *Paper Prototyping* (Morgan Kaufmann, 2003).

WHAT SHOULD I DO BEFORE I START PROTOTYPING?

Before you start prototyping, create app sketches, as discussed in Chapter 6, "Exploring App Concepts." If you haven't done so already, place these sketches in a high-level application flowchart. **FIGURE 7.2** illustrates an application flowchart for a dictionary app; notice how the legend includes symbols for supported gestures. A flowchart provides a holistic view of your app and serves as a blueprint for your prototype. In the early design stages, focus on the "happy paths" that represent typical scenarios, not ones that generate unusual error conditions.[6] Edge cases can be added once you narrow down your concept.

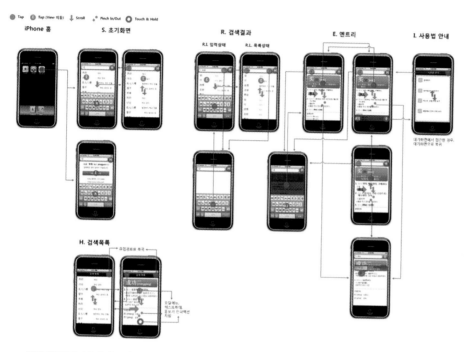

FIGURE 7.2 High-level application flowchart for a dictionary app *(Courtesy of Tony S. Kim)*

Other points to keep in mind when working on your app flows are the following:

- **Streamline, streamline, streamline.**

  As mentioned earlier, mobile users have limited time, so your app flows should be as succinct as possible without compromising usability. To that end, look for ways to combine or remove steps in multistep processes. For example, wizards are great for app setup and other linear processes (e.g., shopping checkout), but they can slow users down when used for frequent tasks, especially those with many optional items.

---

6. "Happy Path," http://en.wikipedia.org/wiki/Happy_path.

- **Provide multiple ways to access information.**

  Users are often faced with dead ends, particularly when drilling down list views, but the app experience can be more fluid. For example, news article views could have cross-links to related articles, but many apps force users to navigate back to the original list view. Similarly, maps that contain points of interest (POI) should allow users to go directly to the POI, instead of requiring them to return to the corresponding list view.

- **Keep users within context.**

  As much as possible, try to keep users within your app. Leaving your app means users will require additional time and effort to reorient themselves, increasing the likelihood that they will not return. For example, many apps force users to visit their web site for help via Safari. Unfortunately, if users can't easily refer to their original problem, the external help may be useless. If users *must* leave your app (e.g., for map directions), at least provide a warning. When users return to your app, they should see the last screen visited, known as "saving state."

NOTE

For a broader discussion on prototyping (not iPhone-specific), consider reading Todd Zaki Warfel's *Prototyping: A Practitioner's Guide.*[7]

Prototyping Approaches

TABLE 7.1 summarizes five different prototyping approaches, from low-fidelity paper prototypes to the iPhone SDK. As the iPhone app space continues to evolve, you may find other approaches well suited to your application space. Be creative—adapt these as needed and formulate your own prototyping strategy. For example, audio can be incorporated into all of the options via a recording or live voice-over.

TABLE 7.1 Alternative iPhone App Prototyping Approaches

Prototype	Strengths	Weaknesses
Paper	Cheap and fast. Good for identifying conceptual, flow, and terminology issues.	Difficult to show low-level interactions; harder to simulate information-rich apps.
Static images on device	Incorporates iPhone form factor. Good for addressing visual issues, e.g., text size.	Limited interaction possible; essentially click through screen to screen.
Interactive on device	Incorporates iPhone form factor and some level of interactivity.	Achieving desired interactivity can require a significant amount of time.
Video	Storytelling approach that provides contextual information essential for location-aware and some immersive apps.	Can be time-consuming if many iterations are needed. Less suitable for usability testing.
iPhone SDK	Code may sometimes be used for the final app design.	Can be costly and less malleable for up-front iterative design.

7. Todd Zaki Warfel, *Prototyping: A Practitioner's Guide* (Rosenfeld Media, 2009).

PAPER PROTOTYPES

Paper prototypes are essentially paper models of your iPhone apps (**FIGURES 7.3–7.4**). They can be used as a communication tool, but they are often developed for usability testing. In these situations the designer or developer plays "computer," hiding and showing user interface elements as needed. In contrast to electronic prototypes, Jared Spool, the founder of User Interface Engineering, describes paper prototypes the following way:[8]

> *We think of paper prototyping as the coarse-grain sandpaper and electronic-version testing as the fine grain. Once we've used the paper prototypes to validate what each screen contains and how it will work, we then move over to the electronic version to fine-tune the look and feel.*

FIGURE 7.3 Paper prototype of a ride-sharing iPhone app
(Courtesy of Alex Jameson Braman, Joseph Lau, and Andreas Nomikos)

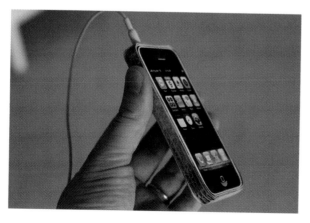

FIGURE 7.4 Paper prototype of an iPhone with the Home screen *(Courtesy of Steven Toomey)*

---

8. Jared Spool, "Looking Back at 16 Years of Paper Prototyping," www.uie.com/articles/looking_back_on_paper_prototyping/ (July 2005).

Benefits

The benefits of paper prototypes range from quick iterations to improved collaboration:

- **Quick iterations**

  Paper prototypes enable you to rapidly iterate and experiment with many ideas. The modest time investment makes it easier to throw away less promising directions.

- **Inexpensive**

  Ordinary office supplies can be used for paper prototypes: Sharpies, Post-its, printer paper. Most important, these up-front paper iterations can reduce costly changes on the development end.

- **Collaborative**

  Paper prototypes do not require any technical skills; thus everyone (users, too!) can participate.

- **Easy to edit**

  You or your users can edit paper prototypes on the fly (e.g., change labels, add screens, add buttons).

Issues to Explore

User experience issues often explored with paper prototypes include

- **App concept**

  Do users understand your app's central concept?

- **Workflows**

  Is the overall navigation clear? Are there too many steps to complete tasks?

- **Information organization**

  Does the current organization match users' expectations?

- **Terminology**

  Are the labels on tabs, screens, and buttons clear?

- **Additional features**

  Over the course of evaluating your app, you may uncover additional features that users need. Users may vocalize these needs, or you may observe them trying to complete tasks not supported in the app. You may also learn which features users *don't* want, which could save valuable development time.

Challenges

As mentioned previously, paper prototypes are less suitable for refining low-level interactions such as transitions, scrolling, and swiping. They may also be less useful for certain classes of apps, such as musical instruments, videos, and games.

HOW TO DO IT

iPhone paper prototypes typically include the "device" and some combination of screens, overlays, and controls. Steps for creating paper prototypes are summarized in this section.

Step 1: Gather materials.

In the previous chapter we listed office supplies that can be used when brainstorming and sketching your app designs; these items are also useful for paper prototyping. In addition, you may want to have the following materials on hand: cardboard, removable tape, glue, correction fluid, and scissors.

Step 2: Determine the form factor.

At some point your designs will have to match the iPhone screen dimensions—320 × 480 pixels (640 × 960 for iPhone 4)—but paper prototypes can be less exact. Using a larger form factor will make it easier for others to interact with the design (e.g., rearrange the layout and write in text fields).

Step 3: Create the prototype.

Your prototype will include a background, the screens, and the user interface controls. As you create the prototype, be sure your scenarios, as discussed in Chapter 4, and application flowchart are readily available.

Background

If your prototype is much larger than the iPhone, you may want to frame your designs with a cutout iPhone made with foam core or cardboard. This frame can help orient participants when usability-testing your app. Alternatively, if your prototype matches the iPhone dimensions, you can adhere it to the device, potentially making it "feel" closer to the real thing.

Screens

Your app screens can be hand-drawn or screenshots. Hand-drawn sketches tend to elicit high-level conceptual feedback, whereas screenshots may lead to low-level visual feedback. If possible, stick with one approach, not half hand-drawn screens and half screenshots. A few notable exceptions are photos, maps, and keyboards: Printing these out will save time, and they'll work fine when combined with hand-drawn sketches.

Prepare the Controls

This section includes tips on building standard controls for your paper prototype.

- **Tab bar**

  Create highlighted and non-highlighted versions of tab states (**FIGURE 7.5**). Use text if you haven't decided on the appropriate tab icon.

- **Keyboard**

  As mentioned earlier, you can use hand-drawn keyboard sketches or screenshots (**FIGURE 7.6**). It's not necessary to have the pressed state for each button, but pay attention to the default colors and special contextual keys such as those for web and email addresses.

- **Sliders**

  Sliders can be created with a tiny piece of construction paper folded over a narrow strip of paper (**FIGURE 7.7**). If you're short on time, you can provide verbal feedback as the user moves a finger back and forth across the slider. This verbal approach can also be applied to progress bars (e.g., "Downloading 1 of 10").

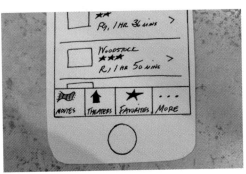

FIGURE 7.5 Paper prototype with a tab bar

FIGURE 7.6 Sample sketch with a keyboard printout

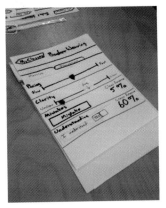

FIGURE 7.7 Example of a slider
(Courtesy of Angela Chiang, Andrew Hershberger, and Charles Naut)

- **Text entry**

  For text entry, participants can write on Post-its or removable tape. Alternatively, they can use a pencil to write directly on the prototype. Be forewarned: Even with good erasing, if participants write too hard, your next user may see what the previous one wrote.

- **Pickers**

  Pickers provide essentially the same function as drop-down lists on web or desktop applications (**FIGURE 7.8**). Given that they can include a large number of items, you may need a long strip of paper to display all of the options. The strip can be folded and tucked away when the user is not interacting with the picker.

- **Highlight**

  Consider creating a highlight cutout that you can move up or down as the user makes selections (**FIGURE 7.9**). Another option is to buy transparent plastic sheets, which come in a variety of colors.

- **Alerts**

  Consider using a different background color for your alerts. Make sure they don't completely obscure content that should be visible underneath (**FIGURE 7.10**).

FIGURE 7.8 Example of a time picker

FIGURE 7.9 Example of a highlight

FIGURE 7.10 Example of an alert overlay

- **Segmented controls**

  Include different states of segmented controls, which are typically used for filters or sorts. Each state can show a different "segment" of the control highlighted. The segmented control in **FIGURE 7.11** lets users sort the list by Popularity, Rating, and Title.

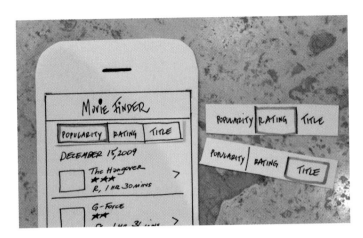

FIGURE 7.11 Segmented control example

NOTE

Apple's *iPhone Human Interface Guidelines* contain details on iPhone controls. In addition, some will be discussed in more detail in Chapter 9, "User Interface Design."

Here are some additional elements you may need to include:

- Loading page indicator
- On/off versions for switches that work like radio buttons
- Check mark for selected items

Word of Caution

As discussed earlier, paper prototypes can improve collaboration and reduce costs. These benefits can occur only if the approach supports rapid iterative design.

With that in mind, try not to go overboard with your paper prototypes. For example, cutting tiny bits of paper for each key on a keyboard probably isn't necessary. Users generally understand how the keyboard works, so you can say things like "Imagine that the keyboard would display the text you entered."

Similarly, if you are preparing a prototype for a study, don't worry if you haven't created every single interface element users may expect—the beauty of paper is that you can always sketch the widget and add it on the fly.

STATIC IMAGES ON THE DEVICE

Once you have refined your overall concept and flows, you may want to create screen captures of your designs and display them on the iPhone. If you link the images with "hot spots," you can offer a more exploratory user experience since no one needs to play the role of "computer" while switching out user interface elements. Moreover, the precise form factor may make it easier to refine visual design details such as type size, layout, and color.

HOW TO DO IT

To start, you'll want to create 320 × 480 images of your app screens. Many drawing programs have iPhone templates built into the software or available for download. Keep in mind that these templates do not have all of the user interface elements in the iPhone universe; developers often create controls that look and feel like standard controls, but they are actually custom-designed and custom-coded. If there's something you need that's not available, be prepared to sketch the desired solution. There are four drawing programs widely used by iPhone UI designers:

- OmniGraffle (see Graffletopia, **www.graffletopia.com**, for iPhone templates)
- Fireworks
- Photoshop
- Illustrator

NOTE
Screens can be hand-drawn, but it may be harder to fit them into the iPhone form factor.

I prefer OmniGraffle and Fireworks since the "page" framework translates well to iPhone screen design. Photoshop and Illustrator are excellent products, but the number of tools and options tends to overwhelm novice users. Three easy ways to view images on the iPhone are via the built-in slideshow, Safari, and LiveView.

Viewing via Built-in Slideshow

The downsides of the slideshow approach are the linearity—you can only swipe forward or back—and the presence of zoom and slideshow controls. On the plus side are speed and simplicity: Save your sketches in an acceptable iPhoto format, then add them to your iPhone photo collection. Be sure to include the status bar (battery and connection information) if it is part of your design.

Viewing via Safari

Another option is to create images with "hot spots" and display these images in Safari. With this approach, users can tap on rows and buttons just as they would with a real app. UNITiD design put together some scripts that enable you to disable zoom and view the images in full-screen mode. An easy-to-follow tutorial can be found on their web site.[9]

---

9. Matthijs Collard, "Prototyping for the iPhone using Fireworks," http://unitid.nl/2009/04/prototyping-for-the-iphone-using-fireworks-cs3/ (April 2009).

LiveView

LiveView,[10] created at IDEO Labs, allows you to view desktop designs from your iPhone (**FIGURE 7.12**). This can help you evaluate the app layout, type sizes, and other visual elements, but it's not possible to interact with the prototype. Additionally, LiveView must be accessed over WiFi, so the geographical range of your testing may be limited.

FIGURE 7.12 iPhone app viewed via LiveView, which was developed at IDEO
(Courtesy of Marcin Ignac)

Word of Caution

Creating on-screen prototypes with static images isn't necessarily more effective than paper prototyping. Static images can't display alerts and control states, so you may need to create a hybrid prototype (e.g., on-screen plus paper overlays). Also, you can't simulate scrolling content with static images, but you can do so with paper.

---

10. Gentry Underwood, "LiveView: An iPhone App for On-Screen Prototyping," http://labs.ideo.com/2009/01/20/liveview-an-iphone-app-for-on-screen-prototyping/ (January 2009).

INTERACTIVE ON THE DEVICE

Given the limitations of static image prototypes, you may prefer more interactive prototyping techniques. Before choosing this route, make sure you've evaluated all of the lower-fidelity options. If some aspects of your app, such as flows and layout, can be worked out on paper, start with paper before committing to an interactive prototype. I'm deliberately using the word *committing* because higher-fidelity prototypes have a tendency to become final designs.

NOTE

Flash is a powerful tool for creating interactive prototypes but you can't view Flash files on the iPhone.

Issues to Explore

You can explore almost any aspect of the user experience; it basically depends on how much time you want to put into the prototype. In contrast to static image prototypes, you can provide forms, transitions, and scrolling content. More important, given the portability of these prototypes, you can get out in the field and walk through your scenarios in context. Although this can be done with paper, the process is much easier with an interactive prototype on the device.

Challenges

Although interactive prototypes are powerful, there are still some aspects that differentiate them from the "real" experience. In particular, you will still likely need to fake the current location information, live data feeds, and the handling of interruptions (what happens when the connection is lost or disrupted?).

HOW TO DO IT

Interactive prototypes can be created with tools like Keynote or PowerPoint[11] (**FIGURE 7.13**), but specialized readers are required to display these on the iPhone.[12] On the other end of the spectrum are custom CSS solutions that are essentially web applications made to look like native iPhone applications. These prototypes can take a significant amount of time, though there are some tools like ProtoShare (**FIGURE 7.14**) that aim to simplify the process.[13] Another solution that holds promise is Briefs, developed by Rob Rhyne.[14] Briefs prototypes run on the iPhone, like actual apps, but take much less time to code and produce. Each "brief" contains a text file that references a series of static images organized into "scenes."

---

11. "How to Mockup Your iPhone App with MockApp," http://mockapp.com/2009/10/12/new-video-demo-how-to-mockup-your-iphone-app-with-mockapp/.
12. "Viewing Your MockApp Mockup on Your iPhone," http://mockapp.com/?s=goodreader.
13. "Native iPhone Prototypes with Protoshare," http://blog.protoshare.com/2009/06/17/native-iphone-prototypes-with-protoshare/.
14. Briefs, http://giveabrief.com/.

FIGURE 7.13 MockApp example of Google Wave *(Courtesy of MockApp)*[15]

FIGURE 7.14 ProtoShare example showing cover flow *(Courtesy of ProtoShare)*

Word of Caution

As mentioned in this section, it is possible to create prototypes that mimic nearly all of your app's features and functionality. This isn't a bad thing as long as the work can be accomplished within a reasonable time frame.

If you're spending an inordinate amount of time prototyping, perhaps you've gone beyond the rapid iterative testing "tipping point." In this case, reconsider what aspects of the prototype can be faked or explained to your audience— the effort required for some user experience elements may outweigh the benefits.

VIDEO PROTOTYPES

Video prototypes are a powerful way to show app usage in context—the actors, the environment, concurrent activities, the passage of time. These contextual elements are particularly important for apps that interact with the real world: location-aware apps, remote controls, cooking aids. Additionally, immersive apps such as musical instruments or games may use video to show their apps in action. Although video prototypes can be used to elicit feedback via usability testing, they are typically created to evaluate and communicate design ideas. **FIGURE 7.15** shows a screen capture from a video prototype created for a caregiver app; the full video is available online.[16]

---

15. "Google Wave iPhone App Demo," http://mockapp.com/2009/10/19/google-wave-iphone-app-demo/.
16. Eldia video, http://vimeo.com/2420799.

FIGURE 7.15 Prototype of Eldia app for caregivers
(Courtesy of Ujjval Panchal, Marcin Ignac, and Yu-Min Chen)

Issues to Explore

Video prototypes are an effective way to explore and document how an app works in the real world. Examples of interactions that may be captured include

- Handling of the device while performing other activities
- Other people who impact the experience
- Interruptions that may influence the user

Harder to Explore

Some issues are less suitable for a video prototype. For example, if you want to explore low-level interactions in great detail, consider creating an interactive prototype that users can walk through at their own pace.

HOW TO DO IT

Video prototypes may seem like a significant undertaking, but the process can be relatively simple:

Step 1. Develop your script.

First, you'll want to develop a script for your video. If you created scenarios as discussed in Chapter 4, it shouldn't take long to write the script. Focus on the scenarios that show how the app is used in a contextual and realistic way. Also, include an introduction to set the stage, for example, who the characters are, where are they located, what their goals are.

Step 2. Sketch storyboards.

If you have already created storyboards for your app, you'll want to adapt them based on your script. You may discover that additional screens are needed to provide a seamless user experience.

Step 3. Create your prototype.

Your prototype can be paper, electronic, or whichever medium you find most effective. Be sure your screens, overlays, and so on are ready before you start shooting video.

Step 4. Film your prototype.

You don't need to purchase an expensive high-end camera to film your prototype. At a minimum, be sure your camera has solid zoom capabilities and a good microphone. If the microphone picks up too much background noise, you may want to rent or purchase a lavalier microphone that can be clipped onto the actor's shirt. Here are some additional video tips:

- Choose realistic locations; seek permission to shoot video as needed.
- Ask the main actor to "think aloud" so viewers know the "whys" behind his or her actions.
- Use a combination of environmental views and close-up app screen views.

Step 5. Edit your video.

There are dozens of video-editing tools on the market. For the purposes of your video prototype, something basic such as iMovie should be sufficient. Some additional editing tips are the following:

- If background information is necessary, remember to start with a voice-over to set the stage.
- Try to keep the final video under five minutes.
- Use fade in/out to indicate the passage of time.

Other Types of Video Prototypes

As mentioned in the previous section, video prototypes can also be an effective way to illustrate how immersive apps like games and musical instruments work. Gogogic, an online and iPhone game developer, uses animatics in its app development process. Animatics,[17] a series of still images displayed in sequence, enable Gogogic to visualize the player experience before diving into coding. Additionally, animatics help prioritize the app requirements. According to Gogogic's CEO, Jónas Antonsson, "At Gogogic, the animatic is king" (FIGURE 7.16).

---

17. "Animatics," http://en.wikipedia.org/wiki/Animatic#Animatics.

FIGURE 7.16 Animatics Gogogic developed for the game Symbol6 *(Courtesy of Gogogic)*[18]

Word of Caution

As mentioned in this section, prototyping should be a relatively rapid process. Sure, you could spend weeks shooting and editing a production-quality video. However, for prototyping purposes, you'll want to "time-box" the effort put into the video.

If the video capture and editing take more than a week, consider an alternative strategy.

Another approach is to animate your scenario with cartoon-like characters as is done with the Xsights iPhone app (**FIGURE 7.17**). Services like GoAnimate provide tools and templates to help newbies create basic animations.

FIGURE 7.17 Animation developed for Xsights app *(Courtesy of Xsights)*[19]

---

18. Gogogic, "Symbol6: How We Created an iPhone Game," http://gogogic.wordpress.com/2009/02/09/symbol6-how-we-created-an-iphone-game/.
19. Xsights video, www.xsights.com/index.php.

NOTE

Marcos Pianelli of Digital-Gourmet created a great app prototype with the iPhone SDK. You can view it on Vimeo: http://vimeo.com/5947546.

THE IPHONE SDK

Prototypes can be developed using the iPhone SDK within Interface Builder. While some design professionals may argue that "working code" is not prototyping, it really depends on the domain and the prototype complexity. For example, paper prototyping would be inadequate for exploring a musical instrument app. In this case, digging into Apple's Audio Library may be the most efficient way to experiment and figure out what's possible.

Almost any aspect of the user experience can be explored, but be careful how far you develop your prototype—if you become too invested in the design, you may be less likely to adapt it based on user feedback. Also, if your prototype isn't fully functioning, it will still be challenging to evaluate features such as location awareness and live data feeds.

HOW TO DO IT

Programming the iPhone user experience is too broad a topic to cover in this book. There are countless books and web sites on the topic. Some titles in the Addison-Wesley family that have been well received include

- *Cocoa Programming for Mac OS X, Third Edition,* by Aaron Hillegass (2008)
- *The iPhone Developer's Cookbook: Building Applications with the iPhone 3.0 SDK, Second Edition,* by Erica Sadun (2009)

Word of Caution

Once you dive into the iPhone SDK, it's typically harder to explore divergent design solutions. Prototyping within the SDK can be time-consuming, so your team may not want to "throw away" hours and hours of development work. As a result, they may be inclined to stick with the first approach and make smaller iterations. Moreover, keep in mind that the UI controls in the SDK may not be as comprehensive as you expect; many seemingly common controls are actually custom-coded.

If your coding skills are limited, you may choose a direction because it's easy, not because it's the best solution. Eventually you may have to make compromises, but this shouldn't happen on day one. In short, use the iPhone SDK for prototyping only if you've explored other options and determined that it is the most appropriate course.

Summary

Prototyping your iPhone app before coding will enable you to explore, evaluate, and communicate your design ideas. Through prototyping, you may uncover ways to improve the app concept, flows, terminology, and low-level interactions such as transitions.

This chapter discussed a variety of prototyping approaches, including paper, electronic, video, and even using Interface Builder and the iPhone SDK. The approach you choose will depend largely on the type of app, your design goals, and the project stage. Whatever you decide, keep these tips in mind:

- Try to explore divergent directions with your prototypes. It will be harder to change course once your app designs are coded.

- You don't have to prototype the *entire* user experience. Prototype only the areas that will help you explore the design issues under investigation.

- Prototypes don't have to be limited to the early design stages—use them to refine app issues that arise in the later stages. ■

CASE STUDY 6

Prototyping at Dan4, Inc.

DAN4 is a design practice dedicated to creating clear and engaging software applications, device interfaces, and multichannel services.

FIGURE CS6.1 Keynote prototype for a messaging platform. A video of the prototype and "how-to" information can be found at www.dan4.com/prototyping.

How do you prototype at Dan4?

We use prototyping essentially three ways at Dan4. First, we see prototyping as a natural part of the design process, allowing us to capture, communicate, and manipulate our ideas—quickly and fluently. In a way, prototyping is designing. For us, creating prototypes is not a tangential task or a project luxury. It is simply good design practice.

Second, prototypes are useful props during user research and user testing. During the early days of a project when we are seeking insights and inspiration, prototypes can help stimulate responses from users that reveal opportunities or risks about a concept. After the research phase, we frequently user-test prototype designs, helping us identify design problems and validate our design decisions.

Last, we always look for opportunities to adapt and reuse our prototypes, for instance, to support formal design specification documents, where the prototypes are referenced during the development process. We've also used prototypes to help with marketing efforts, product demos, and investor presentations.

How do you choose your prototyping approach?

We factor in the usual constraints—time, budget, and scope—but also how the wider development team works and how the prototypes could be reused. For example, we will consider the tools being used, the development approach, workflows, and degree of project formality. From there, we choose the fidelity and the technology for the prototypes.

Can you provide some examples?

While working on a location-based messaging platform for small retailers and franchisees, we wanted to help shopkeepers envision the richness of an iPhone interface. We felt that static, low-fidelity prototypes and mock-ups would not describe the user experience clearly. We opted to create a more experiential prototype, using Keynote [FIGURE CS6.1]. One of the useful things about Keynote for prototyping is that it offers many of the animations and transitions you see on the iPhone through Build Effects. It enables you to mimic the default UIKit transitions and animations and create more sophisticated behaviors involving fades, flips, zooms, ease-ins, and ease-outs that can be developed using Core Animation.

But sometimes low fidelity is fine. During an innovation workshop with a network security systems provider, we spent a half-day creating a very "quick and dirty" prototype. We wanted to communicate the overall product concept but also examine a hunch we had about the practicality of the proposition.

Using photos of pencil sketches, stop-frame animation, an ambient soundtrack, and sounds sourced from the Internet, we created a demonstration that helped the attendees, mostly software developers and managers, quickly gain a common understanding of the concept and an appreciation of the relevance of context of use [FIGURE CS6.2].

Any other advice on iPhone prototyping?

In our experience, it's best to try and start prototyping app concepts as soon as possible. We have found that prototypes are most effective when used to probe the underlying ideas and assumptions around the concept and elicit user insights that help teams figure out where to apply their effort.

Getting early input from others, especially from intended users and customers of the product, provides you with

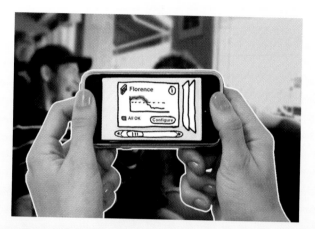

FIGURE CS6.2 Sketch and video prototype for a network security app. A video of the prototype and "how-to" information can be found at www.dan4.com/prototyping.

information to support the early strategic decisions that set the project trajectory and strongly influence the end product.

Often it's better to create several simple prototypes that probe separate aspects of the product. For instance, the essential functionality and overall architecture could be prototyped and tested using paper wireframes or a simple interactive prototype. But the branding, look and feel, and interface behaviors may be better tested using static visual mock-ups or an animated walk-through.

Prototyping at its best is about creating tools that probe the right questions and enlighten the design—as long as it doesn't distract from other project tasks. It's just as important to know what to exclude from the prototype as it is to know what to keep in, always striving toward "as simple as possible, but no simpler." ∎

(Images courtesy of Dan4, Inc.)

CASE STUDY 7

What's Shakin'

MATT PAUL is a founding member of start-ups big and small, such as StreetPrices, SeenON!, and the veritable TiVo of the web, StumbleUpon. Nowadays, as founder of mopimp productions, Matt is focused on the intersections of real time meets rhythm, and location-based services meet game mechanics, but he freely admits that by the time this book comes to print, he might well be working on something else entirely.

How did you get started doing iPhone development?

I first got my feet wet developing for the iPhone in the summer of 2008 at iPhone Dev Camp 2 in which my hack-a-thon team's app, Fwerps, won best app by a group of new/first-time Cocoa and iPhone SDK developers.

What inspired you to build What's Shakin'?

My friend Hunter Peress, an Android developer, and I thought it would be fun to collaborate on a cross-platform mobile app together. We started brainstorming around what we might find fun and would conceivably want to use ourselves. I had been known to dabble in drumming on and off over the last decade, whereas Hunter regularly performs as a hand percussionist; hence percussion was a natural area for us to explore.

The question remained, Could we make a realistic musical instrument that was played via dance and motion? We asked ourselves what instrument would lend itself best to our collaboration. We surmised it would be one that you could hold in your hands like a clave, a wood block, or an *egg shaker*—perfect!

What kind of competitive research did you do?

Over the course of development, I must have tried at least ten competitors. Some had nice visuals, some came with a good selection of instruments to pick from, but none of the lot did justice to the experience of playing an acoustic musical instrument; they simply lacked the responsiveness required. There was definitely an opportunity here to improve the state of the art.

How did you start the design?

Our initial approach was to emulate the sound created when you play an acoustic egg shaker by modeling the individual beads inside and their interactions with the

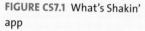

FIGURE CS7.1 What's Shakin' app

FIGURE CS7.2 What's Shakin' app in context

eggshell and one another. We quickly discovered that this approach would prove challenging. Sure, we could make some simplifying assumptions and disregard bead-bead interactions, but it would likely take a lot of time to get things right and a lot of computation to pull off in a realistic manner.

What did you try next?

Soon enough I realized that a hybrid approach leveraging OpenAL in conjunction with the device's accelerometer would be sufficient for our purposes. OpenAL is a cross-platform 3D audio API that allows developers to easily position sounds in 3D space and create sound effects such as the Doppler effect.

OpenAL afforded us plenty of control over the shaker's sound and gave us the ability to modulate it according to the user's style of play. We were even able to expose a parameter on the Settings page that allows the users to vary the number of beads in their egg shaker and produce a more staccato or "slushy" sound accordingly.

Were you able to get user feedback before launching?

First we tested it with our own music—Hunter used it with his Brazilian drums and I tried it while practicing my DJ set. Then we had lots of our friends test the app. On several occasions I would shake along to rehearsals of my roommates' band, The New Up, who practice in the adjacent room to my home office.

All of the feedback we received in-house was great, but I wanted to know how the app would work in the real world—could people hear it in a noisy bar? So I brought an early beta version down to a bar in North Beach. The most concrete takeaway was that the app's parameters needed to be configured a certain way to enable users to show off the app in a loud environment.

How did you know the app was done?

All summer long, my roommates were constantly subjected to hearing this comparison of plastic- versus silicon-based egg shaker technologies; I'm sure it drove them mad. One day, after numerous iterations, they could no longer tell if I was playing acoustic or using the app from the other room without running in to see for themselves—*that* was when I knew we had our emulation down pat and were ready to launch. [**FIGURES CS7.1–CS7.2** show the final app.]

What's next for What's Shakin'?

We're very excited to continue building upon What's Shakin's launch and have made plans to add a greater selection of sounds for users to unlock, the ability for users to record and share their performances with an online community of fellow shakers, and leaderboard rankings and scoreboards so users can boast and brag about their past performances. The pie in the sky for us would be to create a Shaker Hero—esque franchise of games and levels for users to play. ■

Usability-Testing App Concepts

ONCE YOU'VE PROTOTYPED your app concepts, you may reach a crossroads: Should you conduct usability tests now or wait until you have a beta?[1] Developers tend to take the beta route, but you may save time and money by usability-testing your prototype *before* writing code.

This chapter starts with an overview of usability testing and its benefits. We'll look at a variety of usability-testing methods—ranging from "traditional" tests to the RITE method and guerrilla testing—and suggest how to choose the right approach for your app. We'll also discuss beta testing and ways to enhance it with usability methods.

This chapter also includes a case study on REALTOR.com's iPhone app. Here we learn how the REALTOR.com team incorporated paper prototyping and usability testing into the app design process.

---

1. Craig Hockenberry, "Beta Testing on iPhone 2.0," http://furbo.org/2008/08/06/beta-testing-on-iphone-20/ (August 2008).

What Is Usability Testing?

NOTE

The terms *usability testing* and *user testing* are often used interchangeably. User testing may be less preferable since it suggests that users are being tested, when in fact the design is being tested.

Usability testing is an umbrella term for a variety of methods that involve observing users as they interact with a product, typically with a set of predefined tasks (FIGURE 8.1). In addition to evaluating traditional usability metrics—learnability, efficiency, memorability—the sessions can address other user experience concerns. For example, to better understand whether an app meets user needs, you might want to start with semi-structured interviews, as described in Chapter 3, "Introduction to User Research."

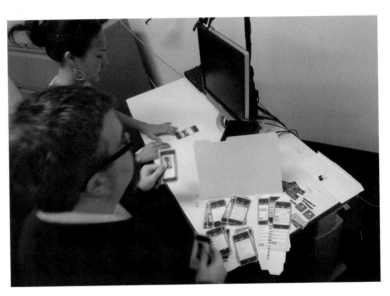

FIGURE 8.1 Facilitator (right) showing a participant (left) a paper prototype for REALTOR.com
(Courtesy of Shohini Solanski, photographer)

Why Usability Testing?

Running usability tests before coding your app can save valuable time and money. If you discover critical user experience issues, it often costs less to change your prototype than to change a fully coded application. Cost savings may also be seen in terms of customer service—fewer user experience issues may mean fewer customer support requests. Perhaps the biggest benefit is increased customer satisfaction. Other important reasons for usability testing are discussed in this section.

HELP RESOLVE KNOWN DESIGN ISSUES

Over the course of designing your app, you may encounter design problems that could benefit from user feedback. These design problems can be low-level (e.g., information layout) or high-level (e.g., user flows). For example, imagine that your team has been exploring two different "Getting Started" flows and is uncertain which one would be more effective. You could create two paper prototypes and evaluate both of them with users.

UNCOVER UNKNOWN DESIGN ISSUES

After several design iterations, you may have a nagging feeling that you missed some critical user experience issues. Even the most skilled designers readily admit that it's challenging to uncover all design problems solely through heuristic evaluations or self-critiques. Of course, you can supplement these methods with internal design reviews, but your colleagues may be too familiar with the app, and thus it will be difficult for them to objectively evaluate it. Usability testing, on the other hand, is an effective way to objectively uncover a wide range of unknown design issues.

SET A BASELINE FOR FUTURE STUDY

Usability testing can be used to establish a baseline for future studies. For example, let's say you conduct a study and discover that only four out of ten participants could discover your app's sharing feature. After redesigning the sharing experience, if eight out of ten participants can now find the sharing feature, you may report that sharing discovery doubled. That being said, be careful when citing causal relationships—your argument will not hold up if your study variables were poorly controlled.

GATHER INFORMATION FOR THE NEXT RELEASE

Once your app is in the App Store, you will receive user feedback through App Store reviews, customer support, and potentially the blogosphere. While these channels are valuable, they may represent a small fraction of your user base. Moreover, the feedback from these channels tends to fall within the realm of "I want feature X" or "I don't like the latest update." This information is valuable, but it usually doesn't tell the whole story behind feature requests and frustrations. Running user tests with a representative cross section of your user base can provide insights into user feedback and guide design improvements for your next release. Keep in mind that it's better to gather this information *before* launching your product.

GET STAKEHOLDER BUY-IN

Companies sometimes run user tests to get stakeholder buy-in for a particular feature or design direction. Although this is a relatively common reason, it's not always a particularly good one. If your colleagues or company executives are questioning your design decisions, they may continue to do so even after usability testing. Before diving into usability testing, I recommend trying to understand the rationale behind stakeholder concerns. If you can address these concerns internally, it's far better than wasting your users' time to resolve company battles.

What If I Don't Have Usability-Testing Experience?

This chapter aims at providing you with the tools and guidance needed to run your own usability studies. If you don't feel prepared after reading this chapter, you may want to look into additional training.

The Usability Professionals' Association (UPA) regularly holds conferences around the world which include a range of practical usability workshops and tutorials. Also, consider reading Jeffrey Rubin's excellent book on usability testing: *Handbook of Usability Testing, Second Edition*, published by Wiley in 2008.

Role of Context

As mentioned in Chapter 3, studies exploring the importance of context in mobile research have produced inconsistent results. Some suggest that field-based studies have more "ecological validity" (the methods, materials, and setting approximate the real-life situation under investigation) and uncover a larger number of critical usability issues,[2] whereas other studies contend that there's little difference between field- and lab-based studies.[3]

In deciding whether to run your tests in the lab or the field, consider the app and the study goals. If you're creating an app where context is a defining aspect of the user experience (e.g., with a location-based app), your tests will ideally take place in the field. However, if you're trying to resolve early-stage flow and terminology issues, you may be able to simulate the context in a lab. In this case you could start with a lab-based paper prototype, then conduct field-based studies in the later design stages. If you are creating an app where context is *not* a defining aspect of the user experience (e.g., with certain stand-alone games), it may suffice to conduct all of your studies in the lab. In short, the field is ideal, but if it's not possible, consider how context affects your app and adapt your approach as needed.

---

2. Christian Monrad Nielsen et al., "It's Worth the Hassle! The Added Value of Evaluating the Usability of Mobile Systems in the Field," *Proceedings of the 4th Nordic Conference on Human-Computer Interaction: Changing Roles* (ACM, 2006), www.usabilityprofessionals.org/upa_publications/jus/2005_november/mobile.html.
3. Anne Kaikkonen et al., "Usability Testing of Mobile Applications: A Comparison between Laboratory and Field Testing," *Journal of Usability Studies* (November 2005).

Usability-Testing Methods

In this section we'll introduce three usability-testing methods: "traditional" usability testing, the RITE method, and paper prototype testing. Later in the chapter we'll delve into the nuts and bolts of running and analyzing sessions.

TRADITIONAL USABILITY TESTING

"Traditional" usability testing is perhaps the most commonly used method. In essence, it involves observing users one by one as they use your product to complete tasks. While they work through these tasks, the participants are asked to "think aloud," which helps the moderator understand the reasons behind the participants' behavior. For example, knowing that six out of eight participants couldn't find a particular button is not as helpful as knowing *why* they couldn't find the button:

- Was it the label?
- The placement?
- The underlying concept?

THE RITE METHOD

The Rapid Iterative Testing and Evaluation method—or RITE method—was coined and authored by a team of designers and researchers at Microsoft. The RITE method has many similarities to "traditional" usability testing: Study participants complete tasks and think out loud. The key difference is that RITE emphasizes rapid changes and verification of the effectiveness of these changes.[4] Instead of the designs being revised at the end of the study, the designs are improved after each participant. Given that the time required to fix problems can vary, the authors of RITE created rules for categorizing issues:

Category 1: Issues that appear to have an obvious cause and an obvious solution that can be implemented quickly (e.g., text changes, relabeling buttons, rewording overlay text)

Category 2: Issues that appear to have an obvious cause and an obvious solution that cannot be implemented quickly or within the time frame of the current test (e.g., difficult new features, current features that require substantial design and code changes)

---

4. M. C. Medlock, D. Wixon, M. Terrano, R. Romero, and B. Fulton, "Using the RITE Method to Improve Products: A Definition and a Case Study," www.microsoft.com/downloads/details. aspx?FamilyID=3b882eb1-5f06-41d9-baba-d39ad13bc3ff&displaylang=en/ (2002).

Category 3: Issues that appear to have no obvious cause and therefore no obvious solution

Category 4: Issues that may be caused by other factors (e.g., discussion guide, interaction with participant, etc.)

Ideally, the RITE user researcher will have experience in the domain and in the problems typically experienced in this domain. If the researcher doesn't have this experience, it may be difficult for him or her to determine if an issue is likely to be a problem for other users.

Second, the product's decision makers should make time to observe user sessions and contribute to the design changes. Without their involvement, it is difficult to evolve the design, which is the essence of RITE. Last, the team should be able to rapidly interpret the results and make design changes, another defining attribute of RITE.

I've used RITE for a variety of software platforms—desktop, web, iPhone—and found it much more efficient than "traditional" usability testing. For example, when testing one app, we discovered a line of text that prevented participants from moving beyond the welcome screen. After we addressed this issue, we were able to press ahead, uncovering more critical conceptual issues. However, RITE does have its limitations. Category 2 issues can be difficult to address within the study timeline (e.g., the solution may not be clear) and may require several days to brainstorm, sketch, and refine the app. To alleviate this problem, try to allocate extra time between sessions, knowing that sometimes even a few days is not enough.

PAPER PROTOTYPE TESTING

Before discussing paper prototype testing,[5] I'd like to address any potential confusion. Paper prototyping falls into a fuzzy area, given that it's a form of prototyping (see Chapter 7, "Prototyping App Concepts") and arguably also a usability-testing method. While it has similarities to "traditional" usability studies and RITE, there are many notable differences. First, paper prototype studies typically include three roles: the moderator, the "computer," and the note taker/videographer. The "computer" is the person who swaps out different screens and user interface controls depending on the research participant's actions. Second, paper prototyping usually includes some level of participatory design, where the user actively contributes to the design. For example, the participant might use a pen or pencil to rename items in a tab bar, or rearrange a layout. As we'll discuss later in the chapter, in these cases you should have paper prototyping materials on hand: Post-its, pens, glue, and so on.

> **NOTE**
>
> Having a three-person paper prototype team may be ideal, but it's certainly not required. I've conducted paper prototype studies where I played all three roles—it's doable but exhausting. If you can pull together a two-person team, I suggest that one person play moderator/computer and the other take notes.

---

5. Carolyn Snyder, *Paper Prototyping* (Morgan Kaufmann, 2003).

Usability-Testing Timeline

If your prototype is ready and your recruiting requirements are relatively straight-forward, you may be able to complete a usability study in less than two weeks. Other factors that may affect your timeline include the usability method and the study context. For example, iterative studies need design time between sessions, and field-based studies require more overall time (extra travel time and slightly longer sessions). **FIGURE 8.2** illustrates the key activities included in most usability studies. The activities occur serially, with the exception of recruiting and discussion guide creation, which often happen in parallel.

NOTE

The high-level activities in **FIGURE 8.2** are essentially the same ones discussed in Chapter 3, "Introduction to User Research," but the execution is different. In particular, there are major distinctions when it comes to the discussion guide and facilitating. These are discussed in the following sections.

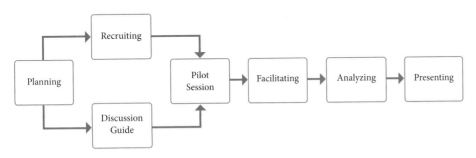

FIGURE 8.2 Usability study activities

Planning Usability Tests

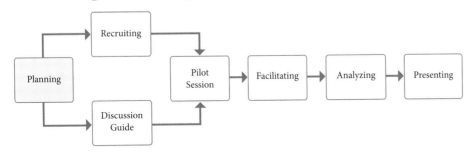

Usability planning often begins with a kickoff meeting with the app's stakeholders—designers, developers, researchers, product managers, customer support. If your team has not participated in usability studies in the past, spend some time explaining the benefits and methods outlined earlier in this chapter. Topics discussed in the kickoff meeting and documented in the test plan typically include[6]

- Purpose and objective
- Study dates and times

---

6. Jeffrey Rubin, *Handbook of Usability Testing* (Wiley, 1994).

- User profile
- Method
- Questions for research
- Roles (moderator, observers, documenter)
- Prototype supplies (if paper prototype)
- Equipment and location
- Report contents

PURPOSE AND OBJECTIVE

Articulating the study purpose and objective will help keep your study focused and ensure that everyone on your team is on the same page. This section includes three examples at different stages in the design process; the app cited helps users find local art events.

Example 1: Early-Stage Research

- **Purpose**

  Evaluate the flows and interaction included in the current app design, with emphasis on finding events and getting directions to venues.

- **Objective**

  Uncover user experience issues and improve designs before development begins.

Example 2: Baseline Before Development Begins

- **Purpose**

  Evaluate the overall user experience of the app design, including flows, interaction design, and lower-level details such as transitions.

- **Objective**

  Uncover user experience issues and improve designs before launch.

Example 3: Feature- or Flow-Specific Research

- **Purpose**

  Evaluate the "share via Twitter" flow.

- **Objective**

  Uncover user experience issues and improve Twitter sharing before launch.

STUDY DATES AND TIMES

Communicating the study dates and times will enable team members to block off their schedules so they can observe sessions. If you're testing "live" code, be sure to communicate the schedule to your development team. Without knowing your plans, they might make changes that could disrupt the study. Ideally, some members of the development team should also observe sessions.

When scheduling the study times, make sure you allocate enough time between sessions. If you're working with paper, you may need some extra time to "reset" the prototype between participants. "Resetting" a paper prototype may involve rearranging the screens or erasing content handwritten on screens. Higher-fidelity prototypes may also need to be reset if participants added or removed content.

USER PROFILE

The user profile, discussed in Chapter 3, may also be used for usability testing.

METHOD

Your usability plan should specify which methods you plan to use and define them as needed. If you plan to gather usability metrics (e.g., task completion times and severity ratings), include them in this section as well as the method for gathering them (manual or automated).

QUESTIONS FOR RESEARCH

Questions for research can cover everything from high-level conceptual issues to low-level app interactions. For example, when conducting a paper prototype study for the art events app, my research questions were designed to shape the app direction and included the following:

- Are prospective users interested in the app concept?
- Does the high-level feature set meet their needs?
- Are they able to navigate between tabs and screens?
- What additional content, if any, do they need on the event detail view?
- What are their impressions of the ad placements?
- Based on what they see that day, would they download the app?

ROLES

The study roles will be influenced by your goals, context, and resources but may include the moderator, the note taker, the videographer, and the "computer" if you're conducting a paper prototype study. As discussed in Chapter 3, your team's user researcher should play the role of moderator. If you don't have a dedicated user researcher, choose a moderator with the following qualities: patience, empathy, flexibility, and assertiveness. If no one on your team meets these criteria, you may want to outsource the moderator role.

When observing users out in the field, keep in mind that the environment will influence the roles. For example, if "the field" means observing a participant using your app in an office, it may be easy to bring one or two team members along. However, if "the field" means following a participant during the morning commute, you may be more nimble on your own.

If team members are observing your study, make sure you explain the observer role. One of the biggest problems I've encountered is observers frequently interrupting user sessions with questions. Observer questions are fine, but it's best to wait until a natural break in the script or the end of the session. Constant interruptions may confuse participants and distract them from the task at hand. Communicating these issues in advance will allow your study to run more smoothly.

PROTOTYPE SUPPLIES

If you're testing a paper prototype and users may contribute to the design, be sure to have supplies on hand. The supplies should be similar to the materials used to create your prototype (e.g., Post-its, pens, extra paper, glue, etc.).

EQUIPMENT AND LOCATION

When conducting studies in a lab, most researchers take notes during the session, supplementing them with audio and video recordings as needed. **FIGURE 8.3** shows a lab setup with two video cameras: one on the iPhone and hands, the other on the participant's face. **FIGURE 8.4** shows the observation room for the same study.

In contrast, if you're conducting your research in the field and the user is constantly on the go, it may be challenging to take notes as you observe. In this case you may want to capture the user's screen with a small mounted camera and record comments through a microphone. More complex setups can include additional cameras as well as wireless transceivers that let the moderator view the participant's screen from a distance.[7] Additional tips on mobile usability-testing configurations can be found on the Little Springs Design web site.[8]

---

7. Antti Oulasvirta and Tuomo Nyyssönen, "Flexible Hardware Configurations for Studying Mobile Usability," *Journal of Usability Studies* (February 2009), www.usabilityprofessionals.org/upa_publications/jus/2009february/oulasvirta1.html.
8. Little Springs Design, www.littlespringsdesign.com/.

FIGURE 8.3 iPhone app usability study, with moderator and participant. The moderator (left) can see the iPhone projected on the large monitor.

FIGURE 8.4 iPhone app usability study observation room. The large screen (left) projects the iPhone screen while the participant is working through tasks; the small screen (right) shows the participant's face. Audio is also streamed into the observation room.

REPORT CONTENTS

Given the rapid pace of iPhone development, most companies seem to prefer lightweight usability reports (e.g., an executive summary with your top findings and recommendations). However, every company is different, so it's a good idea to discuss your reporting strategy in advance. If key members of your team are unable to observe the sessions, you may want to include video and/or audio clips in your report.

Recruiting Participants

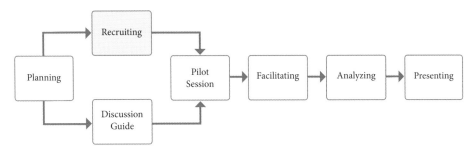

In Chapter 3 we explained how to create a participant screener and discussed several recruiting options—friends and family, recruiting agencies, Craigslist— which are also appropriate for usability testing. As mentioned earlier, don't underestimate the importance of recruiting individuals who match your user profile. Five to eight participants is generally recommended, but recruit twelve participants to account for no-shows and a pilot session.[9]

Drafting the Discussion Guide

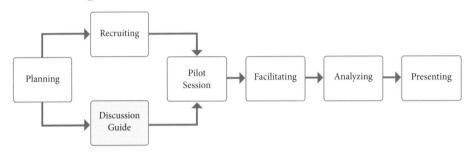

After the recruiting process is under way, start drafting the discussion guide for your study. Discussion guides often differ based on the study and the practitioner style. I've found the following format to be effective for a 90-minute study; there are 15 extra "floating minutes" for getting situated and possible bathroom breaks. Do not exceed 90 minutes, as participants may get tired and lose patience. It's also a good idea to provide water or other beverages.

- Introduction (5 minutes)
- Background interview (15 minutes)
- Tasks (40 minutes)
- Follow-up questions (10 minutes)
- Wrap-up (5 minutes)

INTRODUCTION (5 MINUTES)

TIP

A sample NDA can be found at the Society for Technical Communication's web site, as part of its "Usability Toolkit" (www.stcsig.org/usability/resources/toolkit/toolkit.html).

Provide your name, your company, and information on the process. In particular, explain "thinking out loud" and other method-related information. For example, you might say, "Please describe what you are doing. Imagine that you are talking to a friend who can't see what you're doing." If the app is currently in paper form, it's important to explain how to interact with the prototype (e.g., how to select items and how to enter text). If an NDA (a nondisclosure agreement) or other documents are required, ask the participant to sign them before you begin the study. Finally, inform the participant if team members are observing behind a one-way mirror.

9. Jakob Nielsen and Thomas K. Landauer, "A Mathematical Model of the Finding of Usability Problems," *Proceedings of ACM INTERCHI '93 Conference* (Amsterdam, April 24–29, 1993), 206–13.

BACKGROUND INTERVIEW (15 MINUTES)

Confirm responses from the participant screener and probe deeper as needed. These interviews are a good opportunity to ask participants to *show* how they use related products. For example, when I screened participants over the phone, we discussed the iPhone apps they were using for local event information. When we met in person, I took this one step further and asked them to demonstrate how they used these apps. Try to limit background interviews to 15 to 20 minutes.

TASKS (40 MINUTES)

The number of tasks will vary depending on the app and the estimated task duration. You may have four tasks that take approximately ten minutes each to complete, eight small tasks that require five minutes each, and so on. Whatever the breakdown, try to start with an easy task and provide a natural flow. For example, if you were testing a photo-sharing app, the natural flow might be image capture, image editing, and then image sharing. All of the tasks should relate to the objective outlined in your study plan.

FOLLOW-UP QUESTIONS (10 MINUTES)

Follow-up questions provide an opportunity to step back and understand the participant's impression of your app. Questions that often elicit insightful answers include the following:

- What is your overall impression of what you saw today?
- Do you have any concerns?
- Let's say you wanted to describe the app to a friend; what would you say?
- Is there anything else you wish it could do?
- Would you buy/use the app?

WRAP-UP (5 MINUTES)

Thank participants for their time and contributions to your app. Ask them if they have any outstanding questions, then provide the necessary payment.

FIGURE 8.5 contains an excerpt from a discussion guide created for the previously mentioned art events app. The primary goal of the study was to understand whether prospective users were interested in the concept and whether the initial design met their needs. The prototype medium was paper (FIGURE 8.6), and the sessions were conducted in a conference room in San Francisco, California. Participants were recruited using Craigslist and an online survey. The 90-minute study included three tasks; only one is shown in the figure.

INTRODUCTION

"Thanks for taking the time to meet with me. My company is developing a new product, and it helps if we learn more about people's unique experiences with the technology. First, there aren't any right or wrong answers, so don't worry about giving us 'good data'—it's all interesting to us, no matter how boring you think it is.

"Today's session will be divided into a couple of different sections but will take no longer than 1.5 hours. Before we begin, I need you to sign a nondisclosure agreement."

TASK 1. FIRST-TIME USER EXPERIENCE

"Imagine that your friend told you about a new iPhone app that helps you find local art. Let's say that you download the app to your phone that weekend and decide to try it out. Have you ever been to Ritual Coffee in the Mission? Imagine that you start your day at the café. When you start the app, the following screen appears:" *(Show start screen.)*

Before the participant clicks on anything, possible probes:

- Is this what you expected to see?
- What did you expect? *(if the participant did not expect this content)*
- What would you do next?

UI QUESTIONS

If the participant does not comment, probe into the following before proceeding:

- What do you think about the event information shown? Is anything missing or unclear?
- What do you expect to happen when you click on Sort? *(Note the sort values expected.)*
- What do you expect each of these to do? *(Point to the bottom toolbar.)*

[Tasks 2 and 3 appeared here.]

FOLLOW-UP QUESTIONS

In addition to the follow-up questions described in the previous section, participants were asked:

- Which galleries need to be included to make this useful to you?
- If the service required an account, what would make this most compelling?
- Would the app replace anything you already use?
- Would you be willing to pay for this app?
- How do you feel about ads on this app? What kind of ads do you think would be appropriate?

FIGURE 8.5 Excerpt from the discussion guide for an art events iPhone app paper prototype study

FIGURE 8.6 iPhone paper prototype for finding local art events. An iPhone was used to record audio and photograph participants.

Discussion Guide Tips

To test out your discussion guide, consider reading it out loud as you walk through the user interface. This activity will help you uncover flaws in your guide. For example, you may discover points where you may want the user to pause so you can ask a question. While this solo walk-through is tremendously valuable, it's not a substitute for a "pilot," which is essentially a dry run of the test with a target user. If everything goes smoothly in your pilot, you may be able to incorporate this data into your findings. Otherwise, plan to revise the prototype and/or guide and exclude the data.

Pilot Session

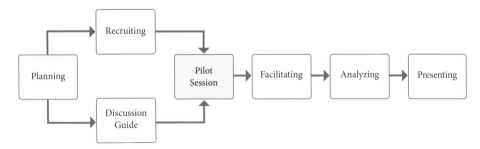

As mentioned earlier, it's critical to run a pilot session to uncover any issues with the prototype or discussion guide. In addition to recruiting a participant based on your user profile, you may want to do a test run with a team member unfamiliar with the app design. Be sure to run the pilot at least a few days before the actual study; that way you'll have enough time to make revisions.

Facilitating Usability Tests

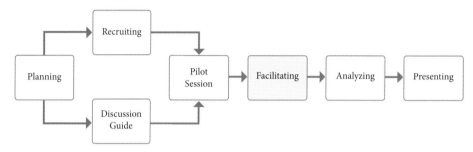

The discussion guide will be instrumental as you facilitate the usability-testing sessions. As mentioned previously, remember it's a "guide"; thus you should adapt as needed. At the same time it's important to know when to draw participants back into the guide. For example, the art events app prototype did not include a companion web site. However, when a participant asked about the web site, it seemed worth exploring, so we discussed this topic further.

NOTE

Tasks can be provided orally, written on paper, or both. I tend to provide both.

In contrast, when another participant started to discuss a feature that was clearly out of scope, I noted the comments and politely moved on to the next task. Additional facilitating tips are discussed in the next section.

BE ENCOURAGING

After presenting users with each task, remain quiet, giving them a chance to orient themselves. Resist any temptation to provide hints or explain what to do next. Provide encouraging verbal and nonverbal feedback such as nodding and smiling.

ASK OPEN-ENDED QUESTIONS

As participants are working through tasks, you may ask open-ended questions to better understand their behavior and comments. Open-ended questions are also an effective way to help participants when they seem confused. Here's an example of this type of dialogue:

Participant: (*Quietly staring at screen*)

Moderator: "What are you thinking?"

Participant: "Well, I was going to tap here, but I'm not sure if it will show more event info."

Moderator: "What do you expect it to do?"

Participant: "I'm not sure. I think it will provide more info on the venue and opening times."

Moderator: "What would you do if you were at home [*or wherever the app is used*]?"

Participant: "I would probably try it and see what happens."

Moderator: "Okay, let's try that."

Participant: (*Taps on selection*)

Moderator: "Is this what you expected?"

Participant: "Yes."

NOTE

If participants try to tap on a feature that has not been defined yet, it's a good idea to ask what they expect the feature to do, then tell them it's not working yet. Knowing their expectations may help shape the feature requirements and design solution.

KNOW WHEN TO STOP

If the participant has been trying to complete a task for a while and seems aggravated, allow some recovery time, then move on to the next task. Sometimes I'll explain what happened and answer task-related questions at the end of the session. When I explain how we intended the app to work, I always add, "Thank you for your help in identifying that problem—your feedback will make the product better for everyone." This reassures participants that *they* weren't the problem; the *interface* was the problem. This exchange may also lead to additional insights.

Analyzing Usability Tests

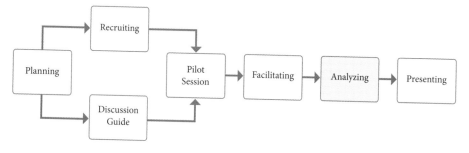

In contrast to up-front user research analysis, which may involve several team members, usability tests are typically analyzed by the user researcher. One reason is objectivity—the app designers may be too attached to their designs; the other is speed. Having your entire team collaboratively analyze each task will take much longer. This doesn't mean that the researcher does not consult with the designers and developers; it just means that the researcher leads the analysis effort. Of course, this assumes you have a dedicated researcher. I've played the role of designer and researcher and have been able to objectively analyze the data, but not everyone can.

Regardless of who leads the effort, consider creating affinity diagrams of your observations, as discussed in Chapter 4, "Analyzing User Research," using your notes as a starting point. Groupings will vary for each app—they can be organized by task, themes, severity, scope. For example, for the art events app, I organized my findings into overall issues and task-specific issues. Similar to the approach in Chapter 4, I tend to summarize the findings in one to two sentences, then provide supporting quotes. If you captured audio or video, you can create short clips to accompany these findings. A few excerpts are shown in the following sections.

NOTE

P followed by a number is shorthand used to refer to participants from the study. The number indicates when the participant was interviewed; for example, P1 is the first participant.

OVERALL ISSUES

Participants expected the app to have a companion web site.

- "I'd rather use the web site when I'm at home since the screen is bigger." (P3)
- "Can I write reviews through the web site?" (P4)
- "Would the bookmarks be the same on the web site?" (P5)

TASK-SPECIFIC ISSUES

Participants expected additional event information.

- "It'd be nice to see the material and dimensions for the artwork shown." (P1)
- "When are the opening and closing receptions?" (P2)
- "Where is the telephone number? I like to call to make sure they're open." (P5)

Presenting Usability Findings

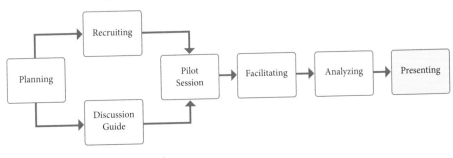

After analyzing your user sessions, consider writing up a Quick Findings report at a minimum. As discussed earlier, Quick Findings typically include approximately five to ten of the most critical issues, sometimes called "top findings," followed by more detailed findings. The extra effort may seem unnecessary at the time, but the document will be a valuable reference in the future.

Although your observations are fresh immediately after the study, it will be hard to remember the details a few weeks later. Once you have your findings documented, share them with the stakeholders who attended the original kickoff meeting.

In addition to sharing insights, you may want to use this meeting time to start brainstorming and prioritizing solutions. Be sure to discuss next steps while the study is fresh in everyone's mind. Unfortunately, as time passes, many teams start to minimize what seemed like critical issues.

Guerrilla Usability Testing

Guerrilla usability testing is derived from *guerrilla marketing*, a term that was coined by Jay Conrad Levinson in his book *Guerrilla Marketing*.[10] Like its marketing counterpart, guerrilla usability testing relies on time, energy, and imagination instead of a big budget. Given its unconventional nature, there aren't any set rules or definitions. In fact, when I was researching user experience organizations that provide guerrilla testing, I found it hard to distinguish their methods from "traditional" usability testing. With that in mind, be aware that practitioners may have different opinions on what constitutes guerrilla usability testing. The next section introduces a few variations that are relatively popular.

COFFEE SHOP TESTING

"Coffee shop" researchers typically go to their local coffee haunt in search of study participants (Starbucks seems to be quite popular). Once they identify an acceptable candidate, they offer the individual coffee in exchange for evaluating their app. These sessions tend to take an exploratory approach; for example, a developer might hand the participant an iPhone with the app and ask, "What would you do when you first open this app?" The location doesn't necessarily have to be a coffee shop. The creator of the What's Shakin' app used a similar strategy at a bar in San Francisco.

---

10. Jay Conrad Levinson, *Guerrilla Marketing* (Mariner Books, 2007).

WALK-UP TESTING

"Walk-up" testing is similar to "coffee shop" testing in the sense that you approach strangers; the main difference is context and duration. "Walk-up" testing usually takes place on the sidewalk or other public place. Given that these people are typically en route somewhere, they may have less patience than coffee shop customers. Ideally, you should provide some type of modest incentive (e.g., a coupon code for your app or an iTunes gift certificate).

COMMON GROUND TESTING

You may have more leeway if you can conduct guerrilla tests in a place where you have something in common with the individuals. For example, when attending a conference for wine professionals, Hello Vino representatives asked fellow attendees to try out their iPhone app prototype. In exchange, they gave each participant a free wine glass charm. Depending on your app, there may be other venues that are suitable for guerrilla usability testing, but please choose the location and approach wisely. Holding interviews in certain locations may be unacceptable for legal or privacy reasons.

Word of Caution

When I suggest up-front usability testing to iPhone developers—that is, "traditional" usability testing—they typically nod their heads but don't seem convinced. However, when I suggest guerrilla methods such as the ones described here, their eyes light up as if to say, "Sure, I can handle that!" I suspect their change in attitude is largely because these nontraditional alternatives seem fast and easy, whereas the other approaches require more planning.

Given that some usability testing is better than no usability testing—not always, but usually—I urge them to at least try one of the guerrilla approaches. But, at the same time, I explain what they're missing by forgoing the traditional usability testing or RITE route.

Representative Users

Without proper screening, it's unlikely that coffee shop or walk-up participants will adequately represent your user base. And, unless they're holding an iPhone, you may not even know if they're iPhone users. Sure, you can stop them on the street and ask, but if you get several "no" answers, you might have saved time by simply recruiting up front. Last, this hit-or-miss approach is clearly a deal breaker if your app is designed for a specialized group, such as doctors.

Adequate Time for Tasks

Nearly all of the guerrilla approaches mentioned imply that someone is doing you a *quick* favor. As a result, chances are you'll keep the study brief, limiting participants' exposure to your app. This might be fine if your app is a game or utility that's typically used for very brief periods of time. However, if you've designed a productivity app with a rich set of features, the value of a guerrilla user test may be minimal. In this case a guerrilla test may be useful for gathering initial impressions but inadequate for uncovering deeper user experience issues.

Ethics and Supporting Documentation

As discussed in the previous section, you should always begin usability studies with an introduction to the procedure, emphasizing that you're testing the app, not the people. Additionally, in many cases companies ask participants to sign an NDA and release forms for using the research and/or photos. You can certainly include these documents when conducting guerrilla tests, but the impromptu nature often leads individuals to forgo these important steps. You may not run into any problems, but do you want to take a chance?

Beta Testing

iPhone beta testing is made possible through Apple's Ad Hoc Distribution system.[11] Based on a series of phone interviews with developers, it's my understanding that most of them find participants through their personal networks, through forums on their web sites, or through social networking services like Twitter. The feedback tends to be unstructured, and the level of detail varies from one participant to the next. This is unfortunate, because beta testing can be very powerful—participants' feedback can be gathered in situ, in context; the participant pool can be geographically dispersed; and feedback can be collected over an extended period of time. To make the most of beta testing, consider enhancing it with some user-centered techniques such as the following ones.

CAST A WIDER RECRUITING NET

The Ad Hoc Distribution system enables developers to include up to 100 participants. Instead of limiting yourself to friends and loyal Twitter followers, create a user profile, as discussed in Chapter 3, and recruit participants who match the profile.

---

11. iPhone Developer Program, http://developer.apple.com/iphone/program/distribute.html.

ASK FOR MORE STRUCTURED FEEDBACK

Include a survey with your beta and consider associating survey questions with specific app tasks. For example, if your beta includes a new email-sharing feature, you could display a brief survey immediately after the user has sent a message. Alternative approaches for prompting users—random, scheduled, event-based— are discussed in detail in the paper "Using the Experience Sampling Method to Evaluate Ubicomp Applications."[12] In terms of tools, there are a number of options for collecting iPhone user data. Haveasec.com can help you gather qualitative data via surveys, and services like Flurry, Pinch Media, and Mobclix use analytics to collect quantitative data (e.g., time on task and drop-off rates).

PROVIDE AN INCENTIVE

Many developers are disappointed when testers fail to follow through on the beta. One way to improve response rates is to provide an incentive after participants submit feedback (e.g., an iTunes gift certificate).

Choosing an Approach

Determining your usability-testing strategy will depend on a variety of factors— the study goals, the app, your team's skill set, the available time and budget. At a minimum, I recommend two studies: one in the early design stage and another in the later stages. If paper is a suitable medium for prototyping your app, consider a paper prototype study for the initial test and a device-based RITE or "traditional" study for the later test.

On the other hand, if paper is not effective for your domain (e.g., musical instruments), you may want to test your app on the device early on and conduct a usability test with your beta in the final design phase. Finally, if your time and budget are extremely limited, consider one of the guerrilla usability-testing methods discussed in this chapter.

Summary

This chapter discussed the benefits of usability testing. In addition to impacting the bottom line—fewer costly iterations on "live" code—usability testing can lead to increased customer satisfaction. Instead of waiting until your users uncover

---

12. Sunny Consolvo and Miriam Walker, "Using the Experience Sampling Method to Evaluate Ubicomp Applications," *Pervasive Computing* (April–June 2003).

issues and vent on the App Store, you can address these issues before even coding your application.

There are many different usability-testing approaches. You were introduced to "traditional" usability studies, the RITE method, paper prototyping studies, guerrilla testing, and beta testing. While each app is different, most apps can benefit from at least two usability tests: one in the early design stage, and another one in the middle to later design stages.

When you start planning your app's usability study, keep in mind the following:

- Some research is better than no research. If you can't run a RITE or traditional usability study, try a guerrilla method or create your own!

- Be as inclusive as possible when planning and running your usability tests. Having your team members on board will make it easier to integrate findings into your app.

- Make sure you pilot your usability study *at least* a few days in advance. This will give you time to adjust the discussion guide and prototype. ▪

CASE STUDY 8

REALTOR.com

CLIFF WILLIAMS has been designing and building user experiences for the web and desktop for the last 15 years. He's currently the interaction design lead for mobile user experiences at Move, Inc., operator of Move.com, Moving.com, SeniorHousingNet.com, Top Producer, and REALTOR.com, the number-one site for home sales.

What inspired REALTOR.com to build an iPhone app?

A big part of searching for a home is being out and about—checking out neighborhoods, going to open houses, touring with an agent. A REALTOR.com iPhone app felt like a natural and useful extension of our web experience.

One of our developers created the spark with a proof-of-concept app. That attracted me and a couple of others at the company. From there we spent whatever extra cycles we could find—between projects, nights, weekends—refining the concept. Eventually it developed enough interest and became an official project (great apps from our competitors helped, too).

How did you approach the project?

Early on it was a mix of open brainstorming and refining the proof-of-concept app. This was a great approach for us because it let big new ideas flow in while we were learning the bounds of the API and the capabilities of the platform.

Once it became an official project, we took a step back to evaluate where we were with the proof-of-concept app, the pool of ideas we had developed, and past user research that might be applicable. This helped us really hone in on a feature set focused on the mobile user.

What were some of the challenges you faced?

As an experienced web designer but first-time app designer, it took a while for me to really get comfortable applying the patterns and principles of the platform. My first attempts were essentially 320 × 480 web sites, not iPhone apps. Data was displayed in long sections that required lots of scrolling. The architecture focused on presenting a breadth of choices at the expense of a crisp, simple workflow. As the app evolved, it became more and more iPhone-y.

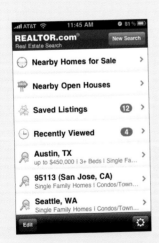

FIGURE CS8.1 REALTOR.com home screen

Were you able to conduct usability tests?

After our first big round of design on the official app, we started thinking about usability testing. Getting a live prototype in time wasn't possible, so I started experimenting with simple HTML prototypes that we could test on a working iPhone. These were effective, but it was difficult to simulate scrolling with fixed-position elements.

We ended up going with a paper prototype that included all of the screens in the app, variations of some key screens, and a handful of bits and pieces that we would overlay at different points. These were created with Adobe Fireworks at 72DPI. Next time I would create them at 300DPI since the printouts weren't that sharp.

Testing netted one big issue (saving your favorite items was confusing) and several smaller ones (clarity of icons and copy). These results pushed us even further down the reduce-simplify-streamline path our designs had been evolving along. [**FIGURES CS8.1–CS8.3** show the final designs.]

Can you describe the usability-testing environment?

Evonne Shea, our project's user researcher, started each session with a brief interview to gather high-level information about the user's current real estate search needs and experiences. Afterward she'd introduce me (the computer) and then move to the adjacent observation room. From there she could observe the participant through a one-way mirror as well as a pair of video cameras—one focused on the prototype, the other on the participant's face. Video was recorded for later analysis and also displayed on a projector in the observation room so team members could watch. We included eight participants in the study. All of them were currently involved in searching for real estate and had some experience downloading iPhone apps.

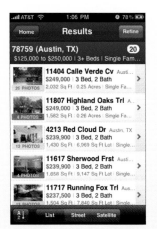

FIGURE CS8.2 REALTOR.com search results

FIGURE CS8.3 REALTOR.com map view

Any additional advice for iPhone app designers?

If you're not developing the app yourself, learn to speak the same language as the folks who are. Read Apple's *Human Interface Guidelines* to start. It will help get the ball rolling on your designs, and it's invaluable as a Rosetta Stone. Check out the online API documentation, too. For purposes of specifications, it's critical to know what the API provides "for free" and what it doesn't.

Another thing that helped me a ton was creating a giant library of screenshots. Download every app that you hear good things about and take screen captures of anything you see that is remotely interesting. Perhaps even more important, take screen captures of the default Apple apps (even the boring stuff, like Settings, is a gold mine). I constantly referred back to this library for best practices on some of the more mundane things and inspiration for big new ones. ■

Feedback messaging; see page 201

UI controls; see page 213

Hierarchy; see page 229

Icon communicability; see page 239

Brand extensibility; see page 256

Branding the user experience; see page 260

Refining Your iPhone App

PART FOUR

Now that you have formulated your app concept, the next step is to look at a variety of ways to refine your design.

In Part Four you will find these chapters:

- Chapter 9, "User Interface Design," includes guidelines for a range of UI issues (navigation, personalization, feedback) as well as best practices for the iPhone UI controls outlined in Apple's iPhone HIG.
- Chapter 10, "Visual Design," explains how to improve your app's visual design, with an emphasis on layout, typography, iconography, and color.
- Chapter 11, "Branding and Advertising," discusses ways to express branding within your app and how to seamlessly incorporate advertising.
- Chapter 12, "Accessibility and Localization," explains how to make your app compatible with VoiceOver, the iPhone's screen-reading software, and delves into alternative localization approaches.

This part tackles these topics serially to simplify the discussion, but your app should consider all of these issues holistically. For example, your accessibility and localization strategies should be considered along with your app's interaction and visual design; you shouldn't wait until the very end to sort out how and where accessibility and localization fit into your design.

189

User Interface Design

AS NOTED IN THE PREVIOUS CHAPTER, first impressions can mean everything. When it comes to your application, its user interface is your first impression. If users can't get past the first screen, they are likely to abandon or delete your app. Once they've had a negative experience, it will be challenging to convince them to try it again.

To prevent this from happening it's important to spend time refining your app's user interface. In this chapter we'll review user interface best practices that can be applied across many app types, covering topics such as the first-time user experience, personalization, and feedback.

Next, we'll delve into specific UI issues not adequately addressed in the HIG, such as when to use a tab versus a toolbar. Finally, we'll discuss back-end requirements that may impact the user experience. Designers often assume that these "invisible" requirements are automatically coded into their apps, but they must be specified in advance.

This chapter also includes case studies on the Sonos and FlightTrack iPhone apps.

User Interface Best Practices

As you refine your app design, the best practices in this section may help focus your efforts. They may be similar to best practices for other platforms, but all of the examples are specific to the iPhone.

1. Be welcoming.
2. Know thy user.
3. Let the content shine.
4. Make selections fast and error-free.
5. Provide appropriate feedback.
6. Minimize the pain.

1. BE WELCOMING

Given that there are thousands and thousands of iPhone apps, it's no small feat when users find and download yours. When they first open it, they are undoubtedly excited to see what it has to offer. Imagine their disappointment when they are dropped into a bare screen with little guidance, forced to complete a long registration process, or confronted with an error message that doesn't tell them what they've done wrong. To help soften the first-time user experience (and retain users!), here are some ways to make your app more welcoming:

- Display "getting started" information.
- Annotate the user interface.
- Provide an *optional* video demo.

Display "Getting Started" Information

Many apps provide a welcome screen that introduces the app in a few brief sentences. This is particularly important in three cases:

- Apps with little or no precedence
- Apps that require certain configurations (e.g., sound turned on)
- Apps that require registration (e.g., Twitter clients)

TweetDeck (shown in **FIGURE 9.1**) welcomes new users and introduces the setup process. Additional information can also be provided for new features that require explanation. For example, Yelp (shown in **FIGURE 9.2**) provides a tip when users open the Scope feature.

FIGURE 9.1 TweetDeck's welcome screen introduces the user to the app and the setup process.

FIGURE 9.2 Yelp provides a tip when users first open the Scope feature.

Annotate the User Interface

Annotations are effective when most of the app functionality is concentrated on one screen. **FIGURE 9.3** illustrates how Postman presents a series of annotations to the first-time user. Notice that there are five concise annotations; many more might overwhelm the user. These annotations go away once users have created their first postcard.

FIGURE 9.3 Postman presents annotations to the first-time user.

Provide an Optional Demo

If your app space is not well defined or the interface is relatively unique, consider offering an optional demo, as Convertbot does (**FIGURE 9.4**). Emphasis is put on *optional* since it can be very annoying to users when they are forced to watch a demo. If you plan to localize your app, keep in mind that video demos should be localized as well.

FIGURE 9.4 Convertbot optional demo

2. KNOW THY USER

The iPhone presents a unique opportunity to create personalized user experiences, yet many apps barely scratch the surface. Information commonly used to personalize the user experience includes the user's name or ID, settings, favorites, and user behavior.

Name

At the most basic level, you can personalize your app with the user's name or ID. In addition to greeting users within the app, as in Flickr (**FIGURE 9.5**), the user's name can be shown when sending app-related messages, such as alerts. This type of personalization is most appropriate when the user's identity is an integral part of the user experience (e.g., social networking apps or multiplayer games). Users may not wish to provide their name if the benefits are not evident.

Settings

The user experience can be personalized with settings, but make sure they are absolutely necessary, not a dumping ground for extra features. Frequently used settings should be within the app; less frequent settings can be stored in the

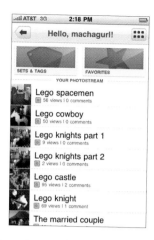

FIGURE 9.5 Flickr welcomes the user on the Photostream page.

iPhone Settings. This distinction is important because users must exit your app to access the iPhone Settings. Additionally, if your app is available on multiple platforms (web, desktop, etc.), make sure the settings are synchronized accordingly. Every app is different, but here are some common settings to consider:

- Font size, especially for news and Twitter apps (e.g., increase/decrease or specify size)
- Sounds (e.g., turn on/off, customize sound)
- Measurement (e.g., miles versus kilometers for location-based apps)
- Default applications (e.g., which Twitter client to launch for Tweets)
- List view (e.g., number of items to display, content to display)
- Recents/History (e.g., on/off, how long to save, how many items to save)
- Tab content (e.g., what appears in each tab, as done in the NYTimes and Yelp apps)
- Screen orientation and autocorrect (e.g., ability to turn off)

Favorites

Favorites (and Bookmarks) enable users to actively save an item to view later. If your app is available on other platforms (web, desktop, etc.), favorites should be synced across all platforms. Favorites are most common in content-rich apps such as news, photos, videos, recipes, and Twitter clients. Yelp provides a seamless syncing experience between its web site and iPhone app. When the user loads Yelp Bookmarks on the iPhone, the app checks for any changes the user may have made via the Yelp web site (**FIGURE 9.6**).

FIGURE 9.6 Syncing Bookmarks on the Yelp app

Behavior

Although settings and favorites are valuable, they can be challenging to manage in the mobile context. In contrast, personalizing the user experience based on user behavior requires no effort. One of the most common examples is the ability to access items using the app history, for example, Recent Searches. Personalization based on user behavior can be taken much further, though it's important to consider user privacy. Some types of personalization (e.g., apps that use Address Book information) may be considered invasive and would require user consent.

3. LET THE CONTENT SHINE

As discussed in Chapter 1, "iPhone Application Overview," one of the defining characteristics of an Immersive application is its focus on the content (e.g., the built-in photo app "hides" the UI controls when photos are viewed).

In January 2008, Edward Tufte lauded this aspect of the iPhone user experience:

> *The idea is that the content is the interface, the information is the interface—not computer administrative debris.*[1]

As much as possible, try to apply this philosophy to your own app. The iPhone screen is tiny in comparison to desktop computer screens; thus every pixel of UI should add value to the user experience.

---

1. Edward Tufte, "iPhone Interface Design," www.edwardtufte.com/bboard/q-and-a-fetch-msg?msg_id=00036T.

At the same time, consider the tasks and their frequency of use. For example, it would be frustrating if controls were hidden in an email app since the user is constantly reading, moving, and deleting messages. Additionally, be clear on how to access the hidden controls. Three common models—tap screen, tap button, and scroll up—are described in this section.

Tap Screen

The "tap screen" model is used when *all* of the user interface controls are hidden and is most appropriate for apps such as photo slideshows, video players, news articles, e-books, and certain Immersive games. **FIGURE 9.7** illustrates how the NYTimes app shows the UI controls when the user first opens an article. When the user starts scrolling (and has presumably seen the controls), the controls gradually fade until they are hidden (**FIGURE 9.8**); they reappear when the user reaches the end of the article. Users may also bring back the controls by tapping anywhere on the screen. This is consistent with the built-in photo slideshow app.

FIGURE 9.7 NYTimes article with controls   FIGURE 9.8 NYTimes article without controls

Tap Button/Zone

The "tap button/zone" model is used when only *part* of the UI controls are hidden. It's most effective when controls are infrequently used and/or space is limited. For example, when GQ users first open an article, the photos are shown (**FIGURE 9.9**). After a few seconds the photos fade into the background and are replaced with a View Media button indicating the number of photos available (**FIGURE 9.10**). This approach may also be used for hiding/showing certain information, such as a legend for movie ratings.

FIGURE 9.9 GQ with media open

FIGURE 9.10 GQ with media closed

Scroll Up

The "scroll up" model is used when the controls directly below the header are hidden until scrolled into view (these are typically one row or less in height). Search is the primary use case, as shown in Tweetie 2.0 (**FIGURES 9.11–9.12**), though it could also be applied to list filters or sort options. Given the minimal cues, this model is arguably for more advanced users.

FIGURE 9.11 Tweetie 2.0 with the Search field shown on "scroll up"

FIGURE 9.12 Tweetie 2.0 when the Search field is not shown

4. MAKE SELECTIONS FAST AND ERROR-FREE

As discussed earlier, the mobile context may make it difficult for users to enter information. Here we'll discuss ways to minimize errors and make users more efficient.

Provide Smart Defaults

Smart defaults can considerably reduce the amount of typing required. For example, the Maps app automatically pre-populates the Start field with the user's current location and the End field with the most recent search (**FIGURE 9.13**).

FIGURE 9.13 The Start field on Google Maps is pre-populated with the user's current location and most recent search.

Include Predefined Lists

Predefined lists are an effective way to minimize text entry if the lists aren't too long. For example, this approach works well with the iBART (Bay Area Rapid Transit) app, given that there are about 40 train stations listed alphabetically (**FIGURE 9.14**). On the other hand, if you were looking up a flight, it would be unwieldy to scan thousands of flight listings. Instead, it would be preferable to search by airline and flight number, as is done in the FlightTrack app (**FIGURE 9.15**).

Suggest Matches

If free-form text entry is required, consider suggesting matches as the user enters the information. This strategy can be effective for apps that search large amounts of unstructured data, such as Google. Suggesting matches can also be helpful when searching user data (e.g., contact lists).

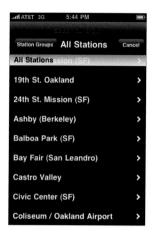

FIGURE 9.14 iBART lists all the BART stations.

FIGURE 9.15 FlightTrack lets users search by airline and flight number.

Store Recent Activity/Selections

If the user has taken the time to enter certain information, consider storing it for future reference. This information may be accessed in a number of ways, for example, by

- Pre-populating certain fields, such as the user's postal code based on his or her location
- Making past selections available in a Recents tab
- Showing History matches as the user types a query

Each of these methods can give users a better experience, simplifying tasks they would otherwise have to do over and over again. For example, when Read It Later users tag items, the app shows frequently used tags (FIGURE 9.16).

FIGURE 9.16 Read It Later provides access to frequently used tags.

Use Voice and Image Recognition

Typing can be significantly reduced if voice or image recognition is used. For example, Google Search lets users vocalize their search queries, and SnapTell lets users search for purchase information using images captured with their iPhones.

5. PROVIDE APPROPRIATE FEEDBACK

As users interact with your app, there may be times when things happen "behind the scenes" that require them to wait a moment. To reassure users during these moments, consider providing feedback in the form of animations, transitions, highlights, or alerts.

Animations

Animations are an effective way to provide feedback for the following situations: downloading content, moving content, and end-of-content indicators.

- **Downloading/processing**

  An activity indicator should be provided when content is being downloaded or processed on the device *and* this activity impacts the user experience. For example, the Voices app displays a full-screen animation as it "transforms" your voice (**FIGURE 9.17**).

  In contrast, the NYTimes app (shown in **FIGURE 9.18**) provides a progress indicator that can be closed, thereby enabling users to continue viewing other content. The full-screen approach should be used only when the app is busy and can't be used for other tasks.

FIGURE 9.17 The Voices app draws red curtains and lowers the "Your voice is being transformed" message when applying voice filters.

FIGURE 9.18 The NYTimes app displays a progress bar by default as articles and images are downloaded, but the user may close it at any time.

- **Moving**

  Move animations help indicate where an object is going and where it came from. For example, they may illustrate content moving between objects (e.g., files between folders) or items moving within a list (e.g., reordering cities on the Yahoo! Weather app). To make your app easier to learn, keep the *interaction* consistent with the built-in apps, but customize the *visual* feedback. For example, the built-in email app shows a letter falling into the target folder (**FIGURE 9.19**), but you might want to show a postcard or other relevant imagery for your app.

- **Bounce**

  The bounce animation indicates when the user has reached the end of a selected screen.[2] Related to this point, it's also beneficial to show part of the last row; that way the user will know there's more information available. **FIGURE 9.20** illustrates how Classics shows part of the next bookshelf at the top and bottom.

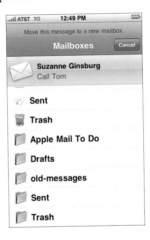

FIGURE 9.19 The Mail app shows an envelope falling into a folder when a message is moved.

FIGURE 9.20 The Classics app shows part of the next bookshelf to indicate additional content.

Transitions

Transitions refer to the visual feedback provided when users move between related screens. Many of the transitions reference real-world metaphors or abstract spatial orientations that help users understand where things reside within an app or how they work. Common transitions include flip, slide, fade, curl, and zoom. As much as possible, try to keep these consistent with the built-in apps.

2. David Barnard et al., *iPhone User Interface Projects* (Apress, 2009).

- **Flip:** Used when accessing Utility app settings or switching between views (e.g., from list to map view). Movement is right to left from the start state and left to right from the end state.

- **Slide left/right:** Primarily used when drilling down lists.

- **Slide up/down:** Often used when a secondary panel slides up along the bottom of the app. For example, Postman uses the slide-up transition when users access the Picture and Styling options (**FIGURES 9.21–9.22**).

NOTE

To see short videos illustrating these transitions, visit http://www.iphoneuxreviews.com/?p=191.

FIGURE 9.21 Postman with the Picture pane hidden

FIGURE 9.22 Postman with the Picture pane shown via slide-up transition

- Fade in/out: Used when viewing media (e.g., entering/exiting a slideshow or video). Also known as "cross-dissolve."

- Curl: Used to access content "under" the current view. Perhaps the best-known example of a curl transition is on Maps (**FIGURE 9.23**).

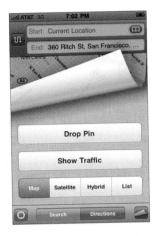

FIGURE 9.23 Curl transition used on Maps

- **Zoom:** Used to maximize/minimize the selected item. For example, the Facebook home screen zooms in or out when users select one of the options.

Text Alerts

Text alerts can be used if visual feedback isn't explicit enough. They can be displayed in-line or on an overlay.

- In-line alert: Displays feedback alongside other content, typically one line at the top of the screen. The alert fades after a few seconds or when the user scrolls down the screen, as shown on Twitterific in **FIGURE 9.24**. This type of alert is appropriate when user acknowledgment is *not* required.

FIGURE 9.24 Twitterific displays a message in-line to indicate the number of new tweets.

- **Overlay alert:** Displayed above a grayed-out screen; the user must dismiss the alert in order to proceed, as shown in **FIGURE 9.25**. This approach is appropriate *only* when user acknowledgment is required and should not be overused since it disrupts the user's workflow.

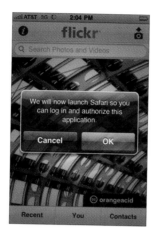

FIGURE 9.25 Flickr provides a modal alert when the user must leave the app.

Sound

Sound may accompany many of the feedback options just mentioned, but use it sparingly. Overuse of sound will annoy users and may lead them to turn off sounds altogether (or worse, they will stop using your app and delete it from their iPhone). Even when used sparingly, sound should not be the primary feedback mechanism. Users may mute their phones in certain situations, and sounds may be difficult to hear in noisy environments.

6. MINIMIZE THE PAIN

When users are engaged with your app, sometimes things will go wrong that are beyond your control (e.g., loss of network connection, limited bandwidth). In these cases try to minimize the impact on the user experience by explaining the problem, maintaining the status quo, and keeping the user informed.

Explain the Problem

Although this may seem obvious, many apps don't explain what's going on when things go wrong. For example, when the network connection is lost, users are often presented with the never-ending loading icon. Instead, it's best to explain the problem in layperson's terms and how it may be resolved. **FIGURE 9.26** illustrates how Epicurious deals with a lost network connection.

FIGURE 9.26 Epicurious provides a helpful message when users are offline.

Maintain the Status Quo

Certain app features may stop working when things go wrong. As much as possible, try to maintain the status quo. For example, in the absence of a network connection, Shazam still allows users to tag songs but postpones the analysis until the network connection is reestablished (FIGURE 9.27). Similarly, instead of providing null results when users try to view network content, ideally your app will cache the last result.

FIGURE 9.27 Shazam doesn't completely break down when offline. Users can still capture the information needed to tag a song, then finish the process when they are back online.

Save Work in Progress

Given that mobile users are frequently interrupted, it's important to save work in progress. Depending on the app, your solution may include a combination of user- and app-initiated features. For example, WordPress provides an auto-recovery feature if users are interrupted by a phone call as well as the ability to explicitly save drafts. Also, a large number of apps save the user's "state," which means they can display the last screen viewed (and the related content) when the user returns to the app. Most Twitter apps even maintain your place in Tweet lists.

Keep the User Informed

If network or other issues impact how the app normally works, keep the user informed. For example, let's say your app provides sports scores. If the user loses the network connection, it would be helpful to indicate the time of the last app update. With this information the user can easily determine whether the scores are current or not.

User Interface Q&A

In Chapter 1, "iPhone Application Overview," we discussed the importance of reading Apple's *iPhone Human Interface Guidelines* (the "iPhone HIG") before you start designing your iPhone app. As you refine your app, consider rereading the iPhone HIG, paying extra attention to Part II, "Designing the User Interface of Your iPhone Application." Here we'll try to address some aspects of the iPhone HIG that could use additional clarification.

WHICH PRODUCTIVITY STYLE SHOULD I USE?

Although there is a definitive Productivity style, many variations have emerged since the iPhone HIG were first written. You may want to explore these alternatives for your app, but keep in mind that diverging from the guidelines may influence whether your app is approved. And, more important, adhering to the guidelines will make your app easier for users to learn and use. Three common variations include tiered tabs, the grid, and top tabs, which we'll cover next.

Tiered Tabs

Tiered tabs are an extension of the standard Productivity style and are commonly used in content-rich apps. In particular, this approach is effective if you want to show subcategories without drilling down lists. FIGURE 9.28 illustrates how USA TODAY uses tiered tabs in a carousel format to show several different sections within the Headlines tab—Top News, News, Money, Sports. Notice how part of the last label, L (for Life), shows, along with an arrow. This provides a hint to users that additional sections are available if they scroll to the right. This row animates the first time, reinforcing that there are additional options beyond the four visible ones.

FIGURE 9.28 USA TODAY uses tiered tabs (along the top) to access the newspaper sections.

Grid Menu

Grid menus can support more entry points than the standard Productivity style. This may be appropriate for apps that have a wide range of features or apps with visual navigation. For example, Facebook has a 3 × 3 grid home screen, and additional pages can be added for Friends or Pages (FIGURE 9.29). This approach can be useful in many apps where more top-level features are wanted. But resist the temptation unless it's absolutely necessary; every feature should be essential and contextually relevant. Also, keep in mind that the grid requires an extra step to move between sections. For example, it takes two steps to navigate from Facebook Photos to Events; it would be one step if a tab bar were used. Other apps that use the grid menu are LinkedIn and Viper.

FIGURE 9.29 Facebook uses the grid style on the home screen.

Top Tabs

Top tabs are similar to the standard ones, except they appear along the top of the app. Apps tend to use this approach to save vertical space, omitting the traditional navigation bar. For example, Yahoo! Finance devotes more real estate to stock information using this model (**FIGURE 9.30**). Although the approach can work well, don't use it unless you have a strong reason.

WARNING!

As mentioned earlier, diverging from the standards may make your app more difficult to learn and use, plus it may be rejected by Apple.

FIGURE 9.30 Yahoo! Finance displays tabs at the top of the screen.

HOW SHOULD I PRESENT TASKS ON THE PRODUCTIVITY-STYLE DETAIL VIEW?

Tasks on the Productivity detail view can be presented in-line, via the toolbar, or some combination of the two. Your approach will depend largely on the type of tasks and the desired navigation model.

In-line

Tasks should be presented in-line when they relate to a specific piece of content on the detail view, as is done on Foursquare (**FIGURE 9.31**). This is particularly effective for compact designs since minimal scrolling is required to see all of the tasks. Showing tasks in-line allows you to display the tab bar in the detail view, providing easy access to other sections of your app.

Toolbar

Showing tasks in the toolbar is effective when the tasks are associated with the *entire* detail view. For example, all of the tasks on AP News (Share, Favorite, and Save) apply to the entire article (**FIGURE 9.32**). That said, AP could have placed these tasks in-line; however, the design would be less successful. The tasks would be less visible if they were shown at the end of the article. And they might get lost at the top since the space is already crowded with an ad and other UI controls. Since the tab bar is not shown along the bottom, two taps are needed to access the other app sections.

FIGURE 9.31 In the Foursquare app, related tasks are placed in-line.

FIGURE 9.32 AP tasks are presented in the toolbar at the bottom of the screen.

HOW DO I CHOOSE THE RIGHT CONTROL?

The iOS has a number of standard controls for making selections. Choosing the appropriate one can be challenging since more than one may apply for a particular use case. As you consider which one to use, evaluate the context and type of information, the number of items, and whether or not maintaining "state," the previous selection, is required.

Action Sheet

Action sheets are primarily used to present options for completing a task, such as sharing content (FIGURE 9.33). They may also be used to request confirmation before completing a potentially dangerous task.

- **Number of options:** Two to seven options, including a Cancel button.
- **Maintains state:** No.
- **Common mistakes:** Excessive color coding. Unless it's a potentially destructive action (which should be red and placed at the top), use white for all options except Cancel. The Cancel button should be dark gray or black and placed at the bottom.

FIGURE 9.33 Action sheet for Tweets on Tweetie

Alert

Alerts float above the app screen and provide critical information. They are shown when something unexpected or urgent has occurred that requires the user's attention, for example, when exiting an app, as shown in the iLike app (FIGURE 9.34).

- **Number of options:** One to two.
- **Maintains state:** No.
- **Common mistakes:** Overuse. Alerts should be used sparingly since they take users out of context and are visually jarring.

FIGURE 9.34 Alert on iLike

Picker

There are two types of pickers: the date and time picker, and the generic picker. The date and time picker provides an efficient way to select a specific date or time (**FIGURE 9.35**). The generic picker can be used to display any set of values (**FIGURE 9.36**). One of the downsides is that the user can't easily see all of the options. If the content is well understood (e.g., a list of countries), this may be fine, but otherwise consider using a table view, which is discussed later in this section.

- **Number of options:** Can show a large number of options.
- **Maintains state:** Yes.
- **Common mistakes:** Including a large set of items that are not well understood. In those cases, the list view may be more appropriate.

FIGURE 9.35 Date picker on FlightTrack

FIGURE 9.36 Meal type on Betty Crocker

Segmented Control

Segmented controls can display different views of similar content. They are typically used when filtering or sorting list views (**FIGURES 9.37–9.38**).

- **Number of options:** Five maximum, though this is dependent on label length.
- **Maintains state:** Yes.
- **Common mistakes:** Placed out of context. The control should be close to the content being manipulated.

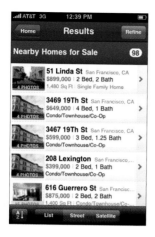

FIGURE 9.37 Segmented control used to change the view on the REALTOR.com app

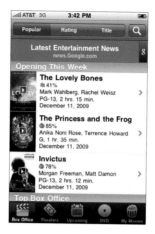

FIGURE 9.38 Segmented control used to sort movie lists on Flixster

Slider

Sliders allow users to choose from a range of values along a single dimension. They are often used in music- and art-related apps (**FIGURES 9.39–9.40**).

- **Number of options:** Start and end points defined within the control.
- **Maintains state:** Yes.
- **Common mistakes:** Ambiguous end points. Best to provide cues on either end as in done in Sketches.

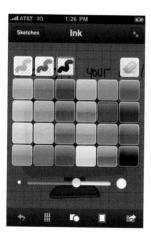

FIGURE 9.39 Brush size selected with a slider on the Sketches app

FIGURE 9.40 Volume selected with a slider on the Pandora app

Switch

Switch controls present two mutually exclusive choices or states (**FIGURES 9.41–9.42**).

- **Number of options:** Two.
- **Maintains state:** Yes.
- **Common mistakes:** Outcome of action unclear because of poor labels.

FIGURE 9.41 Switch used to turn Auto Play on and off on HearPlanet

FIGURE 9.42 Switch used to choose Celsius or Fahrenheit on iThermometer

Table Views

Table views present data in a list with multiple rows; the rows can be divided into sections or groups (**FIGURE 9.43**).

- **Number of options:** Large number possible.
- **Maintains state:** Yes.
- **Common mistakes:** Too many items. Search may be preferable for extremely long lists.

FIGURE 9.43 Table view used to choose a language for Yahoo! settings

Back-End UI Checklist

In addition to creating sketches and/or prototypes of your app designs, consider documenting functional requirements that may impact the user experience. Some important ones include the following:

- **Number of list items**

  The default number of items in a list will vary based on the app, the content, and any parameters. For example, lists with images tend to include fewer items given the row height as well as the time required to display the images.

  On the other hand, the lists in most location-based apps are dynamically limited using distance parameters, though it's still necessary to determine the default (e.g., show ten nearby restaurants). Whatever you decide, make sure you include these requirements in your documentation.

- **Distance parameters**

  In order to display location-based "nearby" views, you need to specify what "nearby" means; is it one mile? Five miles? Ten miles? Does this definition vary if the current location is a city versus a suburb versus a rural area? To adapt to the locale variations, you may want to provide a default but still allow users to change this value via the user interface.

- **Truncation and string length**

  More often than not, the items in your list view will vary in length. For example, one title may fit onto one line whereas another may require three lines. If you want to keep the title to one line, you need to specify this in your documentation. As you formulate your recommendation, consider experimenting with a variety of content scenarios: best case, worst case, and somewhere in between.

- **Loading content**

  If not specified otherwise, each row within a list view loads one at a time. This approach is fine with text-only lists. However, there may be a delay if there are images. To improve the perceived speed, you may want to load the text first, followed by the images. Additionally, make sure your images are optimized for fast downloading.

- **Caching strategy**

  As discussed earlier, caching app content can help maintain the status quo when there are network connection problems. If this situation applies to your app, be sure to outline your caching strategy in your documentation and discuss it with your technical team.

Depending on the app and approach, caching could add significant time to the development schedule. Some apps may also store content on the device. If you go with this approach, keep in mind that the download will be much larger. For example, Betty Crocker stores recipes on the device and takes up a whopping 18.6MB of space, whereas Epicurious accesses most content over the network and weighs in at 3.3MB.

- **Dealing with null results**

    Your documentation should explain how to present the UI when no content is found. For example, you may have headers in your nearby restaurant view that are within a 5-, 10-, and 15-minute walk. However, what happens when there are no restaurants within a 5-minute walk? If you want to hide the header, you should note this in your specification. On a related note, if images are provided for each row in a list but certain list items don't have images, be sure to include a "null" image (a representative placeholder image), as shown in **FIGURE 9.44**.

- **Recents**

    Apps that include a Recents section should specify how many items to store and for how long. In addition, you can let users choose how many items to store and/or let them remove the content. **FIGURE 9.45** illustrates how Yelp lets users remove Recents content.

FIGURE 9.44 NY Art Beat shows a gray image when no image is available.

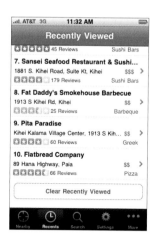

FIGURE 9.45 Yelp lets users "clear" their Recently Viewed list.

Summary

Refining your app's UI may take several iterations before it feels "done." As you work on your refinements, keep this chapter's best practices in mind. Although UI controls may evolve over time, these best practices should be applicable to current and future iPhone apps.

1. Be welcoming.
2. Know thy user.
3. Let the content shine.
4. Make selections fast and error-free.
5. Provide appropriate feedback.
6. Minimize the pain.

In addition to these high-level recommendations, it's important to review the iPhone HIG and make sure your app adheres to the guidelines. If areas in the iPhone HIG are unclear, such as when to use tabs versus the toolbar, review the tips offered in this chapter. And if you are still uncertain which design direction is appropriate, conduct a usability test and make refinements based on user feedback.

To ensure that your app is built as intended, don't forget to spend some time documenting both your "visible" and "invisible" requirements. ∎

CASE STUDY 9

Sonos

ROB LAMBOURNE is the director of user experience at Sonos. He created the Sonos iPhone app with a team of designers and developers at Sonos (**www.sonos.com**) and with Oliver Bayley, an independent UX consultant based in San Francisco.

Sonos is the leading developer of wireless multi-room music systems for the home. The Sonos Multi-Room Music System is the first wireless multi-room music system that lets you play all the music you want all over your house and control it all from the palm of your hand.

FIGURE CS9.1 Sonos Zone Menu

What inspired Sonos to build an iPhone app?

Sonos has had a handheld controller on the market since early 2005. While this product was terrific for its time, it lacked the speed of a touchscreen for entering artist and track searches that are central to the Sonos experience. When Apple released the iPhone, we were able to provide our customers with a touchscreen experience several months before our own new touchscreen controller was due for release. In addition, it was clear that the iPhone was going to be a huge hit, and since Sonos customers and iPhone users overlap demographically, our strategy team saw an opportunity to appeal to the growing number of iPhone customers by providing a Sonos Controller app for them.

Can you describe the design process at Sonos?

Once we have a brief from our product management and strategy teams, we work iteratively to design our products. We start by identifying and understanding our customers. This can take the form of contextual interviews, online surveys, and focus groups. This process leads to user personas and the description of typical day-in-the-life scenarios that we use as frameworks for idea generation. Our user experience design team then sketches designs and makes prototypes that we test with various users.

Was the iPhone app design process different from your typical process?

We were able to work much more quickly with this project than is typical. Apple provides very strong API and user interface guidelines that we used effectively, but the biggest difference was our ability to quickly build and test very thorough prototypes on the real platform.

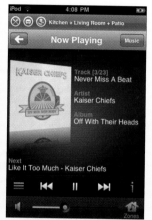

FIGURE CS9.2 Sonos Music Menu

FIGURE CS9.3 Sonos Player

What were some challenges you faced? Do you have any advice for app creators facing similar design challenges?

Our biggest challenge with UI design at Sonos is to ensure that while we offer very powerful functionality, it must be presented in a way that everyone in a home (not just the tech-savvy people) should be able to understand and use. We often decide to limit the scope of designs in order to protect the simplicity of the experience. I think this is a challenge for all app designers—to focus on what is really important. Don't be afraid to cut a feature or simplify a design if you are trying to appeal to a broad audience.

Were you able to conduct usability tests?

We ran usability tests in three stages. First, we tested an early iPhone prototype with 8 to 10 nontechnical family members of Sonos employees. We improved the design

based on their feedback and then conducted further tests in a usability lab with a combination of Sonos customers and iPhone users who didn't own Sonos products. We ran this test with about 15 people. Last, once we had a more complete app, we ran an alpha test in which 30 Sonos customers used the iPhone app to control their Sonos systems in their own homes.

How did usability tests impact the design?

In addition to testing the general appeal of the app, we were able to test the navigation model, the visual design, and any number of details like legibility of text and icons. In our early prototypes we found that the hit areas on the touchscreen were too small for some people, so we made them larger and rearranged some of the UI components to accommodate the changes. We also found that users didn't understand one or two state transitions in the UI, so we made use of Apple's built-in animations to help convey navigation more clearly.

How have your users responded to the app?

Our customers have responded really well on two levels: They are happy they can experience Sonos at a lower cost, which is ultimately good for the sales of our other products, and our users just love the idea of controlling their music simply by taking out their iPhone and launching the Sonos app. [FIGURES CS9.1–CS9.3 show some of the app screens.]

Any other advice for iPhone developers and designers?

Make use of Apple's guidelines, hire good UX designers, focus on simplicity, and always talk to potential users of your product—they won't tell you how to design your product (nor should they), but you will always learn something useful that you can apply to your design. ■

CASE STUDY 10

FlightTrack

MOBIATA creates best-selling mobile travel applications. Mobiata's FlightTrack app has topped the iPhone travel best-seller list ever since the product's launch in November 2008. Benjamin Kazez founded Mobiata in December 2008 and currently serves as president. He has spearheaded the development of Mobiata mobile travel applications such as FlightTrack, HotelPal, and TripDeck.

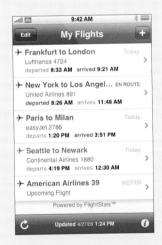

FIGURE CS10.1 My Flights screen

What inspired you to create FlightTrack?

The idea came to me when I was traveling in November 2008. I was at the airport and needed to look up my flight number. After digging through my backpack, I finally unearthed my boarding pass, which was already crinkled and falling apart. At that moment I thought, "Why isn't this on my iPhone?" My iPhone is always in my pocket and easy to access; it would make much more sense to access the info from there. I could use the built-in Notes app, but it would be much better if there was an app that knew my flight number and could automatically update the info if there were any delays. In addition to travelers, I thought this app could be useful for people who are picking others up at the airport.

How did you approach the project?

At first I did a lot of pencil sketches of various user interface possibilities. I spent a lot of time trying to figure out what was the bare minimum needed to find flights. There's not much room, so it was essential to come up with a flight summary that would fit on the screen and not overwhelm users. To this end, I considered what information we could omit from the flight list view based on what the user already knows. For example, I decided to place baggage and aircraft information in the detail view since this was lower priority for most users.

What were some of the design challenges you faced with the detail view?

Based on my own experience, I knew users would be walking around the airport and periodically checking for time and gate number; thus I decided to make this information the most prominent. And around that information are the annotations to the data, such as the terminal and miscellaneous gate details. We went through several iterations of this view. It was a tough challenge since there's a lot of flight data available—scheduled time, estimated time, runway time, gate time, and much more.

What made you decide to allow multiple flights?

From the beginning I knew that I wanted people to be able to track multiple flights at once. On most web sites you can track only one flight, but it's much more useful to allow multiple ones. This way, if you have connecting flights you can see them all at once. Our professional users—taxi drivers and limousine drivers—really value this feature. [FIGURES CS10.1–CS10.3 show a few of the app screens.]

Any advice for designers and developers working on similar products?

Getting external content to work with the iPhone can be a real challenge. We spent a lot of time with our content provider, Flight View, to make sure their data fit well within our application. Many of our competitors weren't taking the time to work through these kinds of details, but they are really important for the user experience. Even though it was a lot of work, going the extra mile really paid off.

How do you stay in touch with your customers?

For the first three to four months I answered all of the support emails and tracked how many users were suggesting certain improvements. When I was ready to plan the next release, I used that as a way to prioritize features. Now we have a dedicated support person—it's crucial to have a connection to your users. Support regularly summarizes user feedback, and we make sure everything is accounted for in our bug tracker. We are constantly asking ourselves why users are requesting a particular feature and how we can improve the design.

FIGURE CS10.2 Flight detail screen

FIGURE CS10.3 Map view for selected flight

What's next for FlightTrack?

A few months after FlightTrack, we released a professional version called FlightTrack Pro that offers more detailed airport delay and closure warnings and synchronization with third-party itineraries. FlightTrack Pro has been localized into English, German, French, and Spanish, and the app works worldwide.

Our HotelPal app enables users to browse and search hotels worldwide with live availability and rates, then secure a room with easy in-app reservations, powered by the Travelocity Partner Network. HotelPal is perfect for last-minute plans, canceled flights, road trips, or just exploring.

Our latest app, TripDeck, offers complete itinerary management for virtually every component of a business or personal trip, including flight information and live flight status, car rentals and driving directions, hotels, meeting times and locations, restaurants, trains, and other related travel details. ■

Visual Design

VISUAL DESIGN ATTEMPTS TO SOLVE communication problems in ways that are functionally effective and aesthetically pleasing.[1] To achieve this delicate balance, designers must understand user goals and user interface elements as well as visual design principles and techniques.

This chapter begins with a discussion of visual structure—grouping, hierarchy, alignment; these are the foundations of effective visual design. We'll spend the remainder of the chapter exploring how color, type, and imagery can reinforce visual structure and create harmonious designs. Emphasis is placed on Productivity- and Utility-style apps, although many of the principles can be applied to Immersive apps as well.

The chapter includes case studies on the USA TODAY, Voices, and Convertbot iPhone apps. These case studies discuss how the designers created visual designs for their apps.

---

1. Kevin Mullet and Darrel Sano, *Designing Visual Interfaces* (SunSoft Press, 1995).

The Importance of Visual Design

Visual design is an integral part of the overall iPhone user experience; however, many apps incorporate visual design *after* the coding is done. In the later stages, the effects are often superficial: a few icons and custom colors. To truly impact app design, visual design should be considered as early as the concept phase. Benefits of effective visual design may include more downloads, improved app usability, and user delight.

ATTRACT USERS

As users browse the App Store and consider what to purchase, your app's visual design will factor into their decision. Sure, there are reviews, text descriptions, and links to demo videos (sometimes), but users will naturally gravitate to the large, colorful screenshots. If users are not inspired or impressed, they may not download your app.

IMPROVE USABILITY

Once users download your app, the visual design benefits will move beyond first impressions. Effective visual designs—coupled with strong user interface design—will improve your app's ease of use. Specific benefits that we'll touch on in this chapter include concept clarity, task efficiency, and readability.

DELIGHT USERS

Visual design can add delight to the user experience. More often than not, certain visual design elements are not required for apps to work, but their absence would make certain apps much less desirable. **FIGURE 10.1** shows how the Voices app adds delight through visual design—the playful icons, the audiotape image, the velvety red curtain, the roving spotlight. The Voices designers could have presented the options in a standard list view, but it would have communicated less personality. (See Case Study 12 on page 248.)

When Should Visual Design Begin?

As mentioned before, visual design should happen as early as the concept phase but it may depend on the app. For example, if you were creating a social networking app with dozens of screens, it would save time (and ensure consistency!) to create a visual design system. A visual design system might use templates or at a minimum rely on a common grid, color palette, use of type, and so on across all screens. The engineering team could also use this system to help create consistent and reusable code.

FIGURE 10.1 The Voices app has several distinctive visual design elements: the playful icons, the velvety red curtain, the roving spotlight.

To create a visual design system, most of the user interface should be defined *in advance*. In this case you may want to create wireframes (black-and-white line drawings) until the user interface is settled, then refine the visual design. If you have an Immersive-style app, it might be difficult to separate user interface and visual design since they are often tightly interconnected, as with iHandy, shown in FIGURE 10.2.

FIGURE 10.2 iHandy app

Visual Structure

Visual structure creates visual pathways that help users move through your designs. Without a clear visual structure, your app may be difficult to interpret or it may be interpreted differently from what you intended. In this section we'll discuss several ways to create visual structure, including

- Grouping
- Hierarchy
- Alignment

GROUPING

Grouping related visual elements reduces complexity and can help users interpret your designs. Groupings are chiefly communicated through proximity, but they may be reinforced with contrast, alignment, and other visual cues. **FIGURES 10.3–10.4** show the Yahoo! Finance stock screens. If you squint at **FIGURE 10.3**, you should see two visual groupings: the stock quote and graph, and recent stock news. What makes this work? Proximity. The stock quote and news form two distinct clusters; they have contrasting background colors, which further reinforce the groups.

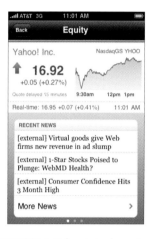 

FIGURE 10.3 Yahoo! stock quote (first pane)

FIGURE 10.4 Yahoo! stock quote (second pane)

In addition to taking the type of information into account, groupings should incorporate the user goals identified in your up-front research. To illustrate, let's examine the eTrade stock screen, which has three groups: the stock quote and price movement, news, and the latest update information (see **FIGURES 10.5–10.6**).

The differences between the Yahoo! and eTrade app groupings are not arbitrary. eTrade is designed for trading, so it's critical to show price movement information with the quote. On the other hand, Yahoo! Finance is used for quick stock lookups—users can't make trades—so the distilled graph view is arguably more appropriate. Before visualizing your groups, consider writing them down in a simple list format. This approach should save time since text edits are easier than visual edits. For example, the Yahoo! stock quote might have these two groups:

Group 1: Stock quote, stock chart, real-time information

Group 2: Recent news, price movement, competitor news

FIGURE 10.5 eTrade stock quote (top)   FIGURE 10.6 eTrade stock quote (bottom)

HIERARCHY

Hierarchy may be used to establish the reading sequence within your designs. Visual elements or groups that are prominent will be viewed first. Prominence is typically achieved by manipulating position and scale.

Position

In the case of the iPhone, elements near the top of the screen are generally more prominent in the visual hierarchy than those near the bottom. To illustrate, consider Urbanspoon's and Yelp's restaurant screens (**FIGURES 10.7–10.8**). Their content is similar, but their hierarchy choices result in very different designs. In particular, Urbanspoon's restaurant ratings and rate buttons dominate the visual hierarchy. As a result, Urbanspoon users are forced to scroll to view the map, which is

FIGURE 10.7 Urbanspoon restaurant screen   FIGURE 10.8 Yelp restaurant screen

problematic given that mobile users typically want quick access to maps. To avoid these user experience issues, make sure your hierarchy matches user needs within the relevant context. And, more important, make sure that every element you choose is essential for the user experience. Even the most well-crafted hierarchy will break down if there are too many elements.

Placing items near the top is not always key to establishing visual hierarchy; the task flow and relationship to other elements must also be considered. For example, Twitterific lets users add contacts, images, and location information to their Tweets (FIGURE 10.9). Although these options are near the top, they may be overlooked since the cursor focus is in the text area. Also, the header is typically used for navigation, so users may not expect additional options in that area. In contrast, on TweetDeck (FIGURE 10.10) the Tweet options are in the lower-right portion of the Tweet form, supporting the natural workflow.

FIGURE 10.9 Twitterific Tweet form   FIGURE 10.10 TweetDeck Tweet form

Scale

Scale is another way to establish visual hierarchy. In essence, larger visual elements attract the eye more than smaller ones. FIGURE 10.11 illustrates how iThermometer uses large text combined with a bright blue background to emphasize the temperature. Its place in the visual hierarchy is reinforced through contrast. Other elements, such as the City, Condition, Wind, and Unit, have smaller type with a subdued blue background. Both groupings occupy the same space, but the temperature is bigger.

Scale can also establish hierarchy *within* visual groupings. For example, All Recipes uses scale and color to draw attention to the recipe name, photo, and rating (FIGURE 10.12). In contrast, the recipe author is displayed in smaller type, suggesting that this information is less important. This makes sense within this context (it's unlikely that users will know the author), but a different scale would be appropriate if it were a celebrity chef.

FIGURE 10.11 iThermometer app

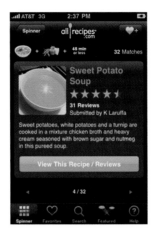

FIGURE 10.12 All Recipes recipe screen

ALIGNMENT

Effective alignment can make your designs easier to understand and more usable. To illustrate, let's look at USA TODAY and the Huffington Post (FIGURES 10.13–10.14). Notice how the headline, section, byline, and body are *all* aligned left in USA TODAY. The photo is right-aligned, but this works since it would disrupt the reading flow if it were left-aligned.

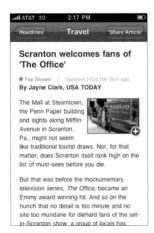

FIGURE 10.13 USA TODAY article view

FIGURE 10.14 Huffington Post article view

In contrast, the alignment on the Huffington Post alternates with each piece of information, forcing users to scan right and left as they read through the article. As you refine your designs, avoid such arbitrary alignment: Every item should have a visual connection with the other items.[2] To play it safe, aim for one alignment per screen. Additionally, consistent alignment across similar types of screens will unify your overall app design.

Color

NOTE

If you need assistance with your palette, consider using a tool like Adobe Kuler (http://kuler.adobe.com), which helps users create color themes. Avoid combinations that are problematic for visually impaired users (e.g., red and black) or color-blind users (e.g., red and green).

We associate color with certain meanings based on our environment (e.g., green = fresh), culture (e.g., red = good luck in China), and personal experiences (e.g., lavender reminds me of my grandmother).[3] As you choose colors for your iPhone app, it's important to consider the relevant environment and culture. Choosing inappropriate colors may send the wrong message or even turn some users away. For example, purple is the color of mourning in Thailand, but it symbolizes royalty in the West.[4] In addition to evoking meaning, color can help reinforce visual structure in the following ways:

- Differentiation
- Emphasis
- Classification

DIFFERENTIATION

Color can be used to differentiate many visual elements on the iPhone. Controls that are often customized by the designer include the navigation bar, list headers, and segmented controls.

NOTE

Chapter 11, "Branding and Advertising," will discuss the relationship between visual design and branding. Often, visual design decisions, such as the color palette, are constrained by the existing brand design.

Navigation Bar

If you want to differentiate your navigation bar from the background, try using contrasting colors. To illustrate, consider the Facebook and Flickr apps, shown in **FIGURES 10.15–10.16**. Facebook has a blue navigation bar and a white background, which calls attention to the brand. In contrast, Flickr uses all white to minimize the user interface, which allows the user to focus on the photos. Both approaches are effective as long as they meet their respective app goals.

---

2. Robin Williams, *The Non-Designer's Design Book* (Peachpit Press, 2008).
3. Donis A. Dondis, *A Primer of Visual Literacy* (MIT Press, 1973).
4. Jennifer Kyrnin, "Color Symbolism Chart by Culture," http://webdesign.about.com/od/color/a/bl_colorculture.htm.

FIGURE 10.15 Facebook

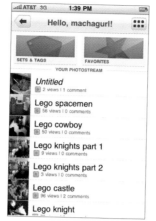

FIGURE 10.16 Flickr

List Headers

List headers are used to differentiate related items. Since they are a guide, not the primary focus, consider using colors with low contrast. For example, let's compare the iLike and iConcertCal apps (**FIGURES 10.17–10.18**). Notice how the dates in the iLike app are readily available but don't compete with the main content. On the other hand, the dates on the iConcertCal app are more prominent than the events themselves. As the user scans the list, the blue bars demand equal (if not more) attention, but users are presumably more interested in the events. If the iConcertCal dates were shown in a color with lower contrast (for example, dark gray), the events would stand out more.

FIGURE 10.17 iLike

FIGURE 10.18 iConcertCal

Segmented Controls

If you choose to customize segmented controls, make sure there's enough contrast to differentiate the segments. Also, keep in mind that Interface Builder lets you alter only the tint; thus you may need to create a custom control to get certain colors. The Whole Foods recipe tab (Overview, Ingredients, Method) is an example of a custom control (**FIGURE 10.19**). Notice how the tan color contrasts well with the green and visually connects with the recipe's background color.

FIGURE 10.19 Whole Foods recipe screen

EMPHASIS

Color may also be used to emphasize certain information or tasks. **FIGURE 10.20** shows how TweetDeck uses red to emphasize Updates and yellow for writing Tweets. Be sure not to overuse your emphasis colors; otherwise the content may be ignored, which defeats the purpose. For example, the Betty Crocker app uses red—a color normally reserved for alerts—for tabs, buttons, icons, and links. Red is synonymous with their brand (the red spoon), but it would be more effective if used sparingly (**FIGURE 10.21**).

Color can also emphasize the primary action on a screen. Amazon uses an orangey-yellow color and arrow icon to call attention to the Sign In button (**FIGURE 10.22**). In contrast, Wells Fargo's Sign On button is difficult to see since it is the exact same color as the background (**FIGURE 10.23**). If you plan to color-code app buttons, carefully consider how they will fit into your palette. Also, make sure your colors don't conflict with the colors used in the built-in apps. For example, green is used to make a call within the telephone, and red is used to end a call.

FIGURE 10.20 TweetDeck

FIGURE 10.21 Betty Crocker

FIGURE 10.22 Amazon

FIGURE 10.23 Wells Fargo

CLASSIFICATION

Color can be an effective way to classify app content. **FIGURE 10.24** shows how USA TODAY uses color to indicate which section you're currently viewing (e.g., green is used for the Money section); these colors correspond to those used on the web site and in the newspaper.

The Huffington Post also tries to communicate its sections by color-coding the headlines. Unfortunately, that solution is much less effective. The colored text may slow readers down as they try to decipher its meaning (**FIGURE 10.25**). If you choose to use color for classification, make sure the approach adds value and clearly indicates what each color means.

FIGURE 10.24 USA TODAY

FIGURE 10.25
The Huffington Post

Type

Type can influence how users interpret and perceive your application. For example, Marker Felt (displayed as **Marker Felt**) may seem friendly and approachable within an art app but informal and unprofessional within a financial news app.

This section discusses several aspects of type—typeface, size, color, and weight—within the context of the iOS.

NOTE

Readers interested in delving even further into type should consider reading *The Elements of Typographic Style*[5] or *Thinking with Type*.[6]

TYPEFACES

If you create your app designs using Interface Builder, you'll notice that the text defaults to Helvetica. This typeface was chosen for its readability and versatility on the iPhone device (the typeface was also immortalized in a film, *Helvetica*[7]). You can override the defaults, but make sure that the selected typeface is appropriate for the task. For example, a whimsical typeface may be suitable for a game but not for reading long texts. Also, apps with long texts, such as the Kindle, tend to use serif typefaces like Times New Roman. Serif typefaces contain structural details on the strokes that connect the letters and make them easier to read; sans serifs like Helvetica don't have these elements.

If you want to use a typeface other than Helvetica, this doesn't mean that all app text must be in the same font. For example, the NYTimes app uses Times New Roman for the headlines and article text but Helvetica for the byline, headers, tab bar, and buttons. Using Helvetica for the byline provides contrast; using it for the other elements ensures readability and conformity with Apple's guidelines. Keep in mind that too many typefaces can add visual noise and make your app difficult to interpret. To avoid this problem, consider limiting typeface usage to one or two families. Variations in type size and weight can help create a visually interesting system using just one family. If further variation is needed or desired, you can also experiment with leading (line spacing) and kerning (the space between letters.)

A complete list of typefaces available on the iPhone is shown in **TABLE 10.1**. Other typefaces can be bundled with your app, but this may increase your app download size.

5. Robert Bringhurst, *The Elements of Typographic Style* (Hartley and Marks, 2002).
6. Ellen Lupton, *Thinking with Type* (Princeton Architectural Press, 2004).
7. Gary Hustwit, *Helvetica* (2007).

TABLE 10.1 Typefaces Available on the iPhone[8]

Typeface*	Styles Supported
American Typewriter	Bold, Light, Condensed, Condensed Bold, and Condensed Light; no italics
Apple Gothic	Plain
Arial	All
Arial Rounded MT Bold	No italics
Courier New	All
Georgia	All
Helvetica	All
Heiti	Light, Medium
Hiragino Kaku Gothic	Plain
Marker Felt	All
Times New Roman	All
Trebuchet MS	All
Verdana	All
Zapfino	All

*Note: Serifs are American Typewriter, Courier New, Georgia, and Times New Roman.

---

8. iPhone Dev Center, "UIFont Class Reference," http://developer.apple.com/iphone/library/
documentation/UIKit/Reference/UIFont_Class/Reference/Reference.html.

TYPE SIZE

Type size on the iPhone is measured in points (e.g., 12 pt, 14 pt, etc.). If you add text in Interface Builder, a default type size is pre-selected for certain elements. For example, text in the navigation bar is 20 pt, and tab bar labels are 10 pt.

If you plan to experiment with type size, make sure the text is readable for the given context and audience. To demonstrate, consider the NYTimes and Ameritrade apps (**FIGURES 10.26–10.27**). Both apps show almost the same number of headlines, but the Ameritrade app is much more difficult to read. The biggest problem is the type size. The text beneath the headline should be at least one point larger than the current one, and more space (referred to as "line spacing" or "leading") is needed between all of the elements (headline, description, time, and line rule).

FIGURE 10.26 NYTimes list view

FIGURE 10.27 Ameritrade list view

Some readers may prefer the Ameritrade app's type size since it shows more headlines. If having four headlines is a requirement, it's possible to increase the font size and show less text after the headline. Another option is to provide default sizes that are readable for the majority of users. If you take that route, be sure to allow users to adjust the type size as needed. Many Twitter clients and news apps provide a type size control on their list and detail views.

TYPE WEIGHT

Another aspect to vary is type weight (a term that's often mistaken as "bold"). As shown in the Yahoo! News example, readers are drawn to the headlines because of the contrast; the headlines are "heavier" compared to the text below (**FIGURE 10.28**). However, if there's little or no contrast, increasing type weight will have minimal impact. The Bloomberg app (shown in **FIGURE 10.29**) adds weight to the headline, time, and date; each demands the reader's attention. If the date and time had less visual weight, the eye would be drawn to the primary content, the headline.

FIGURE 10.28 Yahoo! News

FIGURE 10.29 Bloomberg News

Icons and Other Imagery

Icons are part of the field of semiotics: the general theory and practice of signs. By definition, icons are *physically* similar to an object (e.g., a movie icon might resemble film, not a bucket of popcorn). However, within software, the term *icon* is commonly used for any small image, whether or not it's physically or conceptually similar.

This section reviews a variety of icons in the context of the iPhone user interface—the tab bar, the toolbar, and everything else in between. Before starting, let's review some of the imagery design principles outlined in Mullet and Sano's *Designing Visual Interfaces*.

Immediacy

Icons should be perceived effortlessly; users should not have to pause and interpret them. For example, consider the brush icons in **FIGURES 10.30–10.32**. The first two are immediately recognizable, but the last one requires some interpretation (is it a jar with a brush and pen, or a cup with two straws?). This difference is mostly attributed to the level of abstraction; **FIGURE 10.32** has one too many undifferentiated visual elements to make the icon instantly recognizable.

FIGURE 10.30 Brushes app

FIGURE 10.31 Layers app

FIGURE 10.32 NetSketch app

Generality

Icons should represent a broader class of similar concepts rather than a particular instance. For example, there are three common video icons on iPhone apps: a TV/monitor, a video camera, and a reel of film (**FIGURES 10.33–10.35**, respectively). They all work, but the video camera (the old over-the-shoulder style) may become less general over time. Given the popularity of the iPhone, the Flip, and other small cameras, the prototypical image may evolve.

FIGURE 10.33 Discovery News   **FIGURE 10.34** Consumer Reports   **FIGURE 10.35** Showtime

Cohesiveness

Designing a cohesive system makes icons easier to interpret and understand. Cohesiveness can refer to both style and form. For example, the icons in the Fanball app are stylistically similar, plus they have the same theme: balls (**FIGURE 10.36**). If the MLB (Major League Baseball) tab had a baseball diamond or a bat, the set would have an inconsistent theme. Ideally, your app icons will be cohesive in both respects. On a related note, abbreviations for labels (e.g., NFL) are fine as long as the target users understand them.

FIGURE 10.36 Fanball tab bar icons. The *N* stands for "National"; the sports represented are football, baseball, hockey, and basketball.

Communicability

Communicability refers to an icon's representation within the specified context—the physical, cultural, and social environments. For example, mailboxes often have different cultural references depending on the country. And, even within one country, the references can run the gamut (**FIGURE 10.37**). In such a case it would be wise to draw from the most common mailbox form or explore a different icon approach altogether. Alternatively, as we'll discuss in Chapter 12, "Accessibility and Localization," icons can be localized for each region.

FIGURE 10.37 Mailboxes in the UK *(Courtesy of Frans van Rijnswou, photographer)*

TAB BAR ICONS

Tab bar icons are used in the tab bar within Productivity-style apps. This section reviews standard and custom icons as well as best practices.

Standard Tab Icons

The number of standard tab icons is smaller than most people expect; there are only ten, as shown in TABLE 10.2. As much as possible, try to use standard icons in your app. They are easier for users to interpret since Apple has done the hard work for you—the icons are immediately recognizable, general, cohesive, and communicable. Plus, users have learned their meaning and can transfer that knowledge to your app. As mentioned earlier, be sure to use these as outlined in the iPhone HIG; your app may be rejected if it diverges from the guidelines.

TABLE 10.2 Standard Icons for Use in the Tab Bar[9]

Icon	Meaning	Name
📖	Show application-specific bookmarks	Bookmarks
👤	Show contacts	Contacts
⬇	Show downloads	Downloads
★	Show user-determined favorites	Favorites
✖	Show content featured by the application	Featured

continues

---

9. iPhone Dev Center, *iPhone Human Interface Guidelines:* "System-Provided Buttons and Icons," developer.apple.com/iphone/library/documentation/UserExperience/Conceptual/MobileHIG/ SystemProvided/SystemProvided.html#//apple_ref/doc/uid/TP40006556-CH15-SW15.

TABLE 10.2 Standard Icons for Use in the Tab Bar (continued)

Icon	Meaning	Name
🕐	Show history of user actions	History
•••	Show additional tab bar items	More
⊞	Show the most recent item	Most Recent
👥	Show items most popular with all users	Most Viewed
🕐	Show the items accessed by the user within an application-defined period	Recents
🔍	Enter a search mode	Search
★	Show the highest-rated items, as determined by the user	Top Rated

Custom Tab Icons

Creating a custom set of tab icons is no small feat. In addition to understanding the principles outlined earlier in this section, the designer must be able to formulate an overall system, execute the designs, save them in the appropriate format, and so on.

NOTE

The iOS automatically provides the pressed or selected appearance for items in tab bars, toolbars, and navigation bars.

There are many third-party services (e.g., Glyphish, **www.glyphish.com**) that have developed icons for popular use cases. If you're not comfortable designing your own set, work with one of these services or hire an illustrator. If you choose to design them yourself, be sure to follow the guidelines included in the iPhone HIG:

- Use the PNG format.
- Use white with appropriate alpha and no shadow.
- Use anti-aliasing.
- Create icons that measure about 30×30 pixels.

Additional Tips Not Included in the iPhone HIG

As you browse the App Store, you may see custom tab icons that break Apple's guidelines. For example, Tweetie doesn't provide icon labels, and American Greetings uses a red background instead of black (**FIGURES 10.38–10.39**). Although these apps were approved by Apple, don't assume that yours will breeze through. Also, apps may be rejected if they have icons that are part of the iOS but not sanctioned for third-party usage.

FIGURE 10.38 Tweetie's tab bar

FIGURE 10.39 American Greetings' tab bar

Here are some other tips to keep in mind:

- Use optically equivalent scaling for icons (e.g., circles are slightly larger than squares).

- Always show icons in tabs. Don't leave the space blank; don't use words or arbitrary shapes.

- Provide adequate space between icons and their labels.

- Keep labels concise so they don't run into neighboring labels.

- Display labels in title case (e.g., Title Case); do not use all lowercase (title case) or uppercase (TITLE CASE).

TOOLBAR AND NAVIGATION BAR ICONS

The iPOS also provides a suite of icons that may be used in the navigation bar and toolbar. These icons come in two different styles: bordered and plain. According to the iPhone HIG, the bordered style may be used in the navigation bar or toolbar, but the plain style may be used only in the toolbar. This section examines the standard and custom icons and suggests how to incorporate them into your app.

Standard Icons

TABLE 10.3 includes the standard toolbar and navigation bar icons. Remember, it's important to use standard icons *only* for the actions outlined in the iPhone HIG. Improper usage may make your app difficult to understand. Moreover, misuse could lead to rejection from the App Store.

Custom Icons

Custom toolbar and navigation bar icons are used in many kinds of apps. Regardless of the context, the principles outlined earlier still apply—immediacy, generality, cohesiveness, and communicability. In addition to following the principles, make sure your custom icons do not conflict with the standard ones. For example, the AP News app uses the Trash icon (shown in **FIGURE 10.40**) to *remove* an article from your saved list, but the context implies that the user is *deleting* the article.

FIGURE 10.40 AP News toolbar

Also, try not to conflict with custom icons that have become de facto standards. AP News uses the Star icon for rating an article, yet many apps use the same star for Favorites, which could mislead users. To set expectations, AP News should create an icon that incorporates a star in a different way (perhaps as a series of smaller stars, sort of like an ellipsis). Also, make sure there is adequate space between the icons. Having enough space will make them easier to interpret and will certainly reduce tapping errors (and user frustration with your app).

TABLE 10.3 Standard Icons for Toolbar and Navigation Bar[10]

Icon	Meaning	Name
	Opens an action sheet that allows users to take an application-specific action	Action
	Opens an action sheet that displays a photo picker in edit mode	Camera
	Opens a new message view in edit mode	Compose
	Shows application-specific bookmarks	Bookmarks
	Displays a search field	Search
	Creates a new item	Add
	Deletes the current item	Trash
	Moves or routes an item to a destination within the application	Organize
	Sends or routes an item to another location	Reply
	Stops the current process or task	Stop
	Refreshes contents (use only when necessary)	Refresh
	Begins media playback or slides	Play
	Fast-forwards though media playback or slides	Fast Forward
	Pauses media playback or slides	Pause
	Moves backward through media playback or slides	Rewind

---

10. iPhone Dev Center, *iPhone Human Interface Guidelines:* "System-Provided Buttons and Icons," developer.apple.com/iphone/library/documentation/UserExperience/Conceptual/MobileHIG/SystemProvided/SystemProvided.html#//apple_ref/doc/uid/TP40006556-CH15-SW15.

OTHER CONTEXTS

Icons are not restricted to tab bars and toolbars; they can appear on launch screens, list views, and detail views. App designers have more creative freedom in these contexts since the look and feel may diverge from the iPhone HIG. In many cases the icon illustration style is consistent with the app brand as opposed to the iPhone brand. While the style may differ, the dimensions should still be at least 30 × 30.

Launch Screens

As discussed in Chapter 9, "User Interface Design," some apps use icons in a grid-based launch screen. Perhaps the most well-known example is Facebook, but other apps such as LinkedIn have followed suit (FIGURES 10.41–10.42). Cohesiveness is crucial given that these icons are displayed as a set.

FIGURE 10.41 Facebook launch screen

FIGURE 10.42 LinkedIn launch screen

List Views

List views tend to use icons to quickly communicate the underlying information or concept. FIGURES 10.43–10.44 illustrate how Evernote and Flixster use list view icons. The apps could function without them, but they wouldn't be as aesthetically appealing. Notice how Evernote's icons are much larger than the Flixster ones. This is because Evernote is typically used for spur-of-the-moment thoughts or observations. If users have to fumble around for the right icon, they may lose the chance to capture a photo or other annotation. Additionally, there are only four options; there would be too much white space if the list view had smaller icons.

FIGURE 10.43 Evernote main screen

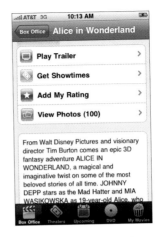

FIGURE 10.44 Flixster view

Detail Views

Detail views often use icons for actions or status indicators. When used effectively, icons can help conserve space and make your app more visually appealing.

Facebook uses icons to incorporate loads of functionality into the profile screen (FIGURE 10.45). Instead of spelling out "comment" as on the Facebook web site, there is a small thought bubble icon. The dimensions are only about 25 × 25, but the surrounding white space should minimize tapping errors. Also, instead of listing the comments, the Facebook app compresses them in a thought bubble, which opens when tapped.

FIGURE 10.45 Facebook news feed

If you choose to incorporate icons in detail views, be sure not to overuse them. Too many icons may create visual noise instead of leaving the page uncluttered and easy to navigate.

Summary

When people think of visual design, images of icons, type, and color palettes come to mind. Although mastering these areas is important, strong visual designs are built upon an underlying visual structure. This chapter introduced several techniques to establish visual structure within your app: grouping, hierarchy, and alignment.

Once your visual structure is in place, you can bring in other visual elements, such as icons and typography, to reinforce the structure and create aesthetically appealing designs. Here are some other tips to keep in mind:

- Your app's visual design should be considered as early as the concept phase. If you wait until after your app is coded, the benefits will be minimal.

- Do not design your app's visual elements in isolation. The layout, typography, color, icons, and other elements must all work together.

- Creating effective icons is very hard and time-consuming. Consider hiring an illustrator—finding an expert will be worth the investment. ■

CASE STUDY 11

USA TODAY

MERCURY INTERMEDIA collaborated with USA TODAY on the design and development of its iPhone app. Mercury has been helping major brands reach their customers through new and emerging technologies for over 15 years. They provide a full range of services, including programming, graphic and UI design, content hosting, and analytics.

How did Mercury Intermedia get involved in the USA TODAY app?

It is a bit unbelievable looking back at it, but the USA TODAY app was our first iPhone app and our first venture into the mobile space. Before we shifted our focus to mobile development, Mercury Intermedia had been working with companies such as *Sports Illustrated*, *Golf* magazine, and several NFL teams creating proprietary, network-enabled desktop applications. What we had been working on in the personal computing space translated incredibly well to mobile. We were very fortunate that USA TODAY saw our potential and gave us a chance to prove ourselves on the iPhone.

How did the USA TODAY brand impact the iPhone app design?

USA TODAY has always been known for large color photos, graphics, and diagrams along with short summarized news articles, all of which translated perfectly to the iPhone. Snapshots proved especially successful, partially because of the unique ability the iPhone gave us to sort voter responses by location through the built-in location services; we often saw more user voting from the iPhone app than from usatoday.com.

FIGURE CS11.1 Progression of the Headlines section

Color-coded sections are also a vital part of the USA TODAY brand identity, and it was critical that we incorporate them into the USA TODAY app gracefully. As in the paper and the web site, we wanted viewers to know immediately when they saw red in the app to associate it with sports and green with money, and so on.

How did the designs evolve over the course of the project?

The Headlines section saw the most evolution throughout the design process [FIGURE CS11.1]. In our early designs, the Headlines article list used an accordion scheme similar to the one in the Weather and Pictures sections. As unique as it was, we quickly realized that it just wasn't easy enough or fast enough to consume a group of headlines quickly, which is what most mobile users demand, so we returned to a more standard headline list view in that section.

Once we decided to move to a list view in Headlines, we had to figure out how to deal with news categorization. Since USA TODAY is a multipurpose application, simply creating a tab bar section for each news category wasn't a viable option. Lumping seven news categories in with four non-news features wasn't ideal, and we noticed in our own iPhone use that anytime content or features were placed behind the tab bar More button, they generally went unnoticed and unused. We weren't willing to sacrifice any of the main sections within the application by burying them behind the More button.

At this point, USA TODAY suggested we try the section slider bar approach. We had seen how successful it was in the original Facebook app developed by Joe Hewitt. Once we locked in on the slider bar approach, we wanted to keep the look and feel of the slider control similar to Facebook's approach. We hoped that by modeling our

FIGURE CS11.2 Photos

FIGURE CS11.3 Snapshots

slider control closely with Facebook's, it would encourage a standard that other applications would adopt and would make it more familiar. To make sure we weren't offending anyone at Facebook, we even emailed Joe Hewitt and got his blessing before moving forward. [FIGURES CS11.2–CS11.3 show some of the final screen designs.]

What's next?

We are constantly reevaluating and looking for better and more effective ways to present information and have several new features and improvements planned for the USA TODAY app. Two of our most requested features, font resizing and offline content access, will be added soon. Users can also expect to see improved subcategory navigation in Headlines as well as a more robust Scores section in the coming year. ■

(USA TODAY icon and application screenshots courtesy of Mercury Intermedia)

Voices

VOICES was created by Taptivate and tap tap tap, one of the leading iPhone app development companies. tap tap tap had apps available the day the App Store launched and has sold well over a million copies of the apps the company has been involved in. They value simplicity and beautiful design, and it shows in their work.

John Casasanta is the founder of tap tap tap. He is a longtime Mac developer and the creator of MacHeist, the number-one Mac software promotion site. Although born a programmer, John's well past his coding prime now and can't be trusted around a compiler these days without the proper supervision.

What inspired tap tap tap to build the Voices app?

Voices was a collaboration between tap tap tap and Taptivate. Taptivate, an iPhone development house, had an early version of Voices and was looking for a publishing partner. They were familiar with our successful app launches and thought we'd be able to make a similar contribution to Voices. In the end, we were very satisfied with the result. Voices quickly became our most popular app, selling over 450,000 copies within its first two months in the App Store.

How did you approach the project?

As with all of the apps tap tap tap has created, we work with people from all around the world. We don't have one office or one central location, so we don't have the limit of having to work with people who live in close proximity to us. As a result, we're able to pool together talented individuals from virtually anywhere.

For Voices, our goal was to try to take a *good* app and make it *great*. This involved assessing any usability issues and reworking many of the graphics in the app. We also redesigned some areas of the app to make them fit with the playful theme. For instance, the playback mechanism was originally a simple progress indicator, but we changed it to have more of a real-world tape deck interface. [FIGURES CS12.1–CS12.3 show how the start screen evolved.]

How have users responded to the app?

They seem to really love it. One of the reasons it's done so well is that it's the kind of app that people are quick to show their friends and family. If you're looking to create a hit app, this viral quality is a major factor that can't be underestimated.

FIGURE CS12.1 Early design of the start screen

FIGURE CS12.2 Later design of the start screen

FIGURE CS12.3 Final design of the start screen

We put a lot of time into polishing the UI, and this didn't go unnoticed, thankfully. There are several other voice-changing apps in the App Store, but most of them have hardly made an impression. I strongly feel that it takes a combination of many things to make for a successful app. You need a solid idea, great execution, and strong marketing, among other qualities. Ignore any of these at your peril.

Any advice for developers embarking on similar projects?

One thing I've always stressed over the years is to col-laborate with others as much as you can. It's extremely rare that someone has the talents to handle all aspects of creating software, whether it's for iPhone, Mac, Windows, the web, or other platforms.

Realize your strengths and weaknesses and choose exceptional people to work with and you'll go *much* fur-ther than you'd ever be able to on your own.

What's next for tap tap tap?

We plan to continue along the same track that we've been on since the App Store opened. We care deeply about making the highest-quality apps and providing great user experiences. Our portfolio consists of a combination of both functional apps and fun apps, and it brings us plea-sure to develop both types.

Our "next big thing" is our take on the ideal iPhone cam-era app; the name of the app will be Camera+. We've been working hard on it for the past several months and it's our most ambitious project to date. We also have several other apps in various stages of development. It's been an exciting ride for us since the iPhone came out, and we're really looking forward to seeing what the future brings. ∎

(Voices icon and application screenshots courtesy of Taptivate)

CASE STUDY 13
Convertbot

MARK JARDINE is the designer and cofounder of Tapbots, the maker of Weightbot, Convertbot, and Pastebot. Mark has been designing for over 10 years. He loves to draw, take photos, and play on computers. His partner, Paul Haddad, has been developing software for the Mac platform for over 17 years.

What inspired Tapbots to build Convertbot?

Convertbot was based on our first app, Weightbot, which launched in late 2008. Around that time the movie *WALL-E* came out in theaters. I was fascinated by the robots in that movie and these robots inspired us to create an app with a robot-like aesthetic and interaction. You may notice that Weightbot resembles Eve from the movie. When it was time to embark on our second application, we wanted to build an application that was really simple and evolved the user experience through design. Converters seemed like a good area since they were a popular category with limited innovation.

How did you approach the project?

Before I start sketching, I try to break apps down into their most simple functionality. What are the interaction points that are required for the app to function? For example, Convertbot had four functions: choose a category, choose what to convert from, choose what to convert to, and enter the value. If I know the main points, then the little details are not as important. [**FIGURE CS13.1** illustrates some of the initial directions.]

How did the design evolve along the way?

Early on we considered using something similar to the wheel on the iPod. We knew it wouldn't necessarily be the most efficient but that wasn't our goal—we wanted to provide a fun experience that people would enjoy. Once I had the design worked out on paper, I immediately switched to the computer. I always start with flat shapes, then gradually build depth into the designs. Depth was really important—there were many iterations to make the app feel like a real robot.

FIGURE CS13.1 Early Convertbot sketches

How did you know when the design was done?

It's typically done when Paul and I can look at it and I say, "Okay, this works." Often I'll put a design aside for a few days and then return to it later. With a fresh set of eyes, I'll notice things I didn't see before. For example, the LED screen in an earlier sketch felt dated [FIGURE CS13.2]—the style was originally from Weightbot. After not looking at it for a few days, I returned to the design and started experimenting with the border. Several iterations later, I removed the thick border and added a much narrower one. This subtle change made the design fresh and gave the LED more room [FIGURE CS13.3].

How did the Convertbot decisions affect Weightbot?

Right after Convertbot was done, we went back and changed the Weightbot borders. Whenever we come out with a new application, we always go back and evolve our other app designs. Basically, the more design work you do, the better you get at it. With every new application we feel our designs improve.

How did you make the Convertbot video demo?

We like to do everything in-house—it's cost-effective and always a good learning experience. For the video demo, I had a decent camera, microphone, tripod, and Final Cut Express. When I took the first shot, the camera was too close to the phone so you could see scan lines. To prevent this from happening, I had to place the camera farther away and zoom in to the iPhone. The phone was in a dock and taped to the table so it wouldn't shift during the demo. Afterward I added sound and a voice-over via Final Cut Express.

What's next for Tapbots?

We are always trying to push our designs. Our latest app, Pastebot, has user-generated content which is very

FIGURE CS13.2 Convertbot with thick border

FIGURE CS13.3 Convertbot with narrow border

different from our other apps. When we designed this app, we incorporated much more of Apple's guidelines since they were the most effective way to achieve our design goals.

What kind of advice would you give to designers who want to create Immersive apps but are afraid to diverge from the HIG?

First, the designer should be capable of creating something that's visually compelling. Second, diverging from the *Human Interface Guidelines* just for the sake of it isn't necessarily going to make your app better. The bottom line is you have to consider your core audience and your goals. We did something completely different since we had specific design goals and a concept behind them. Our applications are part of our story. ■

(Convertbot icon, photographs, and application screenshots courtesy of Mark Jardine)

Branding and Advertising

11

WHEN PEOPLE THINK ABOUT BRANDING their iPhone app, they tend to picture an eye-catching logo that grabs the user's attention. While logos are important for brand identity, you can express your brand in many other ways: through interaction, visual design, sound, voice, a distinct color palette, and more.

Often these in-product brand expressions are far more powerful than external ones. For example, although a strong ad campaign may attract users, over time their brand loyalty will be largely based on the user experience, customer service, and other such factors.

This chapter focuses on ways to express your brand within your app's design. Since I can't cover everything about brand identity, you will find pointers to references and resources to help you learn more about branding strategies beyond the app. This chapter also discusses mobile advertising and ways to integrate ads into your designs.

What Is Branding?

In *The Brand Gap*,[1] Marty Neumeier defines a brand as an individual's gut feeling about a product, service, or company. Although you can't control these feelings, Neumeier discusses how you can *influence* a person's feelings through brand expressions. As mentioned earlier, brand expressions can be within the product itself—interaction, visual, or sound design—or communicated through channels beyond the app. Regardless of where the expression resides, its effectiveness can be measured with the following criteria:

- Distinctiveness
- Relevance
- Memorability
- Extensibility
- Depth

DISTINCTIVENESS

Distinctiveness refers to the qualities that make a brand stand out from the competition. For example, the interaction, visual, and sound design of the Tapbots family of apps (including Convertbot, Weightbot, and Pastebot) are arguably much more distinctive when compared to their competitors. (See Case Study 13 on page 250.) In the absence of this distinctiveness, Convertbot would have been lost in the sea of conversion applications (**FIGURES 11.1–11.2**).

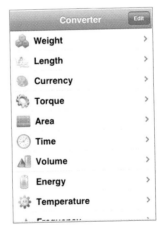

FIGURE 11.1 Convertbot   **FIGURE 11.2** The Unit Converter

1. Marty Neumeier, *The Brand Gap* (New Riders, 2003).

RELEVANCE

Relevance refers to whether a brand expression is appropriate for a given product. To illustrate, compare the concert calendar application icons in **FIGURES 11.3–11.4**. If you covered the app names, which icon would seem more relevant for a concert calendar? Both are aesthetically pleasing, but **FIGURE 11.3** evokes the concert feeling without being overly specific. **FIGURE 11.4** could be misconstrued as a guitar instrument app.

FIGURE 11.3 Live Music application icon

FIGURE 11.4 iLike Concerts application icon

MEMORABILITY

Memorability refers to the extent that people will remember your brand. For example, consider some of the app names within the contact exchange category: Bump, myCard, beamME pro vcard exchange, Smart Contact, and IntroDuse. After hearing them once, which one would you remember most? From my perspective, Bump is hands down the most memorable, as it communicates a somewhat complex concept in a simple way. Additionally, the company extends the bump concept to the application icon (**FIGURE 11.5**).

FIGURE 11.5 Bump application icon

EXTENSIBILITY

Extensibility refers to how well you can extend a brand expression across different media, cultures, and message types. Most iPhone app brands focus exclusively on extensibility across different electronic media—iPhone, web site, email communications—but some brands have more complicated requirements.

Consider Zipcar, the car-share company, which extends its brand across cars and signage as well as an iPhone app. Notice how the Zipcar symbol is barely present in the iPhone app (see the My Zipcar tab), yet the color still makes it feel like a Zipcar product (**FIGURES 11.6–11.8**).

FIGURE 11.6 Zipcar car *(Courtesy of Jacqui Cheng, photographer)*

FIGURE 11.7 Zipcar station *(Courtesy of Harry Hunt, photographer)*

FIGURE 11.8 Zipcar app

DEPTH

TIP

If you want to learn more about branding, another book to consider reading is *The Brand Handbook* by Wally Olins (Thames & Hudson Ltd., 2008).

Depth refers to whether a brand can communicate with individuals on multiple levels. For example, Not For Tourists expresses its brand through its distinctive design: the orange accent, the bold icons, the dark background (**FIGURE 11.9**). Additionally, the brand is expressed through the tone of the reviews and the voice of the user interface text. (See Case Study 4 on page 132.) When users view content outside a specified city, they see a quirky message such as "Not in Manhattan? Well you should be." Not For Tourists could say, "There are no listings in your area," but the formal tone would not suit the brand.

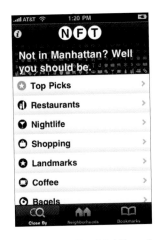

FIGURE 11.9 Not For Tourists' Close By screen

Brand Expressions

As discussed earlier, brand expressions can take several forms, within and beyond your app. This section discusses expressions within the actual product—the name, the trademarks, the user experience design—and effective ways to incorporate them into your app.

NAMING

When the App Store first opened, many apps opted for simple names like the built-in apps (e.g., Calendar and Mail). Simplicity is a positive quality, but it can backfire if many apps have the same name with a nondescript modifier (e.g., Best Camera, Camera Genius, Camera Pro, and so on).

On the opposite end of the spectrum, there are numerous apps with overly complicated names that are impossible to remember. As you brainstorm app names, consider the following seven naming criteria offered by Marty Neumeier:

1. **Distinctiveness.** Does your app name stand out in the App Store, especially from other apps in its category?

2. **Brevity.** Is it short enough to be easily recalled? Will it resist being reduced to a nickname?

3. **Appropriateness.** Does the name fit the purpose of the app? Keep looking if it would work just as well—or better—with another app.

4. **Easy spelling and pronunciation.** Will most people be able to spell the app name after hearing it spoken? Will they be able to pronounce it after seeing it written? A name shouldn't turn into a spelling test or make people feel ignorant.

5. **Likability.** Will people enjoy using it? Names that are intellectually stimulating or provide a good "mouth feel" have a head start over those that don't.

6. **Extendibility.** Does it have "legs"? Does it suggest a visual interpretation or lend itself to a number of creative executions? Great names provide endless opportunities for brand play.

7. **Protectability.** Can it be trademarked? Is it available for web use? While many names can be trademarked, some names are more defensible than others, making them safer and more valuable in the long run.

As you consider app names, remember that space is limited on the device. In particular, app names with more than 14 characters will be shortened with ellipses (e.g., Marble Maze Ultra becomes "Marble...Ultra").

TIP

If you plan to localize your app, make sure the name is appropriate for the target regions. A well-known example of a name that was not considered for localization was a Jaguar model named Mist. In German, *mist* translates to the equivalent of "muck."

If your app has secondary information—parent company, free versus paid, location information—it's important to consider its relationship to the app name. For example, Read It Later is 13 characters long, so the makers decided to place free versus paid information in the application icon (**FIGURE 11.10**). On the other hand, Not For Tourists is 16 characters, and it would be impossible to show the name plus the city. Instead, the icon/symbol is shown in the application icon and the city name is used for the guide below (**FIGURE 11.11**).

FIGURE 11.10 Read It Later application icon

FIGURE 11.11 Not For Tourists application icon

TRADEMARKS

Trademarks identify a company as the source of a product or service. They may take the form of a logo, symbol, monogram, or other visual element. Choosing a trademark form depends on your app name, concept, and branding goals. In most cases you may find that a combination is most effective (e.g., logo and symbol trademarks).

Logos

Logo is derived from the Greek *logos* and is short for "logotype." In essence, logos are letter type customized for a particular company or product name. Although logos can work well within the app navigation bar, they tend to be too large when applied to application icons. Instead of trying to shrink the logo, apps may show the first letter on the application icon. This approach tends to be most effective for established brands; for example, most Facebook users instantly recognize the lowercase *f* (**FIGURES 11.12–11.13**).

FIGURE 11.12 Facebook's logo in the app header

FIGURE 11.13 Facebook's app icon

Symbols

One of the best-known symbols is the old rainbow Apple icon with a single bite taken out of it (most people around the world can recognize the Apple brand even without the company name). If you design a symbol for your app, make sure it's immediately recognizable and can be easily distinguished from those of similar apps. To illustrate, compare the series of Twitter and camera symbols in **FIGURES 11.14–11.19**. Notice how the Twitter clients have distinctive colors and symbols. In contrast, the symbols for camera apps are almost identical, yet they have very different functions: One is an all-purpose camera, another is only for night photography, and the last one is for video. This lack of differentiation makes it challenging for users to identify each one on their Home screens. Moreover, the uniformity suggests that these apps are commodities.

FIGURE 11.14 Tweetie

FIGURE 11.15 Twitterific

FIGURE 11.16 TweetDeck

FIGURE 11.17 Camera Genius

FIGURE 11.18 Night Camera

FIGURE 11.19 iVideo camera

Monograms

Monograms show the first letter of each word in the company or product name. This approach tends to be more common with established brands (e.g., WSJ for the Wall Street Journal), since monograms are difficult to decipher otherwise.

BRANDING VIA THE USER EXPERIENCE

Not all app designs need to be explicitly branded with a trademark. Other approaches worth mentioning are included in the apps described in the following sections.

TweetDeck

TweetDeck showcases its logo and symbol on the launch image, but they're not included elsewhere in the app. However, there are still plenty of cues that indicate it's a TweetDeck app. For example, the yellow Tweet icon has the same visual treatment as the black-and-yellow bird symbol. In effect the creators killed two birds—brand and functionality—with one stone. Moreover, many interactions (e.g., the ability to add columns) are unique to TweetDeck, further reinforcing the brand (**FIGURES 11.20–11.21**).

FIGURE 11.20 TweetDeck's launch image   FIGURE 11.21 TweetDeck's All Friends view

Gowalla

Gowalla shows only its logo on the Passport screen; however, every other screen includes a narrow rainbow-striped bar above the header. This visual element is a subtle form of branding, cuing users that they are within the Gowalla app. Other aspects of the user experience that reinforce the brand include the app's color, icons, language, rules, and stamps acquired when "spots" are visited (**FIGURES 11.22–11.23**).

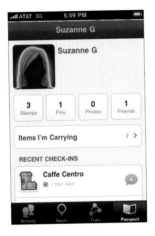

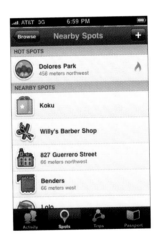

FIGURE 11.22 Gowalla Passport screen   FIGURE 11.23 Gowalla Spots screen

Ocarina

Ocarina, a musical instrument app, shows its product and company name (Smule) on the loading and tutorial screens. Although these brand expressions are not shown while the app is in use, others are embedded within the user experience. For example, the pulsing purple circles and green antenna can be found in several different media: on the App Store page, in the app's launch image, and on the app's web site (FIGURES 11.24–11.25). And, most important, Ocarina's otherworldly sound is like nothing else in the App Store.

FIGURE 11.24 Ocarina launch image

FIGURE 11.25 Ocarina instrument

Mobile Advertising Formats

Apps with large audiences or frequent usage often include some form of advertising, whether it's for their own products, a partner, or a third party. Here we'll discuss some common mobile advertising formats and suggest how to effectively integrate them into your design.

There are three main mobile advertising formats: in-line display, interstitials, and post-roll. Let's take a look at each of these.

In-line Display

In-line ads are shown alongside app content—at the top, bottom, or even within lists (FIGURES 11.26–11.28). The most common place you'll find advertising is along the bottom, since it's the least disruptive yet still figures prominently into the app design. If you choose this ad format, avoid "banner blindness," which means the ad will disappear when the user scrolls. Users are less likely to see or tap on such ad placements.

NOTE

There are many mobile advertising networks that work with the iPhone—for example, AdMob and Greystripe. Additionally, Apple has its own advertising network, iAd (http://developer.apple.com/iad/).

FIGURE 11.26 Ad at the top of Flixster

FIGURE 11.27 Ad at the bottom of NYTimes

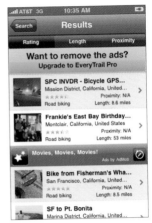

FIGURE 11.28 Ads within EveryTrail

Interstitials

Interstitial ads are typically shown during natural transition points, such as when content is loading. For example, All Recipes shows an ad before displaying certain views (**FIGURE 11.29**). Use this format sparingly within your designs, as overuse may annoy or completely turn away users.

FIGURE 11.29 All Recipes interstitial ad

Post-Roll

Post-roll ads are typically full-screen like interstitials but they're displayed after users complete a specific task. For example, 3D Tower Madness and Words With Friends show a post-roll at the end of the game.

ADVERTISING INTEGRATION TIPS

As you consider which advertising format to incorporate in your app, keep in mind the following advice offered by George Chen, Product Design Manager at Ad Mob:

NOTE

Additional information on these advertising formats and related guidelines can be found at the Interactive Advertising Bureau[2] and the Mobile Marketing Association.[3]

- **Leverage the medium.**

  Ads don't have to be links to web sites or the App Store—they can incorporate music, videos, and maps. Consider creative ways to integrate relevant content given the domain and context of use.

- **Think strategically about placement.**

  Ads are often considered after apps are coded, but they should be part of your design strategy. Incorporating ads into your design strategy will help create an integrated ad experience and lead to increased engagement. For example, Bubble Wrap had significant ad engagement since the ads were shown at the right time and place—at the end of the game and below the game's scoreboard.

- **Optimize landing pages for mobile.**

  If your ad leads to a secondary screen, make sure it's optimized for mobile—users shouldn't have to pinch and zoom to view content. Landing pages optimized for mobile will lead to much higher "conversion rates," meaning users are more likely to complete forms or other actions desired by the advertiser. That said, don't ask users to fill out long surveys or input their credit card number since it will be challenging in the mobile context.

- **Filter ads for your specific audience.**

  Many mobile ad providers allow you to filter ads and ad text via keywords. As much as possible, make sure the ads in your app are appropriate for your audience (e.g., political or religious ads may not be suitable within certain games). Appropriate filtering will benefit advertisers and your users.

Summary

Effective branding combined with a strong user experience is vital if you want your app to stand out from the pack. This chapter introduced several ways to express your brand—naming, trademarks, and the user interface.

---

2. Interactive Advertising Bureau, www.iab.net/iab_products_and_industry_services/508676.
3. Mobile Marketing Association, http://mmaglobal.com/policies.

To have the greatest impact, branding and advertising must be considered in the early stages of your app design. As you develop the branding and advertising strategy for your app, keep in mind the following tips from this chapter:

- Make sure your app name is distinctive yet memorable. Check if the corresponding domain name is available (e.g., **www.yourapp.com**).

- Create a trademark that can be used within different contexts of your app and extended across other media (e.g., web, print, ads).

- If you plan to integrate advertising into your designs, make sure the ads are filtered for your audience and displayed at the right time and place. ■

Accessibility and Localization

AS YOUR APP BECOMES increasingly popular, you may want to expand its reach and translate it into one or more of the 30 languages supported by the iPhone. Additionally, your awareness of accessibility issues may grow over time as visually impaired users struggle with your app and submit feedback. As a result, you may improve your app's screen reader descriptions and incorporate other accessibility enhancements.

If you envision your app heading in either of these directions—localization or accessibility—start designing solutions in the *first* version of your app. If you postpone, you may lose users who could have benefited from those features, and coding them later on may be more challenging.

This chapter starts with a discussion of accessibility on the iPhone, with specific attention to VoiceOver compatibility. We'll spend the remainder of the chapter reviewing ways to localize your app, including built-in and custom solutions.

Accessibility

NOTE

If you are developing an app for government or education use in the United States, chances are you must comply with Section 508, which includes provisions to establish a minimum level of accessibility.[2]

Accessibility is not required by Apple, but there are many strong reasons to create accessible apps. First, accessibility will make your app available to millions of people with visual, hearing, and other impairments. Second, almost all iPhone users, impaired or not, encounter visual or hearing limitations in the mobile context. For example, users have limited attention while driving; thus voice commands can have serious safety and usability benefits.

Finally, Apple has created tools to simplify the accessibility process, so it should not significantly impact your development time.[1] Since the benefits largely outweigh the costs, why wait? In this section we'll discuss ways to make your iPhone app accessible.

BUILT-IN ACCESSIBILITY FEATURES

A number of accessibility features are built into all iOS-based devices. Users can turn these features on in the Accessibility section of the iPhone Settings app (**Settings** > **General** > **Accessibility**); no additional coding is required.

- **Zoom:** Magnifies the entire screen.
- **White on Black:** Inverts the colors on the screen.
- **Mono Audio:** Combines the left and right channels into a mono signal played on both sides. This is an important feature for hearing-impaired individuals.
- **Speak Auto-text:** Speaks text corrections and suggestions as users type.
- **Voice Control:** Allows users to make phone calls and control iPod playback.

VOICEOVER

In addition to the built-in accessibility features, your app can benefit from Voice-Over, the screen-reading technology introduced in iOS 3.0. VoiceOver provides audio descriptions as users tap on UI elements. These descriptions may be entered in Interface Builder, but they should be tested in VoiceOver (you can't hear them within the coding environment).

---

1. iPhone Dev Center, "Accessibility Programming Guide for iPhone OS," http://developer.apple.com/iphone/library/documentation/UserExperience/Conceptual/iPhoneAccessibility/Introduction/Introduction.html.
2. Section 508, www.section508.gov/index.cfm?FuseAction=Content&ID=11.

To use VoiceOver, simply turn the feature on in the Accessibility Settings. Information used to formulate the audio descriptions includes

- **Label:** Describes the UI element; for example, "Add" may be used for the "+" button.

- **Traits:** Describe aspects of an element's state, behavior, or usage (e.g., Button). When combined with a label, a trait may read like this: "Add Button."

- **Hint:** A brief, localized phrase that describes the results of an action on an element. For example, the Facebook "+" button in **FIGURE 12.1** could provide a hint to clarify what content is being added (e.g., "Tapping this control adds a comment"). At the time of this writing, Facebook reads only "Button," which isn't particularly useful.

FIGURE 12.1 Facebook provides limited information for its Comment button via VoiceOver.

- **Value:** The current value of an element, when the value is not represented by the label. For example, the label for a slider might be "Speed," but its current value might be "50 percent."

- **Frame:** The frame (or tap area) of the element in screen coordinates. VoiceOver associates frames with relevant descriptions; the frame is not read to the user.

Additional information you may want to add for VoiceOver includes the following:

- **Nontextual data:** Apps with nontextual data should also provide descriptions in their accessibility labels. For example, Urbanspoon provides the label "Dollar sign, dollar sign, dollar sign" when users tap on the trio of dollar sign icons (**FIGURE 12.2**). While this is a step in the right direction, it would be better to say what the icons mean; for example, three dollar signs could be read as "$15 to $25 per entrée."

When users tap on the Epicurious tab bar icons, they get image names, for example, "0.0_Home_60." This sort of extraneous information is not helpful at all. This problem is exacerbated by the use of nonstandard tab bar icons that require two taps: one for the icon and another for the label (see FIGURE 12.3). If you must customize your icons, make sure you provide useful labels.

FIGURE 12.2 Urbanspoon provides a "dollar sign" label for price images.

FIGURE 12.3 Epicurious provides cryptic labels for tab bar images.

- **Dynamic data:** Apps with dynamic UI elements, such as location-based information, need to update accessibility descriptions on the fly. See the iPhone Dev Center "UIAccessibility Protocol Reference"[3] for implementation details.

- **Table views:** If your app has table views that contain more than one piece of information per row, you may want to aggregate the information into one label. FIGURE 12.4 illustrates how the NYTimes app aggregates headlines and descriptions. If the information were not aggregated, users would have to tap twice to read each article summary.

3. iPhone Dev Center, "UIAccessibility Protocol Reference," http://developer.apple.com/iphone/library/documentation/UIKit/Reference/UIAccessibility_Protocol/Introduction/Introduction.html.

FIGURE 12.4 The NYTimes app aggregates headlines and descriptions.

CUSTOM ACCESSIBILITY SOLUTIONS

Although the iOS has a number of built-in accessibility solutions, it may be beneficial in some apps to create customized solutions. One of the most common ones is the ability to adjust type size within news, blog, or Twitter apps (FIGURE 12.5). If you choose to create custom solutions, make sure they do not conflict with Voice-Over and other features in the Accessibility section of Settings.

FIGURE 12.5 GQ users can choose from four different type sizes.

Internationalization and Localization

NOTE

The terms *internationalization* and *localization* are frequently abbreviated to the numeronyms (number-based words) i18n and L10n. 18 stands for the number of letters between *i* and *n*; 10 stands for the number of letters between *L* and *n*.

Internationalization refers to the creation of products for usage virtually *anywhere*, whereas localization is the addition of features for a *specific* locale.[4] Internationalization is done once; however, localization must be done for each locale. If you plan to make your app available to other locales, their respective needs should be factored into your requirements. Some of these requirements can be handled by the OS; others may need custom solutions.[5] Common issues to consider include language, content, culture, and local laws.

LANGUAGE

Translating your UI into the target language is the most basic form of localization. If you're planning to translate your app into more than one language, consider working with an agency that specializes in localization. In addition to providing the agency with UI text, you may want to show them how the text will appear in the app. If the localization company is aware of potential UI issues (e.g., space constraints), they can take them into account as they complete the translations.

NOTE

Your web site and other support information should also be translated. UserVoice, a customer feedback service, may save time since the service is available in eight languages.

FIGURES 12.6–12.7 illustrate how string length varies in the English and French versions of the Yahoo! app. Notice that there is plenty of room for the Yahoo! News label in English but the French labels barely fit. If you plan to localize your app, it should be designed with the longest-running language in mind (typically German). Also, many non-Western languages are written in a different reading direction and may have their own layout requirements.

FIGURE 12.6 Yahoo! tab bar with English labels

FIGURE 12.7 Yahoo! tab bar with French labels

DYNAMIC CONTENT

If you have localized your app, the UI elements are automatically translated based on the language preference of the user when he or she launches the app. However, dynamic content such as news or Tweets may be updated only periodically (e.g., every hour, minute, or second). Since these translations cannot be embedded in your app, you can associate a feed with a locale or allow users to choose a feed. For example, Thomson Reuters's iPhone app allows users to select a localized News

4. "Internationalization and localization," http://en.wikipedia.org/wiki/Internationalization_and_localization.

5. iPhone Dev Center, "Internationalization and Localization," http://developer.apple.com/iphone/library/documentation/MacOSX/Conceptual/BPInternational/Articles/InternatAndLocaliz.html.

Edition from the United States, United Kingdom, Canada, or India (**FIGURE 12.8**). Similarly, AP News lets users choose a region for its news content (**FIGURE 12.9**). Another alternative is to create an app for each region, though that would increase the development effort.

FIGURE 12.8 Thomson Reuters users may choose a News Edition to view in their app.

FIGURE 12.9 AP users may choose a Region for the app content.

CULTURE

Localizing an app for a particular culture can be a significant undertaking and should be decided early on in the design process. Potential cultural aspects of your app to localize include icons and colors, units of measurement, names and titles, and contact information.

Icons and Colors

As mentioned in Chapter 10, "Visual Design," be sure your app icons and colors are appropriate for the given locale. Choosing inappropriate colors may send the wrong message or even turn some users away.

Units of Measurement

Currency, distance, and other units of measurement may vary depending on the locale. If the unit is changed often (e.g., within a unit conversion app), users should be able to change units within the app. However, if the units are changed infrequently, they should be placed in the iPhone Settings app. For example, the Cocktails app lets users choose a measurement unit within Settings, and RedLaser, a price-scanning app, allows users to choose the currency displayed (**FIGURES 12.10–12.11**). Alternatively, companies like RedLaser could have an app for each locale and include the corresponding currency. However, in this case it is more effective to have a default set based on the user's location, and to give the user the option of changing the currency when traveling to another country.

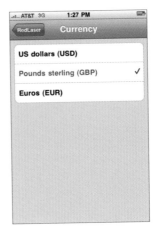

FIGURE 12.10 Cocktails users may choose a measurement unit for cocktail recipes.

FIGURE 12.11 RedLaser lets users choose a currency for prices displayed in the app.

Names and Titles

Name and title fields may vary according to the locale. For example, some UK services include more than 50 titles on their registration forms (e.g., The Baroness, The Viscountess, Field Marshal Lord, and so on). In contrast, U.S. services often omit titles altogether.

Contact Information

Fields required for address, phone, and other contact information vary from locale to locale. You can create a custom solution for each locale or try to develop forms that will meet most locales' needs. This can be challenging if there are significant differences between locales. For example, Japanese addresses have very different fields, groups, and ordering when compared to U.S. addresses. In the following text, compare my address from when I lived in Japan to my current one in the United States:

Japanese address:

T 606 (*postal code*)

Kyoto-shi, Sakyo-ku, Okasaki, Hoshoji-cho 52-2 (*city, ward, subarea, block, and house number*)

Ginsburg Suzanne (*last name appears first*)

U.S. address:

Suzanne Ginsburg

c/o Pearson Education, Inc.

75 Arlington Street, Suite 300

Boston, MA 02116

LOCAL LAWS

Certain types of information may be restricted in a particular locale. Locales may also have laws governing the collection and storage of user data. Resolve these and other potential legal issues before localizing your app.

Summary

Accessibility and localization tend to be priorities for more established apps. However, if you want your app to reach the greatest number of users (which you probably do), you should think about these issues *before* your first release.

Apple has created tools to simplify accessibility and localization so the time and effort required may not be significant. More important, postponing means you may lose users who could have benefited from accessibility and localization.

As you prepare your accessibility and localization strategy, keep these points in mind:

- To make your app more accessible, at a minimum enter the basic descriptions for VoiceOver (label, traits, hint).
- Make sure your app gestures do not conflict with those provided by VoiceOver.
- Localizing your app can be a significant undertaking. Outline your requirements early on so you can plan accordingly. ■

Looking to
the Future

WHEN YOU ARE IN THE MIDST of designing version 1.0 of your app, it may seem impractical to stop and consider what the iPhone and iPhone apps will be like in 5, 10, or 20 years from now. As challenging as it might seem, try to spend time brainstorming future applications and devices. One of my previous employers used to run biannual design brainstorming sessions around a "next-generation" theme. Although many of our ideas were not technically possible at the time (some took 10 years!), it empowered us to constantly push our designs and not get hung up on what the technology of the day could and couldn't do.

Our brainstorms were for web applications, but the same is true for the iPhone. Over time the iPhone hardware, operating system, and app space will evolve. The iPhone of the future may look nothing like the iPhone of today. Additionally, innovations outside of Apple will influence the direction of the iPhone and the overall mobile space. As design professionals, you must constantly monitor industry developments. If you don't keep your eye on the ball, someone else will and you will be left behind.

As you consider what your apps will be like in the future, you may want to refer to some mobile predictions collected by Mobile Trends (**www.m-trends.org**) in early 2010.[1] Here are a few themes inspired by this list.

Handheld Forms Will Evolve

Staying connected will no longer be limited to the iPhone and other mobile devices of today. Scientists and industry pundits predict that wearable computers in the form of eyeglasses, contact lenses, gloves, earpieces,[2] and watches[3] will become more prevalent (**FIGURES F.1–F.2**). These technologies clearly have a long way to go, but why not brainstorm possible applications now? You may come up with innovative ideas that influence your current apps. When the time comes for eyeglass apps, you'll be way ahead of the pack.

FIGURE F.1 Computer attached to eyeglasses *(Courtesy of Georgia Institute of Technology, Nicole Cappello)*

FIGURE F.2 Touchscreen wristwatch for micro-interactions *(Courtesy of Contextual Computing Group, Georgia Institute of Technology)*

Still not convinced? Richard DeVaul, a veteran of the wearable computing field, joined Apple in March 2010. Mr. DeVaul is well known for his MIT PhD dissertation titled "The Memory Glasses," which looks at how wearable computing can provide just-in-time memory support.[4] These innovations might be here sooner than you think.

1. Mobile Trends 2020, www.slideshare.net/rudydw/mobile-trends-2020.
2. Christian Metzger, Matt Anderson, and Thad Starner, "FreeDigiter: A Contact-free Device for Gesture Control," *www.cc.gatech.edu/~thad/p/031_30_Gesture/iswc04-freedigiter.pdf.*
3. Seungyon "Claire" Lee and Thad Starner, "BuzzWear: Alert Perception in Wearable Tactile Displays on the Wrist," *Proceedings of the ACM Conference on Human Factors in Computing Systems (ACM, 2010).*
4. Richard DeVaul, "The Memory Glasses: Wearable Computing for Just-in-Time Memory Support," http://devaul.net/~rich/DeVaulDissertation.pdf.

Mobile Payments Will Become Ubiquitous

Mobile payments will become ubiquitous in the not-so-distant future. As Steve O'Hear of TechCrunch Europe put it, "Everyone will become a walking cash register."[5] We are already starting to see mobile payments integrated into iPhone apps; for example, PayPal has integrated a payment feature into Bump (FIGURE F.3). And Square lets businesses accept card and cash payments via the iPhone or iPad. This trend will only grow in the years ahead as people conduct bank, ATM, and credit card transactions with their phones.

FIGURE F.3 Mobile payments via PayPal

Health Care Monitoring and Delivery Will Improve

Physicians will increasingly provide telemedicine and diagnostics via mobile devices. Today health workers use tools like EpiSurveyor (www.datadyne.org/episurveyor), a platform for gathering and sharing medical data, to help people in Africa, South America, and Indonesia (FIGURE F.4).

In the future, health workers will also be able to use their phones for diagnostics.[6] For example, Professor Aydogan Ozcan and his team at UCLA are developing mobile phone microscopes to help monitor the condition of HIV and malaria patients in undeveloped areas (FIGURE F.5).[7] As mobile diagnostic technologies become more widespread, people will eventually be able to monitor their own health.

---

5. Mobile Trends 2020, www.slideshare.net/rudydw/mobile-trends-2020.
6. "Cellphone Microscope, UCLA," www.youtube.com/watch?v=VH5H6uSQUFE&feature=related.
7. Healthimaging.com, "Cell Phone Imaging Could Improve Health Monitoring," www.healthimaging.com/index.php?option=com_articles&view=article&id=15771 (January 8, 2009).

FIGURE F.4 EpiSurveyor being used for a measles survey in Zambia *(Courtesy of DataDyne)*

FIGURE F.5 Prototype of mobile phone with microscope *(Courtesy of Ozcan Research Laboratory, UCLA)*

Personal health monitoring applications are already being used in the United States, Europe, and parts of Asia. For example, Fitbit contains a 3D sensor that monitors the user's diet, exercise, and sleep. The current customer base tends to be fitness buffs, but these products could also benefit individuals who are at risk for heart disease and other serious conditions.

Environmental Monitoring Will Lead to Scientific Discoveries

Smart sensors will be embedded into handheld devices, which will make new forms of scientific discovery possible. "Crowd sourcing," the ability to aggregate data and uncover patterns, will also become more sophisticated along with deeper mobile penetration. For example, Ushahidi (www.ushahidi.com) was initially developed to map reports of violence in Kenya after the 2008 elections (**FIGURE F.6**). The service has evolved over time and has also been used for monitoring wildlife in Kenya and snowstorms in Washington State.

Privacy Issues Will Come to a Head

As we become more mobile-minded, it won't be long before people start sharing more and more personal information from their mobile devices (e.g., the payment, health, and environmental applications just discussed). As a result, issues surrounding trust and privacy will surely come to a head. When designing apps that encounter privacy issues, you'll need to reassure users that their information is indeed private and secure. At the same time, you'll have to work with other parts of your organization to make sure the messaging within the app is consistent with your company's privacy policy. Without these measures, apps that deal with sensitive personal information are likely to fail.

FIGURE F.6 Ushahidi is a crowd-sourcing crisis information service.

Conclusion

The iPhone and other mobile technologies are evolving day by day. As mentioned earlier, you must constantly monitor the latest developments in the space to stay competitive. Try to attend your local meetups, or create one yourself. If you have the budget, conferences with an international audience are a great opportunity to broaden your horizons. Spend time reading blogs and following iPhone and other industry folks via Twitter. And if you have something to share, consider starting your own blog or presenting at your local meetup.

Good luck building your apps! ■

Index

Footnotes are indicated by an *n* and footnote number.

competitive usability benchmarking,
102–105
concept development, 109, 111
    brainstorming sessions, 113–117
    design-friendly environments,
        112–113
    sketching, 117–127
concepts
    diagrams, 121–122
    paper prototypes, 144
    posters, 122–123
    screens, 123–126
    visual design, 224–225
concurrent activities, 101
connections, troubleshooting, 205
contact information,
    internationalization, 272
content
    Immersive applications, 13
    loading, 216
    reports, 60
    support, 140
    viewing, 196–197
context
    field interviews, 45
    icons, 243
    shadowing sessions, 43
    of use, 40
    users, keeping within, 142
controls
    paper prototypes, 145–148
    segmented, 212, 232
    selecting, 22, 210
    video, 13
Convertbot application, 15, 194, 254
costs
    of paper prototypes, 144
    of research, 42
Craigslist, recruiting from, 60
criticism in brainstorming sessions, 115
cropping images, 32
cultures, 271
curl transitions, 202
cursors, positioning, 22
customizing
    accessibility, 269
    gestures, 22–23, 24
    images, 32

keyboards, 23–27
screens, 149
segmented controls, 232
tab icons, 240
user experiences, 14

D

data
    capturing, 103–104
    presenting, 105
dates, 171
    study, 56
debriefing research sessions, 66
defaults, smart, 199
defining applications, 37
Delete button, 22
demographics, user profiles, 57
demos, optional, 194
depth, branding, 256
design
    best practices, 192–207
    interfaces, 191
    issues, resolution of, 164–165
    issues, uncovering unknown, 165
    prototyping, 138
    tools, creating, 79–86
    visual. *See* visual design
design-friendly environments, creating,
    112–113
Designing Interactions, 137
detail views, 244
    Productivity applications, 7–8
development
    baselining, 170
    concept, 109. *See also* concept
        development
    scripts, 153
    SDK (software development kit),
        156
Device Capabilities Framework, 20
devices, 1
    Bluetooth, 30–31
    cameras, 31–35. *See also* cameras
    compasses, 29–30
    features, 20–21
    interactive prototyping techniques,
        151–152

string length, 216
structures
    hierarchical, Productivity
        applications, 7–8
    of visual design, 225–230
studies
    dates, 56
    dates and times, 171
styles
    applications, 3
    applications, selecting, 16–17
    productivity, 207
subject matter experts, interviews with,
    45
suggesting matches, 199–200
supplies
    for brainstorming sessions, 112–113
    prototyping, 172
support, content, 140
supported gestures, multi-touch
    displays, 22
Suri, Jane Fulton, 140
SurveyMonkey, 61
surveys, 52
    downsides of, 53
Sutton, Robert, 115 n3
swipe, 22
switches, 213
symbols, 258–259

T

table views, 213
tabs
    bar icons, 239–241
    bars, 146
    Recents, 200
    tiered, 207–208
    top, 209
taps, 22
    buttons/zones, 197
    screens, 197
tasks, 175, 178
    action sheets, 210
    adequate time for, 183
    in-line, 209
    productivity styles, 209

team members
    included in brainstorming sessions,
        114
    paper prototypes, 168
    report findings, 76
technology experience, user profiles, 57
templates
    animation, 155
    screens, 149
terminology, paper prototypes, 144
testing
    beta, 163n1, 183–184
    paper prototypes, 168
    tipping point, 152
    usability, 163
    usability, analysis, 179–180
    usability, drafting discussion
        guides, 174–177
    usability, facilitating, 178–179
    usability, guerrilla, 181–183
    usability, methods, 167–168
    usability, overview of, 164
    usability, pilot sessions, 177–178
    usability, planning, 169–173
    usability, presenting findings,
        180–181
    usability, reasons for, 164–166
    usability, recruiting participants,
        173–174
    usability, role of context, 166
    usability, selecting approaches for,
        184
    usability, timelines, 169
text
    alerts, 204
    content support, 140
    entering, 26. *See also* keyboards
    entries, 147
    messaging, 9
thinking big, 118
three dimensional (3D) games, 14
tiered tabs, 207–208
time, 101
    adequate time for tasks, 183
    for brainstorming sessions, 114
    studies, 171

time-boxing effort, 155
timelines for usability testing, 169
Times New Roman fonts, 234
tipping point testing, 152
Tischler, Linda, 115 n4
titles, internationalization, 272
Tognazzini, Bruce, 98
TomTom, 29
toolbars, 209–210, 241
tools
    animation, 155
    design, creating, 79–86
    surveys, 52
Top Findings or Executive Summary
  section, reports, 76
top tabs, 209
touch and hold gesture, 22
touch features, 20–21
    multi-touch displays, 21–27
tracking, 11–12
trademarks, 258–259
traditional usability testing, 167
transactions, 11–12
transcripts, research analysis, 71
transitions, 202–203
translating languages, 270
troubleshooting
    connections, 205
    paper prototypes, 144
    usability testing, 182
truncation, 216
turn-by-turn navigation, 29
TweetDeck, 259–260
Tweetie, 9
Twitter, 192, 259
two-by-two diagrams, 97
typefaces, 234
    sizing, 236
    visual design, 234–237
    weight, 236–237
types
    of prototyping, 142–156
    of sketching, 121
    of video prototypes, 154–155
typical social behaviors (norms), 41

U

UITextInputTraits Protocol Reference,
  26 n5
Understanding Comics, 126
units of measurement, 271
updates
    messaging, 25
    status, 25
up-front research product stage, 55
up-front user research, 42
UrbanSpoon (1.07), 96
USAA application, 33
USA Today application, 246–247
usability
    competitive benchmarking, 102–105
    heuristics, 98
    issues, keyboards, 26–27
    research, 42
    testing, 163
    testing, analysis, 179–180
    testing, drafting discussion guides,
      174–177
    testing, facilitating, 178–179
    testing, guerrilla, 181–183
    testing, methods, 167–168
    testing, overview of, 164
    testing, pilot sessions, 177–178
    testing, planning, 169–173
    testing, presenting findings,
      180–181
    testing, reasons for, 164–166
    testing, recruiting participants,
      173–174
    testing, role of context, 166
    testing, selecting approaches for,
      184
    testing, timelines, 169
    visual design, 224
Usability Professionals' Association
  (UPA), 166
User Experience at Move Inc., 59
user experience (UX) analysis, 93
    applications to include, 95
    benefits of, 94–95
    methods, 95–105

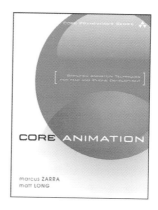

Developer's Library

ESSENTIAL REFERENCES FOR PROGRAMMING PROFESSIONALS

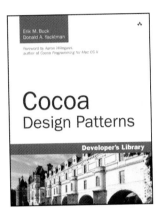

Cocoa Design Patterns

Erik M. Buck
Donald A. Yacktman

ISBN-13: 978-0-321-53502-3

**Cocoa® Programming
Developer's Handbook**

David Chisnall

ISBN-13: 978-0-321-63963-9

**The iPhone™ Developer's
Cookbook, Second Edition**

Erica Sadun

ISBN-13: 978-0-321-65957-6

Other Developer's Library Titles

TITLE	AUTHOR	ISBN-13
Android™ Wireless Application Development	Shane Conder / Lauren Darcey	978-0-321-62709-4
Programming in Objective-C 2.0	Stephen G. Kochan	978-0-321-56615-7
Building Open Social Apps	Chris Cole / Chad Russell / Jessica Whyte	978-0-321-61906-8
Developing Hybrid Applications for the iPhone	Lee S. Barney	978-0-321-60416-3

Addison
Wesley

**Developer's
Library**

informit.com/devlibrary

Developer's Library books are available at most retail and online bookstores. For more information or to order direct, visit our online bookstore at **informit.com/store**.

Online editions of all Developer's Library titles are available by subscription from Safari Books Online at **safari.informit.com**.

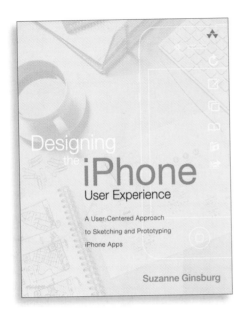

FREE Online Edition

Your purchase of *Designing the iPhone User Experience* includes access to a free online edition for 45 days through the Safari Books Online subscription service. Nearly every Addison-Wesley Professional book is available online through Safari Books Online, along with more than 5,000 other technical books and videos from publishers such as Cisco Press, Exam Cram, IBM Press, O'Reilly, Prentice Hall, Que, and Sams.

SAFARI BOOKS ONLINE allows you to search for a specific answer, cut and paste code, download chapters, and stay current with emerging technologies.

Activate your FREE Online Edition at www.informit.com/safarifree

STEP 1: Enter the coupon code: WBLXAZG.

STEP 2: New Safari users, complete the brief registration form.
Safari subscribers, just log in.

If you have difficulty registering on Safari or accessing the online edition, please e-mail customer-service@safaribooksonline.com